D1533167

REIGNING THE FUTURE

AI, 5G, Huawei, and
the Next 30 Years
of US-China Rivalry

by Dennis Wang

New Degree Press

Copyright © 2020 Dennis Wang
All rights reserved.

ISBN   978-1-64137-376-0 *Paperback*
        978-1-64137-292-3 *Kindle Ebook*
        978-1-64137-293-0 *Digital Ebook*

CONTENTS

——

PREFACE

ACKNOWLEDGMENTS

If you had told me a year ago that I'd soon be writing a book, I would have considered it an impossible feat. However, I have had the pleasure of meeting and knowing some exceptional people over the years who have been incredibly supportive of this project. Our peers very much shape us, and I owe many formative moments of growth and self-discovery to the people below. They are wholly responsible for the crafting of this book.

First and foremost, thank you to Professor Eric Koester of the Creator Institute, as well as Brian Bies of New Degree Press for enabling the publication of this book. Without their support and guidance, this book would not have gotten off the ground.

My parents have also given me an incredible amount of support during this process, offering not only mental support but also helpful tips throughout the writing, editing, and publication stages.

Thank you to Tenzin Choeyang, who has always challenged me to think differently and motivated me to become a more empathetic person. She has been invaluable in offering important critiques of early drafts of my book.

I owe my thanks to my friend and mentor Li Huaxiong for teaching me a new paradigm of thinking and giving me the keys to success during our time in Morocco and Western Sahara.

My professors at Bowdoin College and Duke University have taught me the fundamentals of international relations and technology—many of their ideas you will find in this book.

I would also like to thank the friends and classmates who have given me critical feedback, guidance, and inspiration throughout the editing stages of this book. Their names are listed below. Many of their names have been omitted for reasons for anonymity.

Aiman Xu, Amber Ma, Annie Wang, Bevan Penn, Cecilia Wu, Cindy Wang, Connie Chen, Darren Xie, David Yang, Denis Simon, Gray Gaertner, Harry Yuan, Hieu Nguyen, HongBing Yu, Jackson Yuan, Jonathan Sun, Justin Tandon, Kevin Pu, Li Hua, Lyndon Lee, Mark Lee, Melanie Manion, Millan Welman, Peter Feaver, Prince Sun, Robinson Yu, Rohin Shahi, Simon Sun, Steve Dai, Steve Lu, Steven Cheng, Tianren Zhang, Theo Holt, Tony Guo, William Chang, Yifei Wang, Yunfei Hu, Yunyu Lin.

Furthermore, the publication of this book would not have been possible without the incredible support I received from family and friends on my Indiegogo crowdsourcing campaign. Collectively, the campaign has raised $8,000 to cover the related costs of copy editing, designing, printing, and publishing this book in paperback, audiobook (coming soon), and hardcover editions. The names of contributors are below. Some contributors wish to remain anonymous.

Adrees Lyyaz, Aiman Xu, Ali Zahedanaraky, Andrew Wu, Andy Pu, Annie Wang, Bangxin Xu, Bin Wang, Cao Jun Hua, Cecilia Wu, Yunfei Hu, Conghao Zhou, Connie Chen, Christian Rodriguez, Cui Gui Chen, Daniel Zhu, David Yang, Eric Koester, Eric Lu, Fu Siyuan, Gao Hui, George Hong, George Yang, Hannah Zhuang, Hieu Nguyen, Hillman Han, Hunter White, Jasmine Long, Jason Pei, Jason Wu, Jenny Liang, Jiajia Shen, Jiang Xiaomei, Joe Wang, John Heald, Kelin's Mother, Li Huaxiong, Li Jilong, Li Yunhou, Liam Burnstad, Lily Mu, Lin Tian, Liu Shitao, Lyndon Lee, Ma Suli, Ma Wenbo, Mary Jiang, Moore Miao, Natalie Chen, Pearson Lee, Qi Liu, Rohin Shahi, Samuel Tolbert, Simon Sun, Steve Lu, Steven Cheng, Tao Song, Dennis Wang's Grandfather, Tianren Zhang, Tom Liao, Wang Peng, Wang Biao, Wang Xuguang, Wang Xusheng, Wei Hu, Weiping Yang, Wenning Cai, Wenrui Xu, William Chang, Wu Zhihui, Xinyong Song, Yongwang Li, Yu Hao, Yuan Lixin, Yunyu Lin, Zeng Haowen, Zhang Miaomiao, Zhang Xiangmei, Zhi Sun, Zhu Xiaoqing.

WHY I WROTE THIS BOOK

I was unable to retaliate when, as a child, my classmates branded me as stupid for not speaking English. While they all had different nationalities, many were audacious enough to call me a foreigner. Eventually, I found my escape in reading, beginning with the simplest books. The stories transported me away from the harsh loneliness of my new school in Malaysia. I read everywhere: during recess, at lunch, on buses, and at bookstores.

I appreciated variety and read everything from mystery novels to instructional pamphlets. Fortunately, I found two bookworm friends who supported my language-learning endeavors. As the reading heavyweights of the school, we competed and always tried to out-read one another. In my adventures with *Frog and Toad*, I reflected upon the concepts of individuality and bravery. Seeing myself in *Grandfather's Journey*, a story about cultural change, I better understood my alienation from my classmates.

As a consequence, the stories gave me a deeper understanding of myself and introduced me to the abstract concepts I would later encounter in life. Reading was my passion because it offered moments of introspection and learning that, due to the language barrier, I could not experience with my peers. Books provided an opportunity for ethical, creative, and rhetorical enrichment.

Today, I still treasure the act of reading, owing much of my personal growth to my childhood books. After receiving encouragement from my peers and doing some soul-searching, I embarked on the journey of writing this book both out of curiosity and as a meaningful personal project.

My international upbringing gives me unique perspectives on global issues. Having lived and studied in both China and the United States, I believe I have a fresh viewpoint to share on the topic of US-China relations.

US-China relations are a defining topic of the twenty-first century and also an area of passion for me. Through this book, I hope to inform and inspire others to learn more about this subject. The technological rivalry between the two countries will influence all aspects of our lives. Having studied economics and political science at Duke University and worked at China Central Television (CCTV) and Huawei Technologies, I hope to bring you fresh insights into this issue.

Imagine a Rubik's Cube with its myriad colors and strategies. Why might one person spend a lifetime trying to solve it while another can do so in a matter of seconds? To an observer, the latter individual may seem to display a prodigious mental ability, to solve a seemingly impossible puzzle at such an incredible speed.

Much like understanding global trends in the real world, solving a Rubik's Cube requires a person to have the correct information and a logical paradigm. The champion solver knows all the formulas and shortcuts, requiring little mental power, while the layman will attempt to utilize all their mental energy to solve the puzzle. Changing your approach and way of thinking is much more efficient when solving seemingly tricky challenges. The formulas and shortcuts in the real world involve information that allows you to see through the noise of the consensus, becoming empowered with the ability to participate and contribute meaningfully to important issues.

In writing this book, I hope to play a part in the changing relations between the United States and China by giving my readers new information to navigate the changing world and tackle some of our complex international puzzles. In an evolving, increasingly complex world, innovative methods and paradigm shifts are becoming ever more necessary.

Furthermore, the process of researching and writing this book has been an incredibly empowering experience in and of itself, enabling me to learn so much about the world as well as interact with people from all walks of life. For you, the reader, I hope this book will prove fruitful in providing new and exciting information about an important international issue. Also, I hope that it inspires you to navigate and influence the world as a better informed global citizen.

INTRODUCTION

———

China is a sleeping giant. Let her sleep, for when she wakes she will move the world.

—NAPOLEON BONAPARTE

BANG! Simon and his colleagues kick down the door, bursting into his employee's apartment. Clothes cover counters and chairs, dirty ashtrays lie uncleaned, and leftover cans of beer litter the room. In the dusty dormitory, they can barely make out a figure on the floor, illuminated by the light from the incandescent bulb in the hallway radiating inside. The silhouette is not moving.

Two days have passed since he disappeared in Angola while working for Huawei Technologies. There he is, face down on the floor like a rag doll, arms outstretched and head lopsided. Immediately, Simon and his team spring to action, hoisting the employee by his limbs and hauling him off the floor as they head for the local clinic. In the humid Sub-Saharan night, the team bursts into the shanty clinic of the residential complex.

"No. You must leave. He will die soon," is the grim prognosis the doctor gives Simon and his colleagues.

The clock has almost struck twelve, but the only option for the team is to continue searching. Since that night, Simon has not slept for three days straight, instead taking his patient from hospital to hospital in Luanda. None can help, not even the Presidential Hospital, which has the best facilities in the country. As dawn breaks once again, painting streaks of gold and turquoise upon a blue canvas in the sky, Simon despairs. The employee is indeed on the brink of death.

Simon receives a phone call from the Huawei administration, informing him that it has arranged for a charter flight from South Africa with a doctor on board. Practically ready to collapse, Simon feels a rush of newfound hope.

When the doctor arrives, he takes one look at his patient and states, "He is very ill, but I will take him to a hospital in South Africa."

In the 2000s, this camaraderie enabled Huawei to thrive in the most hostile environments around the world. Upon arrival in South Africa, the employee enters an intensive care unit. Only after fifty-six days in a coma, eighty pounds lost, and many liters of donated blood does he finally recover. His colleagues support the blood transfusion throughout while consoling the employee's family.

This team represents the scrappy and audacious spirit of Chinese companies like Huawei, tackling the frontiers of business in the most brutal environments while China grew economically. Still an obscure company at the time, Huawei began its ascent to prominence by targeting underserved frontiers like countries in Southeast Asia, the Middle East, Africa, and Eurasia.

The company leveraged its ability to provide cheap telecommunications solutions backed by a growing Chinese economy to carve footholds in international markets like Angola. Today, it is one of China's preeminent companies, with increasingly global operations and reaches. Not only has the company beat out its early competitors, but in 2018, it also surpassed Apple to become the world's second-largest phone manufacturer in the smartphone market.[1]

In the future, the global competition for technological dominance will not occur in Silicon Valley or the metropolises of China. Instead, it will be invisible to the casual observer, only found in the jungles and slums of the world. The technological rivalry between the United States and China will hinge on the resourcefulness of both states and their ability to utilize all tools of statecraft. This bilateral relationship between the two countries will be a defining topic in the twenty-first century, potent enough to affect all aspects of our lives.

Underlying tensions between countries define the international political structure, provoking anxiety, uncertainty, and mistrust. As history has shown, governmental entities exist in a brutish environment where the ultimate goal is

---

1   Edwin Chan, "Huawei Overtakes Apple to Become Second Biggest Smartphone Maker", Bloomberg, May 2, 2019, https://www.bloomberg.com/news/articles/2019-05-03/huawei-again-overtakes-apple-as-global-smartphone-market-tanks

self-preservation, where conflicts erupt between actors over resources, glory, and self-defense. Not operating under an international sovereign, countries turn into interest-seeking individuals largely unconstrained in their actions. Even with the existence of the United Nations and other supranational organizations today, states have the faculties to withdraw from agreements and act independently.

While the international community has made tremendous progress since the end of World War II, tensions are nonetheless inevitable. Conflicts now exist in new dimensions, spurred on by the development of new technologies and people's access to information. The integration of technology in people's daily lives has magnified the power of individuals and groups. Massive damage no longer requires the concerted effort of large organizations. Now—more than ever—malicious actors are empowered, unhindered by the boundaries of national borders. Thus, while the frequency of armed conflicts has decreased worldwide, the world remains tumultuous, and we have yet to arrive at a truly peaceful world.

Optimists believe that since the end of World War II, the world has enjoyed a period of stability they have labeled the "long peace," describing an era of unprecedented global integration and prosperity.[2] Accelerating globalization, nuclear deterrence, and the proliferation of democratic regimes characterize today's world. These factors have increased the

---

2   Gaddis, John Lewis. "The Long Peace: Elements of Stability in the Postwar International System." International Security 10, no. 4 (1986): 99. https://doi.org/10.2307/2538951.

costs of international conflict to unacceptable levels, suppressing the ubiquity and intensity of wars. We have entered a peaceful age not seen since that of the Ancient Roman Empire.[3] Scholars like the famous Francis Fukuyama have indeed proclaimed that we have reached "the end of history," believing that Western liberal democracy has triumphed as the final evolution of ideology destined to reach universality in the future.[4]

The United States is currently the leader of the liberal democratic world with its economic, technological, and military supremacy in the international world order. This status quo has led to a lack of global insight within American society. Many hold the view that China is still a stagnant nation, dependent upon an economy fixated on the manufacture of cheap and low-quality goods. It is a country riddled with pollution as the world's factory. Indeed, China had a tumultuous history for much of the twentieth century, buffeted by foreign invasions, civil war, revolution, and disastrous government policies. However, it is changing at a blindingly fast pace today.

China is emerging as an international leader of technology and poised to stand alongside the United States as the home to world-changing innovations and companies. However, will the United States sit still as this Asian economic

---

3   Inglehart, Ronald F, Bi Puranen, and Christian Welzel. "Declining Willingness to Fight for One's Country." Journal of Peace Research 52, no. 4 (March 2015): 418–34. https://doi.org/10.1177/0022343314565756.

4   Fukuyama, Francis. The End of History and the Last Man. London: Penguin, 2012.

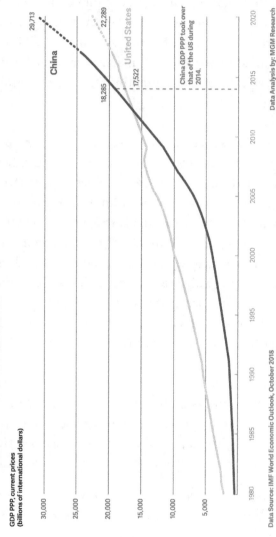

CHINA VS UNITED STATES: GDP PPP COMPARISON

GDP PPP, current prices
(billions of international dollars)

China

United States

29,713

22,289

18,285

17,522

China GDP PPP took over
that of the US during
2014.

Data Source: IMF World Economic Outlook, October 2018

Data Analysis by: MGM Research

Comparison of GDP PPP between the United States and China. *(https://mgmresearch.files.wordpress.com/2018/12/China-vs-US-GDP-PPP-comparison.png)*

juggernaut extends its influence internationally, eroding American primacy? In an environment of constant tension and mistrust in the international system, the United States has reason to engage in a preventative conflict with China, especially in the areas of finance and advanced technology. In terms of economic performance, China long ago surpassed the United States in its gross domestic product (GDP) measured in purchasing power parity (PPP).[5] Often downplayed by the Chinese leadership, PPP measures the purchasing power of different currencies and is a more accurate metric in the context of analyzing US-China relations.

Will globalization contain the tensions that exist in this bilateral relationship? Today's global economic integration is not a rare artifact of the twenty-first century; in fact, globalization has been working for millennia, from the early civilizations to the age of European conquest and colonialism.[6] Finding that the same globalized history is riddled with human suffering, from wars to famines and disease, would not be surprising. Only less than a hundred years ago did sixty million people perish in the horrors of World War II.[7]

---

5   "GDP Ranking, PPP Based." GDP ranking, PPP based (GDP PPP) | Data Catalog, December 23, 2019. https://datacatalog.worldbank.org/dataset/gdp-ranking-ppp-based.

6   Mann, Charles C. 1493: Uncovering the New World Columbus Created. New York: Alfred A. Knopf, 2015.

7   "Research Starters: Worldwide Deaths in World War II: The National WWII Museum: New Orleans." The National WWII Museum | New Orleans, n.d. https://www.nationalww2museum.org/students-teachers/student-resources/research-starters/research-starters-worldwide-deaths-world-war.

Though one may argue that this cataclysmic war and the subsequent end to the Cold War ushered in a new period of liberal institutionalism led by the United States, championing the triumph of the Western democratic model, exceptions exist. We are seeing a resurgent Russia and China and internal forces of populism and nationalism worldwide that threaten to undo these achievements. Is the twenty-first century indeed a new era or merely a blip in the unfortunate history of human conflict?

American politicians on both the left and right of the political spectrum agree that China is the number one threat to US preeminence in international politics. A failure to address or reconcile with China's rise will prove incredibly dangerous to American interests. You might be surprised to learn that China has already surpassed the United States in various areas of technology. Once following a model of "copying," China has slowly shifted into a model of domestic innovation, according to prominent technologist Kai-Fu Lee.[8] The country—armed with a market of 1.4 billion people and direct government backing for research—has become a fertile testing ground for the application of next-generation advances like artificial intelligence, big data, and fifth-generation telecommunications. Effectively, the country has "leapfrogged" other technologically advanced countries.[9]

With the development of technology, we are living in an increasingly winner-takes-all world. In the future, we will

---

8   Lee, Kai-Fu. AI Superpowers: China, Silicon Valley, and the New World Order. Boston: Houghton Mifflin Harcourt, 2018.

9   Ibid.

see "haves" and the "have-nots" of technology, especially in the areas of artificial intelligence.[10] Lacking the capital, entrepreneurial ecosystem, and access to a large market and pool of data, countries may find the task of catching up to the United States or China challenging. They may find themselves dependent on technologies, services, and standards developed by the two countries, made more pronounced by people's increasing dependence on the convenience of technology. Cities like San Francisco and Shenzhen will become the digital hubs of the world as they find themselves in a positive feedback loop of innovation, providing vast amounts of wealth and productivity for their respective countries.

Having studied economics and political science at Duke University as well as having worked at China Central Television and Huawei Technologies, I have always found US-China relations to be one of my main interests. I have conducted interviews with various stakeholders and experts on this topic, which I present to you along with original stories, information, and analysis. I divide this book into two parts:

- Part 1 contains Chapters 1 and 2. From the Opium War to China's rise, this part introduces the historical relationship between China and the United States, detailing the storms of history that have led to the current state of affairs in the twenty-first century.
- Part 2 encompasses Chapters 3 through 13 and analyzes China's technology industry and game-changing innovations of the twenty-first century. I discuss these innovations in the context of international relations.

---

10   Ibid.

In this book, I will present several new insights on the technological rivalry between the United States and China:

- China's technological rise is unprecedented and tipping the balance of power in the twenty-first century.
- "Weapons of Mass Destruction" such as artificial intelligence, big data, and 5G are changing the nature of statecraft. No longer will countries rely solely on economic or military hard power in international politics.
- 5G and Huawei stand front and center in the current tension between the two countries during US President Donald Trump's administration. Huawei was able to rise to prominence as a result of its unique culture and international reach.

The next frontier of US-China technological competition is not limited by artificial intelligence, big data, or 5G; rather, it includes fields of technology that we cannot yet envision.

This book will appeal to anyone interested in US-China relations and technology, from students to business professionals, policymakers, and more. Now let's begin!

PART ONE

CHAPTER 1

INTERNATIONAL FORCES

———

Peace is an armistice in a war that is continuously going on.

—THUCYDIDES

ONE CENTURY AGO TODAY

Only rats, mud, stench, and death existed on the battlefield. Diseased and deprived of sleep, these boys who had once dreamed of glorious war found nothing more than perpetual fear. They longed for a warm meal, for it could be their last. Polishing their weapons nervously, the young men passed the time in the shadow of the impending cataclysm. The belligerents dug rows of trenches on the eastern theater, but the first ones were the most dangerous. Thousands subsisted in these abysmal conditions, with sickness claiming the lives of more than those who dared wander into the no man's land. These walking corpses were haunted day and night by the menace of sudden death.

Shortly after Serbian nationalists assassinated Archduke Franz Ferdinand and his wife in 1914, all hell broke loose. Within two months, Europe had divided itself into two camps: the Triple Entente (led by Austria-Hungary, Germany, and Italy) and the Allies (consisting of Great Britain, Russia, and France).[11] Young men bid farewell to their families in search of glory and camaraderie, eager to serve their nation in what British statesman Herbert Henry Asquith once characterized as "an obligation of honor which no self-respecting man could possibly have repudiated."[12]

As they left their homes, the soldiers anticipated a quick and glorious war. However, the bloodshed between 1914 and 1918 would become one of the most brutal conflicts Europe had ever known, claiming the lives of twenty million.[13] Soldiers lucky enough to survive returned to their homes disoriented and disillusioned as the lost generation of the twentieth century, mere silhouettes of their former selves.

How did this conflict snowball into one of such large proportions? Long before the war, vital forces were already at play in the international political system. The start of World War I was shaped by the changing power structure between countries in Europe leading up to the conflict.

---

11   World War I (1914-1918), n.d. https://www2.gwu.edu/~erpapers/ teachinger/glossary/world-war-1.cfm.

12   Twamley, Zachary. A Matter of Honour: Britain and WWI. Point Pleasant, NJ: Winged Hussar Publishing, LLC, 2016.

13   World War I (1914-1918), n.d. https://www2.gwu.edu/~erpapers/ teachinger/glossary/world-war-1.cfm.

A hundred years before the archduke's assassination, Napoleon Bonaparte and his legendary Grande Armée marched across the continent but were cut short at Waterloo. The conclusion of the Napoleonic Wars proved seminal in defining the political norms before WWI. European heads of state, in response to Napoleon's defeat, assembled at the Congress of Vienna, where they devised a new political order to define peace and cooperation in the postwar world.

The delegates, through working groups, banquets, and balls, negotiated a new status quo characterized by a balance of power between states. They redrew borders, created buffer zones between countries, and formed alliances to prevent states from gaining hegemonic power in Europe. They believed they could maintain peace by distributing power between countries so that no single country would be incentivized to take military action against another. Effectively, states are kept in check by their relative strength, enabling peace and cooperation.[14]

Though the Congress of Vienna redefined the international power structure, it did not alleviate the tensions that continued to escalate through to WWII. Europe was a bonfire ready to be set ablaze. Powers existed in a state of fragile coexistence tensions and distrust. Domestically, sentiments of nationalism and militarism bloomed throughout Europe, increasing the antagonism and suspicion between countries. During this time of unbounded national ambition, states

14   Boundless. "Boundless World History." Lumen, n.d. https://courses.lumenlearning.com/boundless-worldhistory/chapter/the-congress-of-vienna/.

engaged in a game of military one-upmanship. The Austrians feared the Russians, the Russians feared the British, and the British feared the Germans.[15] Each country began to modernize, expanding its military in response to the others, unraveling the balance of power established at the Congress of Vienna.

SIMILARITIES

Today's world ominously resembles the prelude to the conflicts that struck Europe in the early twentieth century. It is characterized by changes in the balance of power, increasing nationalism, and the development of game-changing technologies:

- Balance of Power: US unipolarity is waning in the world, and resurgent countries across the globe are growing economically. Among the rising countries is China, which threatens to tip the balance of influence from the West to the East, drawing discontent and worry from Western policymakers. The country's rise has even been described by former White House strategist Steve Bannon as an "existential" threat to the United States.[16]
- Nationalism: Statesmen are also championing attitudes strikingly similar to popular discourse of the pre-WWI

---

15 Kennedy, Paul M. "WWI and the International Power System." International Security 9, no. 1 (1984): 7. https://doi.org/10.2307/2538634.

16 Wu, Wendy. "Steve Bannon Helps Revive US Cold War-Era Committee to Target China." South China Morning Post, March 26, 2019. https://www.scmp.com/news/china/diplomacy/article/3003283/cold-war-back-steve-bannon-helps-revive-us-committee-target.

world—one of populism, nationalism, and romanticization of national prestige. Donald Trump and Xi Jinping are salient examples, as both pledge to return the United States and China to a presupposed state of former national glory.

- New Technology: Today, the world is also developing new technologies at a dizzying pace. Countries like the United States, China, and Russia are developing next-generation fighter jets, nuclear delivery vehicles, and cyber capabilities. The landscape of war indeed looks incredibly different than in 1917. Instead of new technologies like the tank, machine gun, or poison gas, the world is also experiencing a new type of warfare.

BALANCE OF POWER

Like the start of WWI, today's world is characterized by new spheres of influence as a result of the shifting balance of power. China is becoming an increasingly assertive country internationally, supported by its ballooning military and economic capabilities. The United States, therefore, has less and less control over China's actions in specific parts of the world. Much like Germany's rise vis-a-vis the United Kingdom, China's economic rise compared to the United States is disconcerting.

As countries begin to develop their own spheres of influence and threaten the preeminent position of a powerful country, flashpoints can become more prevalent.[17] An area with a high

---

17   Allison, Graham T. Destined for War: Can America and China Escape Thucydidess Trap? London: Scribe, 2018.

propensity for Thucydidean conflict is the South China Sea, where experts believe that China already has enough of a military foothold to prevail against the United States.[18] The United States' predominant position as the world superpower is waning, and countries like China are able to enforce their own authority, which the United States will suffer prohibitive costs to defend against. Much like the assassination of Archduke Ferdinand, a simple spark can ignite war. In the South China Sea, for example, a military error (say, the collision of ships) can bring the United States and China into military conflict.[19] Areas such as the South China Sea—where spheres of influence intersect—are ripe ground for conflict.

One may argue that since the end of WWII, the creation of supranational organizations such as the United Nations has decreased the likelihood of war. However, history will tell us that both the United States and China have violated international laws to protect their spheres of influence. The United States, going against international law, carried out its invasion of Grenada in 1983 to solidify its control over the Caribbean. Similarly, China has continued its military expansion in the South Sea despite losing a case settled by

---

18 Townshend, Ashley, Matilda Steward, and Brendan Thomas-Noone. "Averting Crisis: American Strategy, Military Spending and Collective Defence in the Indo-Pacific - United States Studies Centre." Averting Crisis: American strategy, military spending and collective defence in the Indo-Pacific - United States Studies Centre, n.d. https://www.ussc.edu.au/analysis/averting-crisis-american-strategy-military-spending-and-collective-defence-in-the-indo-pacific.

19 Allison, Graham T. Destined for War: Can America and China Escape Thucydides Trap? London: Scribe, 2018.

the International Court of Justice at the Hague regarding the UN Law of the Sea. Other events in history also point to the downfall of international institutions such as the start of the Korean War (due to the Soviet boycott of the UN Security Council) and the start of WWII (a failure of the League of Nations).

Thus, despite popular belief, countries are not necessarily constrained by international norms—the national interest and relative power take central importance in decision-making. This lack of respect for supranational institutions harkens back to the Concert of Europe, created by the world powers after the fall of Napoleon as a mechanism to foster international peace and the balance of power. The Concert of Europe was designed by the European countries as a mechanism to curtail conflict. However, when the constraints became inconsistent with the reality of power relations, the institution became ineffective, deteriorating as Europe descended into world war.

In the future, as countries rise around the world and US influence wanes, we will see greater intersections of spheres of influence, creating more uncertainty around conflicts. Indeed, in addition to the rise of China, other countries are growing economically, threatening to displace the economic status of traditional countries in the West. Collectively known as the BRICS countries, they include Brazil, Russia, India, China, and South Africa. Political scientists claim that as countries around the globe become more powerful, we are moving from a world of unipolarity—dominated by US influence—to a world characterized by multipolarity, with many sources of influence across geographic areas.[20] Will our multipolar world, similar to the multipolar Europe before WWI, be the source of another great conflict?

Indeed, we are already seeing diminishing US influence at key international forums. US President Donald Trump is using the "America First" model, backing out of treaties such as the Paris Climate Agreement, UNESCO, and NAFTA, among others; additionally, the United States is threatening to undermine its solidarity with its traditional European allies in NATO. Countries' lack of participation in international institutions set the stage for World War I and II. As the world becomes multipolar and the United States increasingly fixates on "containing" the "China threat," the future of international relations is truly unstable.[21]

Despite international economic integration, conflict may still be inevitable. The world before WWI was also globalized, with European imperial domains spanning across the world. Despite globalization, war might be more favorable for the reigning economic hegemon.[22] Between 1905 and 1908, the British Admiralty contemplated using its centrality in the world financial system to inflict damage on rivals—namely, Germany and the United States—threatening to

---

20   Boxhill, Ian. From Unipolar to Multipolar: the Remaking of Global Hegemony. Kingston, Jamaica: Arawak, 2014.

21   Pan, Chengxin. "The 'China Threat' in American Self-Imagination: The Discursive Construction of Other as Power Politics." Alternatives: Global, Local, Political 29, no. 3 (2004): 305–31. https://doi.org/10.1177/030437540402900304.

22   Angell, Norman. The Great Illusion. New York: G.P. Putnam's Sons, 1910.

displace British power.[23] One can parallel this attitude with the US attitude in the twenty-first century, with the United States accusing China of economic malpractice, initiating what in the media has been called the "trade war." Similar to WWI, conflict in today's multipolar world may prove disastrous.

MILITARY ADVANCEMENTS

Fritz Haber was a prominent German chemist during WWI. Growing up exceptionally gifted, he entered the world of academics contrary to the will of his parents. Little did they know that this decision would send ripples throughout the world. He was the one who introduced to the world to poison gas, first used against the Allies at the Battle of Ypres during WWI.

As a British chemist once reflected, "a casualty from gunfire may be dying from his wounds, but they don't give him the sensation that his life is being strangled out of him."[24] During this time of unbounded national ambition, Germany was experiencing a newfound interest in the natural sciences. Haber entered his professional life during this prime time, making many contributions to the world of science—and, ultimately, winning the Nobel Prize in 1918

---

23 Evans, Richard J, and Harold James. "Debate: Is 2014, like 1914, a Prelude to World War?" The Globe and Mail, June 19, 2017. https://www. theglobeandmail.com/opinion/read-and-vote-is-2014-like-1914-a-prelude-to-world-war/article19325504/.

24 Haber, L. F. The Poisonous Cloud: Chemical Warfare in WWI. Oxford: Clarendon Press, 2002.

for synthesizing ammonia from nitrogen and hydrogen gas.[25] With modernizing technology, the range of human conflict has increased. During WWI, Haber's innovation of poison gas was thought to be a war-winning weapon by the Germans, completely undermining the traditional defenses of their adversaries.[26]

During Haber's time, other technologies such as the machine gun, poison gas, and armored tanks also changed the way wars were fought forever. The physical landscape of war evolved into one characterized by attrition warfare, as these technologies gave belligerents a defensive advantage—each side dug deeper and deeper into their trenches. In the twenty-first century, technologies continue to change the world. Albert Einstein may be correct in his omen of "I know not with what weapons WWIII will be fought, but WWIV will be fought with sticks and stones." Today, cyberattacks can cripple entire networks, and countries have already stockpiled enough nuclear weapons to destroy our world many times over. Indeed, we might not live to see a fourth world war after the third.

The development of technology increases a country's hard power, tipping the balance of power in its favor. Haber's introduction of chemical warfare during WWI gave the Germans an advantage, and this poison gas was soon also

---

25 "The Nobel Prize in Chemistry 1918." NobelPrize.org, n.d. https://www. nobelprize.org/prizes/chemistry/1918/haber/biographical/

26 "Weapons on Land - Poison Gas." Canada and WWI, n.d. https://www. warmuseum.ca/firstworldwar/history/battles-and-fighting/weapons-on-land/poison-gas/.

used by the Allies during the conflict. Today, an arms race is ongoing between the most powerful nations of the world. In the 2018 American Nuclear Posture, the US government supported the modernization of its nuclear arms, in response to the Russian improvements in its nuclear arsenal. Not only will the United States be modernizing its nuclear force, but it will also develop small-scale tactical nuclear weapons in response to the Russian threat.[27]

Between China and the United States also exists a technological competition in the twenty-first century. China is becoming the world leader in research, technology, and innovation, already submitting more patents each year than the United States. The technological development of this Asian giant has inspired insecurity in the United States, prompting a hawkish attitude in both Democrats and Republicans.

The changing balance of power brought by technological development is causing tectonic shifts in the international power structure, moving us toward a world with no clear center of gravity. Currently, the United States claims the preeminent position in the world as a powerhouse of military and R&D spending. However, in the near future, our world may move into a state of multipolarity while each country develops technologically, creating an international system more prone to conflict—similar to the multipolarity of the world during WWI.

---

27 "Nuclear Posture Review." Department of Defense, February 2018. https://media.defense.gov/2018/Feb/02/2001872886/-1/-1/1/2018-NUCLE-AR-POSTURE-REVIEW-FINAL-REPORT.PDF.

During that time, countries armed with new technologies bought into the illusion that they could have an offensive advantage in war, with a particular benefit for the side that attacks first. With new technologies today, a similar case might occur, destabilizing the world.

NATIONALISM

Similar to 1914, today's world is also characterized by domestic ambition, nationalism, and populism exhibited throughout the world. We have populist and nationalist leaders running some of the world's most powerful nations. From Donald Trump to Xi Jinping, Shinzo Abe, Narendra Modi, the list goes on. These leaders want to return their countries to their former glories, appealing to the great masses of people who have felt disenfranchised from the ever-interconnected international system.

The Nobel scientist Haber, among other prominent thinkers of his time, facilitated the dissemination of German wartime propaganda, supported by the nation's grand illusions and its aggressive stance in foreign relations. Propaganda fanned the flames of German nationalist fervor, lulling many middle-class citizens into enthusiastic support of the war.[28] For example, Haber, while caught up in the nationalist sentiments of the time, committed himself to the notorious "Manifesto of the 93," signed by some of Germany's greatest scientists, writers, and artists. This document rebutted

---

28   Stern, Fritz. "Fritz Haber: Flawed Greatness of Person and Country."

Angewandte Chemie International Edition 51, no. 1 (August 2011): 50–56.

https://doi.org/10.1002/anie.201107900.

the wartime propaganda of the Allies and denied German wrongdoing in the war, claiming that German militarism and national identity were indeed essential to each other.

Many similarities could be found between China in the twenty-first century and Germany in the twentieth. Both countries share spectacular economic and military growth, threatening to displace the power of the reigning hegemon. However, domestically, the masses of both countries share similar sentiments of nationalism. China has grown increasingly nationalistic, driven by the victimization narrative painted by the CCP. Through a series of "patriotic education" and an ideology based around the "century of humiliation," the party-state paints itself as oppressed throughout society. The CCP, then, claims the responsibility to revive the country's former glory.

The countries in WWI started the conflict in search of glory. The United States and China are particularly guilty of this motive, as the state leaders of both countries have pledged that they will return their country to its former glory, with Trump's "Make America Great Again" and Xi's "China Dream" and "National Rejuvenation," among other slogans.

As the world's two biggest economic and military juggernauts, the domestic rhetoric between the two countries is a destabilizing force. When the spark of conflict occurs between the two, the domestic attitude of citizens has the power to force politicians to adopt hardline policies toward the other country, which will lead to a greater damaging of US-China relations. Indeed, we are seeing the start of this spiraling conflict ever since Trump adopted a warlike policy toward

China, starting the trade war. As perceptions change between the countries, distrust will be further exacerbated, leading to games between the two countries that are not beneficial to either side.

HUMAN NATURE AND THE HUNGER GAMES

Her father died in a mine explosion when she was eleven. Since then, she has had to keep her family from starving to death, forced to provide for her mother and sister using the hunting and gathering knowledge her father taught her. She is sixteen years old, with straight black hair, gray eyes, and olive skin. Living in the impoverished coal-mining region of District 12, Katniss Everdeen, in a heroic act to protect her sister, volunteers herself to participate in an annual game in the Capitol where boys and girls from the ages twelve to eighteen compete in a televised battle royale to the death.

Using whatever is at their disposal in the arena, the contestants are tasked with finding every possible way to survive, using deception and skill to outmaneuver, outlast, and ultimately kill other contestants if necessary. In case you have not read or watched the *Hunger Games* series by Suzanne Collins, it is a story about death, romance, and drama in the dystopian nation of Panem, featuring the heroine Katniss Everdeen.

What does Suzanne Collins' *Hunger Games* book have to do with US-China relations? The key lies in human nature. According to Thomas Hobbes, author of *Leviathan* and one of the founding fathers of political philosophy, society, as run by human nature, is "solitary, poor, nasty, brutish, and short."[29] The world he described is like the world of *The Hunger Games*. Individuals are required to fend for themselves in an arena without laws—anything is fair game. Individuals need to do their best to survive in this world, forging alliances with other contestants not in friendship but out of necessity.

To understand why the United States and China might engage in conflict in the twenty-first century, we must think of the international political system as the world described by Hobbes. In the international relations theory of classical realism (which Hobbes helped contribute to), states engage in conflict just like the contestants inside *The Hunger Games*. Humans go to war for four reasons: competition over scarce goods, the desire for security, glory, and for the sacrifice of something greater than themselves.

In the modern-day, scholars have coined the term structural realism (or neorealism), which posits that states exist in a state of international anarchy, similar to Hobbes' world. Prominent Harvard international relations scholar Kenneth Waltz theorizes that states exist in a state of "anarchy" in the international system. This view asserts that the world lacks a global sovereign authority able to constrain the actions of states. As the world lacks authority, individual rational states are primarily concerned with their own survival, engaging in self-help behavior by developing their military or economic prowess. Thus the natural state for countries is to develop their offensive and defensive capabilities. States distrust each other and engage in games of one-upmanship as they try to

---

29   Hobbes, Thomas. Leviathan. S.l.: Ancient Wisdom Publication, 2019.

respond to each other's military developments, creating a balance of power.

As part of structural realism, states engage in self-help to preserve their survival, reacting against developments made by other states, which is why, throughout the world, military budgets remain an important aspect of statecraft. Though weapons are never physically used against individuals or other states, the existence of these weapons in a state's arsenal shows others that state's resolve and ability to fight a battle when it actually comes. This balancing of perceptions and relative powers has dictated much of the phenomena in international politics. A state with weaker relative military capabilities could see its diplomatic clout weaken against states that are more militarily and economically powerful.

At the bargaining table, often the countries with the greater relative ability come out on top. For this reason, the United States has been successful in defining much of the postwar world order. As the sole remaining superpower after the fall of the Soviet Union, the United States has used its international dominance to craft a world order favorable to itself. Today, what is accepted as norms internationally in terms of institutions, policy, political culture, media, and even pop culture is often based on the American model. Through this supremacy, the United States enjoys further benefits that it can use to strengthen its country and provide a better standard of living for its citizens.

The idea of structural realism is very much prevalent in the case of WWI. After the fall of Napoleon, the European powers existed in a precarious balance of power. However, this balancing created a race to amass more relative advantages, triggering an arms race between countries. Fueled by the domestic passions of militarism and nationalism, war was made incredibly likely between the European powers. According to British statesman David Lloyd George, who lived during WWI, this Great War "was won not on the merits of the case, but on a balance of resources and of blunders." In his view, the relative hard power of nations decided the outcome in favor of the Allies because their "reserves of manpower, of material and of money at the command... were overwhelmingly greater than those possessed by the vanquished."[30]

We will see that structural issues may drive the United States and China toward war in the twenty-first century.

DISRUPTION TO THE INTERNATIONAL SYSTEM

China is disrupting the global system, which is currently based on liberal institutionalism backed by US hegemony. The economic rise of China and other emerging states plus the decline of Western countries is rendering the future of liberal institutionalism uncertain.

For one, China's increasing prominence is moving us toward a world with multiple poles of power. The country and other emerging states are developing their own spheres of economic and military influence. At the intersections of these spheres lies conflict. Here, states will be more likely to engage

---

30 Lloyd, Lloyd George David. War Memoirs of David Lloyd George. London: Nicholson & Watson, 1934.

in what is described as "self-help behavior"—such as through arms buildup—leading to cases of increased tensions and situations in which no party leaves unscathed.

The United States will no longer be able to enforce order in all areas of the world. An example of the waning US sphere of influence is the South China Sea, where China has already gained a powerful military foothold. Rather than being the "benevolent suzerain rule-giver to the world," China is becoming more assertive, challenging the United States in this region.[31]

Furthermore, China is changing the narrative surrounding liberal institutionalism. The country has mounted a major public relations offensive, investing billions of dollars worldwide to improve its public image.[32] By obstructing free speech and promoting its own narrative around the world, China is weakening the merits of the traditional Western and US narratives. Chinese officials know that wars do not need to be fought or won with guns. Media and culture can also be extensions of warfare.

The country has a deeply rooted ambition of upsetting the liberal world order. Xi Jinping views his country's rise as

---

31   Dreyer, June Teufel. "The 'Tianxia Trope': Will China Change the International System?" Journal of Contemporary China 24, no. 96 (2015): 1015–31. https://doi.org/10.1080/10670564.2015.1030951.

32   Shambaugh, David. "China's Soft-Power Push." Foreign Affairs. Foreign Affairs Magazine, September 3, 2015. https://www.foreignaffairs.com/articles/china/2015-06-16/china-s-soft-power-push.

a path of restoration.[33] This view is indicative of the belief that instead of simply "rising" to be among the other great powers of the world, China wants to return to its former civilizational glory as being the preeminent country. This view also explains China's increasingly aggressive stance in the South Sea, as well as the ambitious scope of its economic projects such as the Belt and Road Initiative. Both endeavors echo China's civilizational heritage of Silk Road trade and ocean navigation. In the future, we may continue to see more Chinese projects in line with this rhetoric of national rejuvenation.

THE PELOPONNESIAN WAR

The year is 431 BCE, and the Spartans have summoned the Corinthians to the Spartan assembly. The topic of discussion is Athens and the threat it poses. After much debate between Spartan policymakers and the Corinthians, the warlike city-state sends its best fighting men to stymie Athens' rise to power in Greece. This historical conflict, known as the Peloponnesian War, is a seminal event crucial to what prominent Harvard scholar Graham Allison termed the "Thucydides Trap."[34]

Ancient Greek historian Thucydides, in his *Histories of the Peloponnesian War*, chronicles the conflict between the two preeminent Greek powers, writing his book "not as an essay

---

33 Xiang, Lanxin. "Xi's Dream and China's Future." Survival 58, no. 3 (March 2016): 53–62. https://doi.org/10.1080/00396338.2016.1186978.

34 Allison, Graham T. Destined for War: Can America and China Escape Thucydides Trap? London: Scribe, 2018.

to win the applause of the moment, but as a possession for all time."[35] During Thucydides' time, the conflict between Sparta and Athens was considerable, involving alliances and participation by numerous Greek islands as well as between the Athens-led Delian League and the Sparta-led Peloponnesian League. At the end of the fighting, Sparta reigns supreme, occupying Athens' government and ushering in turmoil in the city-state's domestic politics. Ultimately, this conflict shaped the Greek world due to its incredible economic costs and political changes, terminating the golden age of Athens.

The structural factors at play at the onset of the Peloponnesian War have been most beneficial to the study of international relations and US-China relations. The "Thucydides Trap," a term coined by Harvard professor Graham Allison, posits that the propensity for armed conflict to occur is high when a rising power threatens the position of the dominant influence. In Allison's words, "Thucydides went to the heart of the matter. ...When a rising power threatens to displace a ruling power, the resulting structural stress makes a violent clash the rule, not the exception."[36] Due to "the rise of Athens and the fear that this instilled in Sparta," conflict was inevitable between the two city-states.[37]

Using the Peloponnesian War as a basis, Allison continues to analyze other historical conflicts where a rising power

---

35 Thucydides. History of the Peloponnesian War. Place of publication not identified: Franklin Classics Trade Press, 2018.

36 Allison, Graham T. Destined for War: Can America and China Escape Thucydides Trap? London: Scribe, 2018.

37 Ibid.

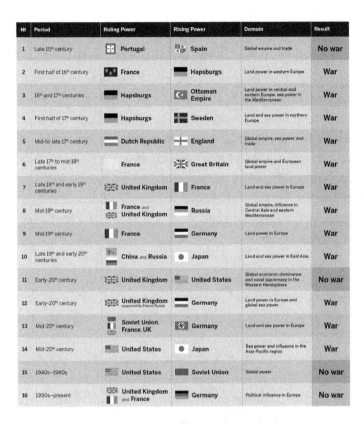

№	Period	Ruling Power	Rising Power	Domain	Result
1	Late 15ᵗʰ century	Portugal	Spain	Global empire and trade	No war
2	First half of 16ᵗʰ century	France	Hapsburgs	Land power in western Europe	War
3	16ᵗʰ and 17ᵗʰ centuries	Hapsburgs	Ottoman Empire	Land power in central and eastern Europe, sea power in the Mediterranean	War
4	First half of 17ᵗʰ century	Hapsburgs	Sweden	Land and sea power in northern Europe	War
5	Mid-to-late 17ᵗʰ century	Dutch Republic	England	Global empire, sea power, and trade	War
6	Late 17ᵗʰ to mid-18ᵗʰ centuries	France	Great Britain	Global empire and European land power	War
7	Late 18ᵗʰ and early 19ᵗʰ centuries	United Kingdom	France	Land and sea power in Europe	War
8	Mid-19ᵗʰ century	France and United Kingdom	Russia	Global empire, influence in Central Asia and eastern Mediterranean	War
9	Mid-19ᵗʰ century	France	Germany	Land power in Europe	War
10	Late 19ᵗʰ and early 20ᵗʰ centuries	China and Russia	Japan	Land and sea power in East Asia	War
11	Early-20ᵗʰ century	United Kingdom	United States	Global economic dominance and naval supremacy in the Western Hemisphere	No war
12	Early-20ᵗʰ century	United Kingdom supported by France, Russia	Germany	Land power in Europe and global sea power	War
13	Mid-20ᵗʰ century	Soviet Union, France, UK	Germany	Land and sea power in Europe	War
14	Mid-20ᵗʰ century	United States	Japan	Sea power and influence in the Asia-Pacific region	War
15	1940s–1980s	United States	Soviet Union	Global power	No war
16	1990s–present	United Kingdom and France	Germany	Political influence in Europe	No war

The 16 cases of the Thucydides Trap throughout history. (*https://www.belfercenter.org/thucydides-trap/resources/case-file-graphic*)

threatened to displace a ruling power. Twelve of these cases resulted in war, and only four instances avoided conflict— albeit requiring "huge, painful adjustments in attitudes and actions on the part of challenger and challenged alike."[38] Does this historical trend paint a grim outlook for the future of the relationship between the United States and China?

---

38   Ibid.

At a large banquet hall in Seattle stands Chinese President Xi Jinping. On his way to Washington, D.C., Xi is in the city of Seattle to broadcast an optimistic message to US decision-makers. With Washington state sending more than $20 billion in aircraft and agricultural products to China in 2014, as well as being home to tech behemoths like Microsoft and Amazon, the Chinese president is in town to express a message of positivity. He hopes to convey the friendly ties between China and the United States and boost the confidence of enterprises on both sides of the Pacific for the future of bilateral trade.[39]

Present at the banquet were also former Secretary of State Henry Kissinger, then-Secretary of Commerce Penny Pritzker, and numerous other individuals from the state government and the National Committee on United States-China Relations. In his speech, Xi stressed that there is "no such thing as the so-called Thucydides Trap in the world," hoping that the two countries can build a "new model of major-country relationship that features non-conflict, non-confrontation, mutual respect, and win-win cooperation."[40]

---

39   Xin, Zhou, Wendy Wu, and Kinling Lo. "Xi Jinping Sounds Long March Rallying Call as US Trade War Tensions Rise." South China Morning Post, May 21, 2019. https://www.scmp.com/economy/china-economy/article/3010977/xi-jinping-visits-rare-earth-minerals-facility-amid-talk-use.

40   "Speech by H.E. Xi Jinping President of the People's Republic of China At the Welcoming Dinner Hosted by Local Governments And Friendly Organizations in the United States." Ministry of Foreign Affairs of the People's Republic of China, September 25, 2015. https://www.fmprc.gov.cn/mfa_eng/wjdt_665385/zyjh_665391/t1305429.shtml.

Who's Rebalancing Whom?

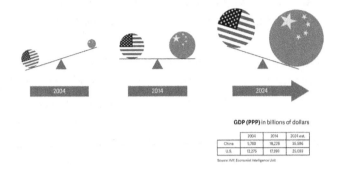

GDP (PPP) in billions of dollars

	2004	2014	2024 est.
China	5,760	18,228	35,596
U.S.	12,275	17,393	25,093

Source: IMF, Economist Intelligence Unit

Comparison of the relative weights of the United States and Chinese economies. (*https://www.belfercenter.org/thucydides-trap/resources/whos-rebalancing-whom*)

However, fast forward to 2019, and the situation between China and the United States seems grim. We can see a bipartisan hawkishness in the US government regarding China, and this sentiment was not alleviated by the election of Trump in 2016. In fact, since the start of the official trade war in June 2018, the United States has taken more hardline measures against China. History may not be deterministic, but it may be the best way for us to predict the future, and the omen of Thucydides has perhaps already started playing itself out.

Both countries have fallen deeper into the Thucydides Trap at the time of this writing in 2019. The conflict seen on the news has revolved around trade. However, in fact, at the core of the trade tensions actually lies issues of technology rivalry and the balancing of technological capabilities. The real issue is the structure of agreements between the United States and China, rather than the trade deficit itself. According to realist international relations, countries naturally focus on building their technological power, rising vis-a-vis adversaries. This phenomenon is at play in China's Thucydides Trap.

For many years, the United States witnessed an unanticipated growth in China. According to Professor Peter Feaver of Duke University, the United States, during the Reagan and H.W. Bush administrations, did not enact proper policies to contain the country's rise. The United States, at the time of China's "reform and opening up," miscalculated that the country would eventually undergo political liberalization as a result of the introduction of economic freedoms by the Chinese government.[41] China today remains economically liberal but politically authoritarian.

The United States is just beginning to realize the threat of competition by China, coined the so-called "China threat." Under the Trump administration, the country has started to impose a series of restrictions on the country.

"It is a massive national security issue to the West," Bannon said, in a phone interview on Saturday with the South China Morning Post. "The executive order is ten times more important than walking away from the trade deal. [Huawei] is a major national security threat, not just to the US but to the rest of the world. We are going to shut it down."[42]

---

41   "The President Takes On China, Alone." The New York Times. The New York Times, May 15, 2019. https://www.nytimes.com/2019/05/15/podcasts/the-daily/trump-china-trade-war.html.

42   Mai, Jun. "Steve Bannon Says Killing Huawei More Important than Trade Deal with China." South China Morning Post, May 23, 2019. https://

Unlike during the Peloponnesian War, conflict today is not fought with weapons to kill; rather, war consists of many new dimensions. States now have many more resources at their disposal, with greater control in economics, technology, and media. The Thucydides Trap, in the twenty-first century, will, therefore, encompass factors much greater than simply military standoffs through conventional weapons. For warfare to move beyond limits, it must become a complete military "Machiavelli" as the future battlefield will be beyond the battlefield.[43] The structural stresses caused by the Thucydides Trap will drag China and the United States closer and closer to a conflict that transcends boundaries.

Due to nuclear deterrence, the taboo of warfare, and the audience costs of direct military conflict, flashpoints between China and the United States will be largely invisible. Conflicts will manifest themselves in different ways, such as through the trade war. Other dimensions include the cyberspace, innovation, ecology, culture and media, space exploration, and many others. In a globalized world where actors are interdependent, the significance of boundaries is merely relative—the efficacy for international political competition has the potential to seep into many aspects of our lives.[44]

---

www.scmp.com/news/china/diplomacy/article/3011145/steve-bannon-says-killing-huawei-more-important-trade-deal.

43   Qiao, Liang, Al Santoli, and Xiangsui Wang. Unrestricted Warfare. Brattleboro, VT: Echo Point Books & Media, 2015.

44   Qiao, Liang, Al Santoli, and Xiangsui Wang. Unrestricted Warfare. Brattleboro, VT: Echo Point Books & Media, 2015.

Effectively, this situation can be represented by a three-dimensional chess game, with a struggle for victory on multiple layers of conflict.

Like Katniss Everdeen in *The Hunger Games*, countries exist in a state of anarchy in the international system. Each state faces off with the others, joins in on alliances, and develops its own hard power advantage vis-a-vis potential adversaries. This world is characterized by inherent distrust and the need for political survival, for the strong do what they can and the weak suffer what they must.[45] WWI occurred because of the structural stress imposed by this international system. Seeing how the conflict will play out between China and the United States will be interesting.

---

45   Thucydides. History of the Peloponnesian War. Place of publication not identified: Franklin Classics Trade Press, 2018.

CHAPTER 2

DOMESTIC FORCES

———

Our responsibility is to rally and lead the whole party and the Chinese people of all ethnic groups, take up this historic baton and continue working hard for the great renewal of the Chinese nation, so that we will stand rock firm in the family of nations and make fresh and greater contribution to mankind.

—XI JINPING

We will make America strong again. We will make America proud again. We will make America safe again. And we will make America great again.

—DONALD TRUMP

GUNS, OPIUM, AND TEA

Lord George Macartney and his entourage, weary after having braved the oceans for almost a year, finally set foot on the emperor's summer quarters. With as much order and pomp as they can muster, the entourage parades up the stairs to a small wooden palace, marching up the eight significant steps to the structure. They clutch the many gifts and wares in hand and wait in the sizzling summer heat as sweat drips down their brows. Only after many hours do their wills waver, and they return to their quarters.[46]

During the following days, mountains of gifts are exchanged between the English and the Chinese. English wares include rugs, wool, and many scientific and mechanical wonders that the nation had to offer—backed by its burgeoning industrial might. China provides many of its coveted goods such as velvet, silks, jade, porcelain, and tea. However, despite this outward show of pomp and friendship, Macartney's China expedition is doomed for failure.

Central to this encounter between the East and West were the contradictions in culture and expectations. Macartney departed Portsmouth, England, aboard three ships in 1792 to start his expedition in the hopes of negotiating with China to open up long-term trading opportunities for the English East India Company.[47] For the Chinese, on the other hand, this visit was simply an ordinary foreign embassy, which arrived in Beijing to give gifts to the great Qing Empire.

46   Platt, Stephen R. "How Britain's First Mission to China Went Wrong." China Channel, May 18, 2018. https://chinachannel.org/2018/05/18/macartney/.

47   Peyrefitte, Alain, and Jon Rothschild. The Immobile Empire. New York: Vintage Books, A Division of Random House, Inc., 2013.

An artistic rendition of Macartney's embassy. *(https://upload.wikimedia.org/wikipedia/commons/e/e4/LordMacartneyEmbassyTo-China1793.jpg)*

The Qing officials, dressed in long robes made of silk and decorated with motifs of animals, wearing red hats with hair tied up in queues, greeted Macartney and his priest interpreters. The two parties negotiated at the emperor's summer residence (Yuanming Yuan), a majestic oasis representing the zenith of Chinese imperial garden and palace design 800 acres in size.

A sticking point for Macartney's embassy is a matter of ceremony. Notably, Macartney insisted that he would not perform the "kowtow" to the Qianlong emperor. Despite his great admiration for the prosperity and civilization of the Qing Empire, he viewed Qianlong as an equal to the King of England, entitled only to the same show of respect. He insisted that he not prostrate himself before the emperor so as to distinguish powerful England from a small tributary state like Korea. Faced with the stubborn Macartney, the Chinese officials agreed.

A particular expectation was, for example, that Chinese tributary states like Vietnam and Korea come to the throne not to impress but to give gifts in exchange for legitimacy. By prostrating oneself to the powerful Qing empire, foreign visitors, in reality, strengthened the Qing's right to rule China. By recognizing the supremacy of China—the eminent power in Asia—the ambassadors would recognize the dominance within their own smaller countries. Lord Macartney and his entourage did not hold these expectations.

The day arrives when Macartney has an appointment with the Qianlong emperor. Macartney enters his hall, carrying above his head a jewel-encrusted golden box containing a letter from King George III. By his account, he ascends the steps to the throne and kneels on one knee as agreed, instead of performing the kowtow. Qianlong's eyes are "full and clear, and his countenance open," much to the surprise of Macartney, who expected a "dark and gloomy" demeanor.[48]

Macartney feels overcome by the elaborate spectacle of the audience tent, with its rich tapestries, carpets, and lanterns, "disposed with such harmony," he later writes in his journal. This encounter reflects what he describes as "that calm dignity, that sober pomp of Asiatic greatness, which European refinements have not yet attained."[49]

---

48   Platt, Stephen R. Imperial Twilight: The Opium War and the End of Chinas Last Golden Age. New York: Vintage Books, 2019.

49   Ibid.

However, Macartney has no idea how deeply he offended the emperor with his negotiations. Shortly after his embassy with the Qianlong emperor, the emperor sends an edict expressing his "great displeasure" with the British, declaring that he will no longer show them any new favors and that they will be escorted out of Beijing.[50]

"When foreigners who come seeking an audience with me are sincere and submissive, then I always treat them with kindness," Qianlong writes. *"But if they come in arrogance, they get nothing."* Macartney's and all of Britain's requests are doomed.[51] *Trade, to Qianlong, is in exceptional hands, and he sees no need to change more than a century of precedent to please one country. In words that will sting the British for a generation, he adds, "Strange and precious objects do not interest me. ...We possess all things. I set no value on objects strange or ingenious and have no use for your country's manufactures."*

Our Celestial Empire possesses all things in prolific abundance and lacks no product within its borders. There is, therefore, no need to import the manufactures of outside barbarians in exchange for our own produce.

—QIANLONG EMPEROR

Since imperial times, the Chinese have viewed the outside world as barbaric, including Macartney and his company

---

50   Ibid.

51   Platt, Stephen R. "How Britain's First Mission to China Went Wrong." China Channel, May 18, 2018. https://chinachannel.org/2018/05/18/macartney/.

from England. China was the center of the universe, and it demanded the respect fitting for its wealth and abundance. European countries had, throughout the nineteenth century, wished to gain access to Chinese goods but were abrogated by the Chinese. The West's frustration with China's nonconformist attitude continues today, with countries like the United States condemning the Asian giant's trade policies. Similarly, the United Kingdom in the eighteenth century was increasingly frustrated with its trade deficit with China. Driven by the country's obsession with tea—one of China's main exports—the trade gap was seen as problematic by British policymakers.[52]

During this time in the 1800s, tea was the rage in the English market; however, the East India Company struggled to find a product that would pique the interest of Chinese traders—that is, until they discovered the utility of opium. British traders soon arrived in troves to Canton with ships loaded with opium, slowly fueling an epidemic that would engulf China. The East India Company was able to supply the drug to China backed by its host country's vast colonial domain. The English had finally found a good that the Chinese wanted—and the Chinese wanted it on an unprecedented scale.

The opium crisis would spur the emperor to appoint viceroy Lin Zexu to eradicate this national malady. Lin quickly arrested Chinese opium dealers, demanding that foreign firms turn over their stocks with no compensation. When they refused, he stopped trade altogether and forced the merchants to surrender their opium, where Lin destroyed some total of

---

52   Black, Jeremy. British Foreign Policy in an Age of Revolutions: 1783-1793. Cambridge u.a.: Cambridge Univ. Press, 1994.

1,000 tons in a process that took twenty-three days. Tensions slowly rose until a series of events led to the United Kingdom firing upon Chinese civilians, using gunboat diplomacy, and starting the country's century of humiliation.

NATIONAL HUMILIATION

China's humiliating defeat during the First and Second Opium Wars was a wake-up call for the country's intellectuals. Despite having existed for thousands of years, the nation had never experienced its cultural history being threatened to this extent. This event was the start of China's Century of Humiliation (百年国耻), forever printed in the Chinese historical and political psyche.

The Opium Wars were started by Western nations that wished to exploit China's abundance of resources. Their incursion is truly a seminal moment in Chinese history—a dividing line between the country's imperial past and revolutionary future. Aroused with nationalism in the face of foreign invasion, intellectuals within the country advocated for a series of new political and technical modernizations to catch up with the advancements of the West. Only by modernizing could the country protect its people, culture, and resources.

The self-strengtheners were a group of individuals who, appalled by the intrusion of British influence over China, envisioned a stronger homeland. They dreamed of national rejuvenation propelled by the integration of new technological knowledge so that the country could fend off the West's gunboat diplomacy. However, they were mostly unsuccessful, as China plunged into even darker depths after the first two Opium Wars.

As head of the Grand Secretary during China's Self-Strengthening Movement, Woren believed Westerners were evil. They should not teach Chinese youth because they "not only set fire to the [Yuanming Yuan] and destroyed it but also indiscriminately murdered civilians."[53] He continued by writing that Westerners "have always been [China's] enemies," causing "humiliation [that] [was] unprecedented."[54]

After a terrible defeat by the British during the First Opium War, Chinese leaders were forced to sign a series of so-called "unequal treaties" that put the country into greater subservience to the West. The very identity of the Chinese civilization was at risk. The unequal treaties were only the start of the series of humiliations that China experienced. Later in the century, China would experience higher numbers of foreign incursions as well as internal revolts.

After the end of the Opium Wars, China underwent other historically significant events such as the Taiping Rebellion, defeat during the Sino-French War, defeat in the First Sino-Japanese War, the British Invasion of Tibet, and many more. All these events resulted in losses of resources, culture, and territory for the Chinese government. Most importantly, these setbacks stung the ego of Chinese society; with China having once been a great civilization, these humiliations were unthinkable.

---

53   Atwill, David G., and Yurong Y. Atwill. Sources in Chinese History: Diverse Perspectives from 1644 to the Present. Upper Saddle River, NJ: Pearson/Prentice Hall, 2010.

54   Ibid.

The Chinese view of imperialism. *(https://www.wikiwand.com/en/Century_of_humiliation)*

Not until the end of WWII and the ascent of the Chinese Communist Party over the Nationalist Party (that fled to Taiwan) did the country slowly regain its footing. In the 1920s, Chinese nationalists began spinning the arrival of Western gunboats as the cause of all the country's problems. Chairman Mao also blamed Western aggression for China's decline. And so emerged the narrative of China as a victim that can still be heard today, even as the country casts off its loser status.[55] China turned the Opium Wars into a founding legend of its struggle for modernity. The Century of Humiliation serves as the basis for much of China's political rhetoric and Chinese nationalism. The Chinese pride themselves on the country's long history and centrality in world affairs. After the rise of the Communist Party, the country started to regain its footing on the international stage. The Chinese, instead of calling the country's meteoric surge the "rise of China," see it as the "return" of China.

Any future developments and conflicts between China and the West (especially the United States) should consider the historical memory of the Chinese. Nationalism arising from history can be a constraint or catalyst for political decisions. When a state is faced with a tough political choice, for example, nationalism may force the government to adopt hardline or hawkish attitudes in its foreign affairs. Domestic nationalism is an attitude that needs to be balanced by political leaders.

---

55 "Be Careful What You Wish For." The Economist. The Economist Newspaper, n.d. https://www.economist.com/books-and-arts/2011/10/29/be-careful-what-you-wish-for.

Anti-Japan protesters shout slogans as they march outside the Japanese embassy in Beijing. *(https://www.economist.com/node/21563301/all-comments)*

Notably, in recent history, events concerning tensions between China and its East Asian neighbors have sparked dramatic events in Chinese cities. Vigilantes and mobs took to the streets in protest of the installation of missiles in South Korea, boycotting Korean goods. In another case, during a time of animosity between China and Japan over island territory disputes, Chinese mobs took to the streets to smash Japanese-made cars.

In the age of Xi Jinping, Chinese nationalism is on the rise. State-sponsored patriotism is very much a resource dispensable to the state, and in no way is it in short supply. In the context of US-China tensions, nationalism is a tool used by both the Chinese party-state and US governments, galvanizing the public to strengthen its resolve.

The Chinese people may see political pressure from the United States as a new form of attack by a foreign power, evoking memories of the humiliation that the country suffered during the Opium War. Not only is the United States a foreign power, but it has also fought two wars with China in the last century: the Korean and Vietnam Wars. Chinese citizens are starting to discuss more the relevance of these two wars in public discourse amid the current tensions between the two countries (in Chinese, called the War to Resist America and Aid Korea 抗美援朝战争).

How will political leaders from both sides of the Pacific reconcile with Chinese nationalism, and will the hardline attitudes of citizens become a roadblock in reconciliation? This question remains to be answered by experts.

CHINA DREAM

Soldiers marching in steady unison, the only sound ringing throughout the city the dramatic thundering of their boots. Like a pendulum, the sound rings out with a rhythmic beat. The soldiers keep their faces held high with a fair and stoic complexion. In the distance, one can hear the hum of tanks and trucks.

At Tiananmen Square, the country's newest technologies are on show, first to be seen by the world. From modern autonomous drones to missiles to intercontinental ballistic missiles able to deliver nuclear payloads around the world, the country's next-generation weapons are on proud display, showing the might of the new China under Xi Jinping. The parade is a real manifestation of the China Dream, representing China's new power in technology, with many of the new weapons domestically developed. It signals that China will no longer allow itself to be bullied by other nations.

"On the bank of the Yellow River, gather the fine sons of the Chinese people;

To liberate mankind, to defend our motherland, we'll carry out our duty...

Like the Yellow River, surging and sweeping forward, drive the Japanese invaders out of our land!"

The chorus booms as the parade marches through Tiananmen Square, the same place where, seventy years ago, Mao Zedong declared the founding of the People's Republic after having driven out the Japanese. The sun is blinding in the blue sky, yet the soldiers remain unblinking. They salute in perfect unison, each with one white-gloved hand raised to their helmet and the other hand firmly gripping their weapon. As the military band continues to blow into their horns and sing, the audience gawks in awe at the country's newfound military might, collectively taking a breath as the Chinese flag is flung out and slowly raised by the flagbearer on the flagpole. Everyone begins to sing.

"Arise, ye who refuse to be slaves;

With our very flesh and blood Let us build our new Great Wall!...

Brave the enemy's gunfire march on!

March on! March on! March on, on!"

Time is suspended at the final loud sound of the gong of the last beat of the anthem. The pomp and drama of the moment only amplifies the tension as Xi takes to the podium on Tiananmen Gate, addressing the audience. This place is where Mao once stood, declaring the founding of the People's Republic. Seventy years later, China is celebrating its seventieth anniversary of the victory over Japan during World War II. Present are over thirty heads of state and leaders of government, such as the likes of Russian President Vladimir Putin, South Korean President Park Geun-Hye, South African President Jacob Zuma, and many more.[56]

Before this grand parade, roads were shut down, public transportation was closed, hospitals restricted their activities, the stock markets closed, and parts of the city center were even placed under martial law by the government. Macaques and falcons were sent out to remove bird nests to hinder the possibility of a bird collision with a plane.[57] Domestic satellite televisions stopped airing entertainment programs, and China Central Television only broadcast programs and films about WWII. To reduce air pollution and ensure blue skies for the parade, half of Beijing's cars were barred from the streets, and nearly 10,000 industrial factories in Beijing

---

56 Cgtn. "China Releases List of World Leaders Attending V-Day Parade." CGTN America, September 8, 2015. https://america.cgtn.com/2015/08/25/china-releases-list-of-world-leaders-attending-v-day-parade.

57 "Trained Monkeys and Eagles Ensure Flight Safety for V-Day." Trained Monkeys and Eagles Ensure Flight Safety for V-Day – People's Daily Online, September 1, 2015. http://en.people.cn/n/2015/0901/c90000-8944059.html.

and areas near and far (Hebei, Tianjin, Shanxi, Inner Mongolia, Shandong, and Henan) suspended or cut production to reduce emissions.

This parade was the quintessential indicator of China's rising nationalism. After taking power in 2013, Xi solidified himself as the country's de facto ruler, espousing his trademark "China Dream." The China Dream is a dream of a Chinese renaissance, stressing economic, political, and cultural renewal, founded upon the party-state's rhetoric surrounding its founding legend of the Century of Humiliation and the unification of the country under the Communist banner at the end of WWII.

In the field of economics, China has undergone a number of reforms since the Reform and Opening Up period of the 1970s and 1980s, spearheaded by Deng Xiaoping. The open endorsement of capitalism by policies would have been an unthinkable act before the time of Deng. In the twenty-first century, the ideology of the CCP has fundamentally changed, lowering the constraints on government policies and rhetoric. The government now has greater freedom in promoting progressive private-sector policies, causing an explosion in economic growth.

Today, we can also see a resurgence in interest over Confucianism not only as a way to counter Western criticisms of the country's political system but also as a source of pride in China's ancient culture and the longevity of its philosophy. The China Dream is genius in its ambiguity. Though the conventional Western interpretation of the China Dream is a returning of China to the center of the world as the Middle Kingdom (translation from Chinese 中国), it also indicates a new age in China where individuals are now allowed to dream again after Mao's dark era, with a return of traditional Chinese values immortalized through the work of Zhuangzi (i.e., the Butterfly Dream Parable) and Confucius.[58] However, the central theme of national rejuvenation remains and continues to stay consistent with the trend of China's increasing interest in bringing back Chinese imperial culture, so much of which was lost and buried during the tumultuous period of the Century of Humiliation.

"Nation," as defined by the Oxford dictionary, is "a large body of people united by common descent, history, culture, or language, inhabiting a particular country or territory." Consequently, the definition of "nationalism" is the belief that one's nation is more significant than another's.

One can consider modern Chinese nationalism to be the perversion of patriotism—the devotion to one's country and culture, politics notwithstanding. The party has ramped up its rhetoric of national rejuvenation and the China Dream. From the perspective of Chinese nationalists now, criticisms of the Chinese Communist Party by outsiders become criticisms of China itself, five thousand years of history and all. Even intellectuals who are wholly Chinese and patriotic are afraid of public retribution from their peers by speaking out. Instead of offering legitimate thoughts and analyses on the

---

58   Chai, Winberg, and May-lee Chai. "The Meaning of Xi Jinping's Chinese Dream." American Journal of Chinese Studies 20, no. 2 (2013): 95–97.

country's future, these intellectuals self-censor in the fear of public backlash in a trial by the populace.

If ethnic Chinese people face backlash from their peers, what is the response to foreign criticism? Within the US-China bilateral relationship, international media coverage has lost credibility in the eyes of Chinese nationalists. These nationalists are very supportive of the China Dream, fighting against so-called foreign forces, fixating on territorial disputes and historical conflicts with other countries.

Indeed, Chinese nationalism can be exhibited by a belief of superiority in not only the political system but also "descent, history, culture, or language." Hence it has engulfed the meaning of Chinese patriotism. The Chinese Communist Party, through its campaign of propaganda and nationalistic education, has long since changed the discussion around what it means to love one's country. Due to the exaltation of the China Dream, anti-nationalism has become antigovernment, and antigovernment is now also antipatriotism. Necessarily, for one to love China and its history, one must also like the party, as the two have become inseparable.

The belief in Chinese cultural and historical exceptionalism will become a significant issue in US-China relations. How will the two countries manage this critical bilateral relationship without invoking the pains, and subsequent nationalism, of the past? Criticism of China should not be conflated with a wholesale attack on other aspects of the country. Currently, the intellectual critique of China's governance system is becoming less and less objective.

CHINESE STABILITY

A contributing factor to Chinese nationalism is the stability of the Chinese state. For the past twenty years, it has enjoyed steady economic growth, providing better living standards for its over one billion citizens. The government has imposed greater censorship to homogenize thoughts as well as defined new international norms and institutions, crafting its own world order. The growth in China's economy and its capacity for governance is enviable. So far, Chinese society remains resilient and stable.

Some scholars scrutinize China, arguing that the end game of Chinese communism will soon begin.[59] These scholars also believe that the CCP must embrace genuine systematic democratic change lest it experience a revolution. However, the country's stability is not necessarily made weaker by an authoritarian system. An authoritarian state can enjoy economic growth and stability. In fact, economic growth and stability create the performance legitimacy that buttresses regime support. Chinese authoritarianism is indeed viable even under conditions of advanced modernization and integration with the global economy. Stability and authoritarianism can coexist, and performance-based legitimacy and nationalism are supporting the Chinese state.

Instability in China may not cause the emergence of democracy. On the other hand, it can, in fact, cause the country to become more authoritarian. China's high-ranking officials

---

59   Shambaugh, David. "China's Soft-Power Push." Foreign Affairs. Foreign Affairs Magazine, September 3, 2015. https://www.foreignaffairs.com/ articles/china/2015-06-16/china-s-soft-power-push.

have no interest in the argument that democratization will lead to stability, as convincing as it may sound to the democrats of the world.[60] The government's insecurity regarding instability can actually lead to increased authoritarian oppression. Democracy, in certain instances, can even be a catalyst for instability. Using cases from the Middle East, we see that the introduction of democracy to weak states leads to power struggles characterized by regionalism and ethnic conflicts.

Chinese nationalism and the stability of Chinese society intertwine to make a highly resilient nation, bounded by not only historical roots but also by the country's economic and political advancements. The result is a society ready to face the challenges and responsibilities of being one of the most prominent nations in the world. It is also a society ready to face the pressures from the United States for being number two in the world.

THE ROLE OF PROTESTS IN CHINA

While an observer might believe that China's authoritarian system suppresses all forms of protests, certain ones are, in fact, welcomed by the government and embraced by citizens.

Contrary to popular belief, a high level of activism exists in China. Based on statistical data, scholar Wenfang Tang asserts that trusting the central government makes people

---

60   Nathan, Andrew J. (Andrew James). "Authoritarian Resilience." Journal of Democracy 14, no. 1 (2003): 6–17. https://doi.org/10.1353/jod.2003.0019.

in China protest more.[61] This counterintuitive phenomenon reveals citizens' comfort with the central government. They likely see Beijing as an authority figure that protects citizens' interests. To have this point of view, citizens must first be confident that CCP bureaucrats care about the country and that they have the authority to create change. The citizens thus feel confident challenging their local officials, knowing they have the support of the central government. If they are not supportive of the regime, they may take issues into their own hands rather than appealing to the government.

On the other hand, the party is also supportive of protests. According to Yongshun Cai, the government is faced with a dilemma: concession leads to "more resistance" and repression "damages the regime's legitimacy."[62] Therefore, it differentiates between the local government and the central government to direct the populace's frustration away from the core. Not only does this strategy retain the central government's legitimacy, but it also is a mechanism for information collection on societal grievances.

In other words, CCP leaders concede the legitimacy of its lower echelons while maintaining the authority of higher echelons. The Center, by siding with rebellious citizens in opposition to local governments, paints itself as a responsible

---

61   Tang, Wenfang. "The 'Surprise' of Authoritarian Resilience in China." American Affairs Journal, February 20, 2018. https://americanaffairs-journal.org/2018/02/surprise-authoritarian-resilience-china/.

62   Cai, Yongshun. "Power Structure and Regime Resilience: Contentious Politics in China." British Journal of Political Science 38, no. 3 (2008): 411–32. https://doi.org/10.1017/s0007123408000215.

guardian; yet, at the same time, it retains a firm grasp on the local governments. This strategy of intentional irresponsible management empowers citizens, giving them a sense of control and democratic participation. Indeed, based on surveys done by Yun-han Chu, citizens trust the central government more than their local government.[63] The differentiation between the local and central, alongside intraparty condemnation of local irresponsibility, could be a form of psychological control that allows the central leadership to solidify its rule. In reality, the central party has the efficacy to manage local governments before citizens point their problems.

Not only does the CCP welcome protests, but citizens openly embrace them as the status quo. Citizens are "emboldened by what often seems to be a genuine belief" about their rights, spurring them toward activism.[64] Criticizing the scapegoat that is their local government, citizens vent their grievances without inhibition by using the concept of "rightful resistance."[65] Thus citizens see protests as a norm that is acceptable in Chinese society. With the spread of new technologies, they are now more empowered to police problematic behaviors of their local government. By not censoring these voices of local dissent online, the CCP also shows its support for local activism.[66]

---

63   Chu, Yun-han. How East Asians View Democracy. New York: Columbia University Press, 2010.

64   Obrien, Kevin J., and Lianjiang Li. "Rightful Resistance." Rightful Resistance in Rural China, n.d., 1–24. https://doi.org/10.1017/cbo9780511791086.003.

65   Ibid.

66   King, Gary, Jennifer Pan, and Margaret E. Roberts. "How Censorship in China Allows Government Criticism but Silences Collective Expression."

The central government maintains the status quo by standing atop a mountain, watching the tumultuous relationship between the lower government and its citizens. However, how long will this status quo last? As scholar Kevin O'Brien mentions, low-level protests may "presage the stirrings of a more far-reaching counterhegemonic project."[67] How will the government respond when the center is faced with protest? Will the current situation in Xinjiang lead to developments reminiscent of the Tiananmen Square incident when the Center is directly challenged? How will the government deal with the rightful resistance of radical left-wing students? Time will test the resilience of the Chinese party-state.

CHINESE COMMUNIST IDEOLOGY

Since Deng Xiaoping, Chinese politics have become less ideologically driven. Some observers, as a result, may argue that ideology doesn't influence politics. However, one needs to understand that the issue of ideological legitimacy is very real for the CCP. The relationship between ideology and action does not always have to be explicit.

To prove that it is the rightful leader of China, the CCP has to justify its ideological base. One striking example is the "Resolution on Certain Questions in the History of Our Party

---

American Political Science Review 107, no. 2 (2013): 326–43. https://doi.org/10.1017/s0003055413000014.

67   Obrien, Kevin J., and Lianjiang Li. "Rightful Resistance." Rightful Resistance in Rural China, n.d., 1–24. https://doi.org/10.1017/cbo9780511791086.003.

since the Founding of the PRC," in which it "reaffirms that [Mao's] ideology remains 'the valuable spiritual asset of our party' and that 'it will be our guide to action for a long time to come.'"[68] The creation of this document indicates the party's need to regain ideological footing after the tumultuous Mao years. Only then can it continue its program of economic opening-up without ideological incoherency, as such reforms would have been seen as apostasy during the Mao years.

William Joseph argues that "ideology is woven into the political fabric of every society," which is especially true of Chinese society, where the country is run by a single-party state.[69] As author Robert Dahl expresses in his book *Democracy and its Critics*, an authoritarian government that is like a "guardian" in nature could, in fact, be very robust, such as the Republic of Venice.[70] However, I would add that such a government must be guided by an ideological glue that informs action and inspires loyalty. In the case of China, the government interprets and adjusts the concept of Marxism to suit its interests. Indeed, especially convenient is when "Marx's theory is incomplete or ambiguous in many places and could be 'applied' in contradictory ways without manifestly infringing its principles."[71] Ideology gives identity and a political platform for a group. Similar to how political

---

68   Joseph, William A. Politics in China: an Introduction. New York: Oxford University Press, 2019.

69   Ibid.

70   Dahl, Robert A. Democracy and Its Critics. Johanneshov: MTM, 2019.

71   Kolakowski, Leszek. Main Currents of Marxism: Its Origins, Growth and Dissolution. Oxford: Oxford University Press, 1978.

parties cannot survive in a multiparty state without a solid ideological platform, an authoritarian state cannot win the loyalty of its people if its identity is surrounded by ambiguity. Only with an ideology will citizens better understand, connect with, and trust the ruling regime. In China, therefore, Marxism acts as a particularly useful ideology; the government can use it for regime legitimization as well as take advantage of its ambiguity and malleability to justify various societal changes.

Does public opinion exist in China? At the outset, one could easily reply in the positive: yes, there is public opinion in China; besides, why wouldn't there be a general opinion? However, I question the notion of Chinese public opinion itself. To what extent is public opinion created by the populace? And how much ownership do they have over this "public" opinion?

For one, nationalistic rhetoric is rife in Chinese media, and the outside observer would assume that the people of China are highly politically conscious—that public opinions over certain political matters exist. Anything and everything in China can be politicized. I would, on the contrary, argue that despite a widespread publicity campaign, the people of China, in fact, do not have a public opinion over matters of politics.

If people are indoctrinated since birth to think a certain way, their deeply entrenched beliefs will remain throughout their lives. Such is the case with the populace in China. Public opinion has been warped by the state so much so that it should no longer be considered "public" opinion.

Instead, the term "state-imposed view" is more fitting. As this state-sponsored opinion gets passed down through generations, it becomes a state religion, unchallenged and informing how people live their lives. After all, do we call religion "public opinion?" Oftentimes, religion is regarded as the truth.

State-imposed opinion is an echo chamber, presenting the illusion that people have freedom over their opinions. Given mechanisms such as social media, mandatory school education, and censorship, people in China do not have access to the plethora of information that people in the West receive. Further, those with different views may self-censor for fear of retribution or ostracization from their peers. Indeed, we can see a high degree of similarity between the ideological preferences of the party and its people.[72]

Furthermore, the actions of the state have the chance to define the opinion of people. As scholars Jennifer Pan and Yiqing Xu posit, the geographic influence of China's Reform and Opening Up period has the propensity to sway citizens' views on the economic policy of the government.[73] Thus, do the people of China really have a public opinion? Perhaps they are only influenced by the control of the party-state.

---

72   Ji, Chengyuan, and Junyan Jiang. "Enlightened One-Party Rule? Ideological Differences between Chinese Communist Party Members and the Mass Public." Political Research Quarterly, 2019, 106591291985034. https://doi.org/10.1177/1065912919850342.

73   Pan, Jennifer, and Yiqing Xu. "Chinas Ideological Spectrum." SSRN Electronic Journal, 2015. https://doi.org/10.2139/ssrn.2593377.

MAKE AMERICA GREAT AGAIN

China is not the only country striving for national rejuvenation. Across the Pacific is another powerful country, led by a new, audacious, and loud-spoken leader who pledges to return his country to its historical greatness. Under the banner "Make America Great Again," US President Donald Trump is no different to Xi Jinping in his nationalist, populist rhetoric. Rooted in this nationalism is the belief of American exceptionalism. Just like China looks back to history to inform its place in the world, the United States, too, has its founding legend.

Having just won the war against the United Kingdom, the United States was a young and ambitious state, founded by a new breed of fearless men and women who voyaged across the ocean in search of a new life. These people, according to Alexander Tocqueville, were so enamored in the radical ideas of equality and liberty that they would "rather be equal in slavery than unequal in freedom."[74] Indeed, the new United States of America was truly a cauldron of liberty and ambition unbounded, an inheritor of European ingenuity yet unrestricted by a monarchy and filled with a continental destiny that spurred it to action.

While Chinese exceptionalism looks back to its 5,000 years of uniquely continuous civilization, Americans see the United States as the first new and modern nation.[75] Indeed, Alexander Hamilton in the late eighteenth century suggested that

---

74 Tocqueville, Alexis de, Arthur Goldhammer, and Olivier Zunz. Democracy in America. New York: Library of America Paperback Classics, 2012.

75 Callahan, William A. "Dreaming as a Critical Discourse of National Belonging: China Dream, American Dream and World Dream." Nations

the United States had come up with a new and unique form of "political science" as an innovation in governance, different from other democratic forms of government of the past.[76]

Another example of American exceptionalism can be seen in interpretations of the United States' role and position in the world. Throughout history, the United States has used its exceptionalism views as the impetus for foreign policy decisions. Speaking on the greatness of US political ingenuity, John L. O'Sullivan argues that the birth of America "was the beginning of a new history, the formation and progress of an untried political system, which separates us from the past and connects us with the future only."[77] The United States sees itself as a new and innovative country, destined for greatness due to its position of taking the first step into a new age. The United States saw itself as different from monarchist Europe yet continued to hold the European belief of cultural superiority over the other parts of the world. Therefore, it justified engaging in imperialism over different parts of the world.

What do domestic attitudes and rhetoric have to do with the current relationship between China and the United States in the twenty-first century? Different from the international

and Nationalism 23, no. 2 (March 2017): 248–70. https://doi.org/10.1111/nana.12296.

76 Hamilton, Alexander, James Madison, and John Jay. The Federalist Papers. New York: New American Library, 1962.

77 Wilsey, John. "'Our Country Is Destined to Be the Great Nation of Futurity': John L. O'Sullivan's Manifest Destiny and Christian Nationalism, 1837–1846." Religions 8, no. 4 (2017): 68. https://doi.org/10.3390/rel8040068.

structural issues discussed in the last section, domestic forces within China and the United States can draw the two countries closer and closer into conflict. Take, for instance, a flareup in places like the South China Sea. Due to sentiments of nationalism between the two countries, politicians on both sides of the Pacific will be pressured to take antagonistic or hardline stances rather than conciliatory attitudes lest they put their domestic credibility in danger. The South China Sea is seen by China as an ancient and historical right, while, to the United States, it goes against its values of freedom and democracy.

Xi and Trump will be hard-pressed not to go against their political platforms and risk their credibility and status as strongman politicians in their respective countries. After all, how can China overcome the Century of National Humiliation and fulfill the China Dream by backing down to Western influence in an area where China believes it has a historic right? For the United States, with the widespread consensus around the Western democratic world order and the so-called "End of History," how can it allow China to grow its influence internationally as a fundamentally nondemocratic and authoritarian regime? Thus, in addition to international structural forces and the balance of power, as described in the first chapter, ideology, nationalism, domestic sentiment, and norms can also force the two countries into conflict.

Another danger in domestic politics is the beliefs of politicians themselves. The prevailing national sentiment and public discourse in the two countries can force upcoming politicians to genuinely hold hardline and nationalist policies. In the United States, for example, public opinion, the education system, the media, and the electoral system can inherently create politicians who have hardline policies against China. A common complaint of Chinese individuals and students living in the United States is that they believe the ordinary American holds unreasonably antagonistic attitudes toward China and its political system, perhaps a remnant of Cold War propaganda and the spinning of China as the new scapegoat in the media.

Thus, individuals who become politicians may become hostile toward China. When these people enter fields of politics or business, holding a stakeholder position in global affairs, the United States may be drawn into conflict with China. In China, on the other hand, politicians can still fall victim to its rhetoric. One must remember that the Chinese Communist Party is the largest political party in the world, with over eighty-eight million members.

In China, party membership does not necessarily mean that you have to be a politician. Instead, those who excel in various areas of the industry are welcomed to apply to join the party—like teachers, businesspeople, etc. Becoming a party member in China is an incredibly competitive process, with only the most capable of applying getting to join. Contrary to popular conception in the West, membership in the Chinese Communist Party is not as politically involved as it seems. By joining the party, an individual can gain various social benefits from the government as well as a higher level of social status; furthermore, having party membership allows one to progress faster up the ladder of business (which is especially important if someone works in a state-owned enterprise).

However, the institution of party selection itself is a process of ideological training and indoctrination. Individuals need to pass exams, do thought analysis, and study the government rhetoric of the period, such as Xi's trademark ideology of Xi Jinping Thought of Socialism with Chinese Characteristics for a New Era. Compounded by the fact that only a slim 2 percent of party cadres involved with politics progress up the party hierarchy, the institution itself places those with certain ideological elements in positions of power. Therefore, the process involves the same tunnel vision that may exist on the American side, as well as the type of domestic ideological inertia that is putting the two world powers on a collision course. This internal echo chamber of public local opinion, political rhetoric, and nationalism is making the relationship between China and the United States precarious. Internally, the world is indeed looking a lot like that before the start of World War One, one led by political strongmen and fired-up passions of the masses, calling for hawkish foreign policy.

At the start of the twentieth century, intellectual leader and Indiana Senator Albert J. Beveridge was on the campaign trail. He gave a speech regarding his views on the United States' position in the world and how it should conduct its foreign policy:

It is a glorious history our God has bestowed upon His chosen people; a history heroic with faith in our mission and our future; a history of statesmen who flung the boundaries of the Republic out into unexplored lands and savage wilderness; a history of soldiers who carried the flag across blazing deserts and through the ranks of hostile mountains, even to the gates of sunset; a history of a multiplying people who overran a continent in half a century; a history of prophets who saw the consequences of evils inherited from the past and of martyrs who died to save us from them a history divinely logical, in the process of whose tremendous reasoning we found ourselves today.[78]

ALBERT J. BEVERIDGE

The domestic rhetoric between the two states, as well as their respective history in foreign affairs, pits them against each other. From the US campaign in the Middle East and the Philippines to Manifest Destiny and the Marshall Plan, the country has had a history of influencing global affairs with its technological, military, and political clout. This influence is justified through its exceptional founding and history and the belief of its destiny of shaping the world in various dimensions.

A similar case exists in China. In recent history, the country's government has become more assertive internationally, from the One Belt One Road project to the Asia Infrastructure Investment Bank (AIIB) to territorial disputes in the East and South Seas, the country is becoming stronger in the international stage.

Domestic rhetoric is forcing the two countries into a game of chicken. Neither party is willing to back down, lest it lose face in front of its local audience, which has put the two countries in a constant game of one-upmanship. When a spark ignites, and the two countries engage in all-out conflict,

---

78 Beveridge, Albert. MARCH OF THE FLAG: Beginning of Greater America. Place of publication not identified: FORGOTTEN Books, 2016.

		Player 2	
		Compromise	Don't compromise
Player 1	Compromise	(0,0)	(-1,1)
	Don't compromise	(1,-1)	(-10,-10)

A game of chicken. (*http://www.gametheorystrategies.com/2011/08/03/ normal-form-games/*)

neither side will win. In this cauldron of domestic opinion, the concoction will be highly poisonous.

The rhetoric in both countries has set the precedence of expansionism, and the shared ambitions of both China and the United States may collide in the future. In the past, the two states have explored expansionism through the use of technological and economic advantages, coercing other countries through military or financial means. Now the omen of national rhetoric is manifesting itself on the global stage, with the two inching closer and closer to a conflict in the twenty-first century. In this century, a similar theme will play out internationally but much of the battle will be invisible to the human eye and happen behind the scenes.

Recent developments in the second decade of the twenty-first century have continued to undermine the relationship between the United States and China. Since becoming president, Trump has not only decreased the soft power of the United States on the international stage by pulling the country out of supranational organizations like UNICEF but also alienated the Chinese.

Trump was the one who declared the so-called trade war against China, imposing various forms of economic attacks. Not only has this move hurt the economies of both countries, but it has become useful fodder for Chinese nationalism. The Chinese government and its people believe that the United States and some of its Western allies are co-conspirators, attempting to suffocate China. When put in the context of the Century of Humiliation, the US campaign against China invokes crucial historical memory within China. Chinese state media China Central Television (CCTV) has started broadcasting more programs of the Korean War, rallying Chinese people to bear the brunt of US attacks.

On the other hand, Americans are gaining a steadily worse view of China. While China's soft power has never been durable in Western countries due to ideological differences as well as the memory of the Cold War, the echo chamber of US public opinion has created a tyranny of the majority in American society. The dominant thought within main-stream US discourse is that China is an "evil" country that must be contained and that it has been cheating the United States for several years. One of the effects of this view is the demonization of Chinese nationals (such as students, researchers, business people, and others). Thus, recent events have made the domestic opinions of both countries toward each other deteriorate. The two countries might not be able to work together to foster a more positive relation-ship for a while.

The international stability offered by a U.S-led world order will inevitably become a relic of the past, even if China fails. We are returning to a world in which realism dominates, reminiscent of the lead-up to WWI. Today's world is characterized by national competition, nationalism, powerful new technological advancements, and spheres of influence. Though Chinese hegemony is not guaranteed, the country's ambitions will send ripples through the international community. We already see the escalating tensions between the United States and China, with the opening salvo being the trade war. We are entering a volatile time.

In this struggle, the deepest and longest-lasting is the competition in the field of science and technology. With the further development of digital technologies such as AI, 5G, IoT, cloud, new materials, and quantum computing, human beings are welcoming in the fourth industrial revolution; science and technology affect all military, economic, security, and financial fields. The struggle is also for the development and leading power of the long-term comprehensive strength of the two countries.

PART TWO

CHAPTER 3

CHINESE TECHNOLOGY: A Boom of Development

The Chinese entrepreneurs have thrived, in part, because they created companies able to change as China changed.

—EDWARD TSE

FLYING MACHINES

Sporting a pair of dark rectangular glasses and a small tuft of chin stubble, Frank Wang does not come across as a remarkable multibillionaire. However, under his signature golf cap lies an incredibly brilliant and philosophical man, who stands at the forefront of China's entrepreneurial and technological rise. From a young age, Frank has been in love with flying objects, perhaps because of the influence of his engineer father.[79]

---

79 "Frank Wang." Yo! Success, August 20, 2016. https://www.yosuccess. com/success-stories/frank-wang-dji-technology/.

He used to pour over learning about model airplanes during his spare time, dreaming that one day he would be able to create these flying machines. However, with a less-than-stellar academic performance during his high school years, he was unable to land a spot at his dream schools of MIT and Stanford, instead ending up at the Hong Kong University of Science and Technology, where he set out to study electrical engineering.

Frank found his calling in his university years and devoted everything to his passion, skipping classes and often staying awake until the break of dawn, designing and creating flight-controller systems. In 2006, Frank and a couple of his friends decided to move their dormitory workshop to the nearby manufacturing hub of Shenzhen, where they lived in a three-bedroom apartment, collectively working on these systems out of Frank's meager funding from his university scholarship.[80]

Thankfully, according to Frank's professor Li Zexiang, "good performance [at work] was not necessarily comparable with good grades." Li now owns 10 percent of Frank's company, serving as its chairman. Indeed, in the West, this company would be known as DJI (Dajiang Innovations Science and Technology Co.), famous for its unmanned aerial vehicles. DJI currently holds 70 percent of the drone market.[81] Part of

80   Chiu, Karen. "The Story of Drone Pioneer DJI." Abacus, October 2, 2018. https://www.abacusnews.com/whois-whatis/dji-dominates-world-drones/article/2128689.

81   Borak, Masha. "World's Top Drone Seller DJI Made $2.7 Billion in 2017 · TechNode." TechNode, July 24, 2018. https://technode.com/2018/01/03/

DJI's strength derives from its location. Situated in China's manufacturing hub, Shenzhen, DJI is close to its factories, allowing it to design a part in the morning and build it for testing in the afternoon. In 2017, the company reported revenues of $2.83 billion.[82]

In the annals of technology, a company like DJI cannot often grab a dominant position in a market as fast as it did, taking technology from the hobbyist to mainstream. It was the first company that integrated a camera with a multirotor copter.

Widespread commercial use is already well underway: drones broadcast live aerial footage at the 2018 Golden Globes; relief workers rely on them to map the destruction left behind by Nepal's 7.8-magnitude earthquake; farmers in Iowa are using them to monitor cornfields. Facebook will be using its UAVs to provide wireless Internet to rural parts of Africa. DJI drones are even being used by professionals on the sets of *Game of Thrones* and the newest *Star Wars* film.

CROSS THE RIVER BY FEELING FOR THE STONES

Frank's achievements would not have been possible if he were born in a previous generation. Once controlled by political hardliners who firmly believed in a centrally planned economic system, China was once an economically backward

---

worlds-top-drone-seller-dji-made-2-7-billion-2017/.

82 Wang, Ying. "Drone-Maker DJI to Develop More Industry Applications." China Daily. China Daily, January 27, 2018. http://www.chinadaily.com. cn/a/201801/27/WS5a6bd252a3106e7dcc1371b0.html.

country. Not until the country's economic liberalization in the 1980s did entrepreneurs like Frank start to spring up throughout the country, propelling China to become the technological juggernaut it is today.[83]

The classic story takes place in the sleepy fishing village of Shenzhen, where fewer than 30,000 inhabitants once lived, scattered about in various small clusters. After being deemed the first Special Economic Zone by the central government in 1980, Shenzhen experienced an urban and economic explosion of epic proportions. The city is now known as Asia's Silicon Valley, home to twelve million people and technology giants such as DJI.[84] No one calls Shenzhen their hometown, simply because the city is so young.

As high-tech entrepreneurship continues to become an ever more critical economic driver, the Chinese government is increasingly aware of the need to promote such bases of entrepreneurship and technological development. Deng Xiaoping, China's paramount leader during the latter half of the twentieth century, famously stated that the country should "cross the river by feeling for the stones," referring to a pragmatic approach of economic reform through experimentation. The government created many crucibles of economic liberalization like Shenzhen, allowing market economics to

---

83   Chang, Weih, and Ian C. Macmillan. "A Review of Entrepreneurial Development in the People's Republic of China." Journal of Business Venturing 6, no. 6 (1991): 375–79. https://doi.org/10.1016/0883-9026(91)90026-a.

84   "Shenzhen, China Population." World Population Statistics, n.d. https://populationstat.com/china/shenzhen.

pull the country out of its fiscal rut. As a result, the private sector began to grow.

Today's China is more entrepreneurial. New policies sharply contrast the government's pre-1978 rhetoric, creating an optimistic outlook for entrepreneurs. In a *Xinhua* article titled "China Advocates Entrepreneurial Spirit to Boost Innovation," the government officially affirms the importance of entrepreneurs, pledging to give a "long-lasting boost to mass innovation and entrepreneurship."[85] Furthermore, the country's "11th Five-Year Plan" (between 2006 and 2010) echoes a similar government sentiment, identifying the need to build China into an "innovative state."[86]

The open endorsement of capitalism in such policies would have been an unthinkable act before the time of Deng. In the twenty-first century, however, the ideology of the CCP has fundamentally changed, lowering the constraints on government policies and rhetoric. The government now has greater freedom in promoting progressive private-sector policies. Though the party continues to be politically authoritarian, its opening-up policies have greatly benefited the Chinese economy.

---

85   Bo, Xiang. "China Focus: China Increases Science Education to Boost Innovation." Xinhua, September 1, 2017. http://www.xinhuanet.com/english/2017-09/01/c_136574669.htm.

86   Zheng, Yongnian, and Minjia Chen. "China Plans to Build an Innovative State." China Policy Institute, June 2006. https://www.nottingham.ac.uk/iaps/documents/cpi/briefings/briefing-9-china-innovative-state.pdf.

In research conducted by Farhat Rasool, several elements catalyze entrepreneurship:[87]

- The existence of a stable government, ensuring confidence among the general public regarding the continuity of government policy toward the small, medium, and large business.[88]
- Government expenditures. Individuals are more likely to invest and participate in riskier business activity due to expansionary fiscal policy. Alternatively, direct government spending on entrepreneurship initiatives may have a positive benefit.[89]
- The education level of the population. The level of education of a country's citizens can influence the prevalence of the country's private-sector entrepreneurship activities.

Other research conducted by Rolf Sternberg and Sander Wennekers points to more elements that indicate possible prerequisites for entrepreneurship:[90]

---

87 Rasool, Farhat, Ahmed Gulzar, and Shaheen Naseer. "Drivers of Entrepreneurship: Linking With Economic Growth and Employment Generation (A Panel Data Analysis)." The Pakistan Development Review 51, no. 4II (January 2012): 587–606. https://doi.org/10.30541/v51i4iipp.587-606.

88 Ibid.

89 Ibid.

90 Sternberg, Rolf, and Sander Wennekers. "Determinants and Effects of New Business Creation Using Global Entrepreneurship Monitor Data." Small Business Economics 24, no. 3 (2005): 193–203. https://doi.org/10.1007/s11187-005-1974-z.

- The stage of economic development of a country. The prevalence and impact of entrepreneurial activity differ between countries in different stages of economic development.[91]
- The social capital of enterprising individuals. Venture capitalists use social relationships to deal with risk, as personal connections have a "moderating" effect on investment selection.[92] Furthermore, as early-stage entrepreneurs have weaker access to venture capitalists, their connection with angel investors become essential. Angel investors are often found through personal relationships.[93]

THE EXISTENCE OF A STABLE GOVERNMENT

Government stability is crucial for economic growth.[94] In the context of the Chinese party-state, the government has continued Deng's policy of economic liberalization. Hence entrepreneurs do not have to continually adapt to the changing

---

91   Ibid.

92   Batjargal, Bat, and Mannie (Manhong) Liu. "Entrepreneurs' Access to Private Equity in China: The Role of Social Capital." Organization Science 15, no. 2 (2004): 159–72. https://doi.org/10.1287/orsc.1030.0044.

93   Li, Changhong, Yulin Shi, Cong Wu, Zhenyu Wu, and Li Zheng. "Policies of Promoting Entrepreneurship and Angel Investment: Evidence from China." Emerging Markets Review 29 (2016): 154–67. https://doi. org/10.1016/j.ememar.2016.08.011.

94   Rasool, Farhat, Ahmed Gulzar, and Shaheen Naseer. "Drivers of Entrepreneurship: Linking With Economic Growth and Employment Generation (A Panel Data Analysis)." The Pakistan Development Review 51, no. 4II (January 2012): 587–606. https://doi.org/10.30541/v51i4iipp.587-606.

rules of the game, becoming more confident in risk-taking.[95] Given the trajectory of progressive policies in the twenty-first century, entrepreneurs are also optimistic about future business opportunities and incentives.

GOVERNMENT EXPENDITURES

One form of government expenditures are tax breaks for entrepreneurs. The "Notice of the State Administration of Taxation on Income Tax Preferences for Start-up Investment Enterprises" offers a significant tax reduction for small businesses. This policy has encouraged entrepreneurship, according to Changhong Li, by increasing the total monetary amount of angel investors' contributions in high-tech fields.[96]

Another form of government expenditure is the creation of innovation parks. As part of the Sparking Program, high-tech parks were created, providing facilities and office space for new companies. These parks serve as incubators for young companies, not only giving them access to physical facilities but also synergizing connections with other firms in the park. According to Junbo Yu, innovation parks have experienced rapid growth in the last twenty years, contributing a

95   He, Canfei, Jiangyong Lu, and Haifeng Qian. "Entrepreneurship in China." Small Business Economics 52, no. 3 (May 2018): 563–72. https://doi.org/10.1007/s11187-017-9972-5.

96   Li, Changhong, Yulin Shi, Cong Wu, Zhenyu Wu, and Li Zheng. "Policies of Promoting Entrepreneurship and Angel Investment: Evidence from China." Emerging Markets Review 29 (2016): 154–67. https://doi.org/10.1016/j.ememar.2016.08.011.

significant share of industrial output and becoming magnets for foreign direct investment.[97]

EDUCATION LEVEL OF POPULATION

The demand and supply of relevant business education can influence a country's number of entrepreneurial projects.[98] Demand refers to the interest and preferences of individuals for business education, while supply refers to the availability of relevant training and educational programs.

A demand-side example is the *Xinhua* article "China Advocates Entrepreneurial Spirit to Boost Innovation," which encourages university students to engage in entrepreneurship.[99] By promoting the appeal of self-employment, the government can change the youth's preferences, increasing the demand for entrepreneurship.

A supply-side example is the government's initiative of allowing children to learn science at a younger age. According to *Xinhua*, these curriculum changes are aimed at "populariz[ing] science and technology" to "boost innovation among the

97 Yu, Junbo, Roger R. Stough, and Peter Nijkamp. "Governing Technological Entrepreneurship in China and the West." Public Administration Review 69 (2009). https://doi.org/10.1111/j.1540-6210.2009.02095.x.

98 Lin, Song, and Zhengda Xu. "The Factors That Influence the Development of Entrepreneurship Education." Management Decision 55, no. 7 (2017): 1351–70. https://doi.org/10.1108/md-06-2016-0416.

99 Bo, Xiang. "China Focus: China Increases Science Education to Boost Innovation." Xinhua, September 1, 2017. http://www.xinhuanet.com/english/2017-09/01/c_136574669.htm.

public."[100] By having educational opportunities to learn about innovative fields, youth may continue to engage in science and technology, possibly becoming entrepreneurs in the future.

SOCIAL CAPITAL

Social capital is the network of relationships between individuals that are conducive to business activity. According to Shanshan Qian, personal connections can complement an entrepreneur's lack of capital and information, giving them a competitive edge.[101] For instance, a well-connected individual will have better access to industry-specific insider information and sometimes even venture to fund. The informal capital market has become the most important source of equity capital for startups, supporting the early stages of businesses.[102] Indeed, according to a study done by Dejin Su, personal connections in business and government are positively correlated to venture performance. With China's continued economic growth, government expenditures, and increasing prevalence of business education, entrepreneurs may naturally gain stronger and more extensive connections.[103]

---

100 Ibid.

101 Qian, Shanshan. "The Role of Guanxi in Chinese Entrepreneurship," n.d. http://www.diva-portal.org/smash/get/diva2:530871/FULLTEXT02.pdf.

102 Li, Changhong, Yulin Shi, Cong Wu, Zhenyu Wu, and Li Zheng. "Policies of Promoting Entrepreneurship and Angel Investment: Evidence from China." Emerging Markets Review 29 (2016): 154–67. https://doi.org/10.1016/j.ememar.2016.08.011.

103 Su, Dejin, Qixia Du, Dongwon Sohn, and Libo Xu. "Can High-Tech Ventures Benefit from Government Guanxi and Business Guanxi? The

STAGE OF ECONOMIC DEVELOPMENT

Due to economic development, China's countryside experienced a boom in entrepreneurship. The share of business activities in rural household income rose from 8.1 percent in 1983 to 14.9 percent in 1988. This increased private sector activity was allowed by economic opening-up, playing an enormous role in increasing citizens' income.

The prevalence of high-tech entrepreneurship will increase as China continues to modernize its economy. For instance, the government recognizes the need for innovation to becoming the primary driver of growth, as mentioned in the "National Mid- and Long-Term Scientific and Technological Development Plan Guideline." Reducing the economy's reliance on low value-added goods export, China hopes to move toward an economy focused on consumer spending and innovation. This economic shift will increase the demand for entrepreneurship in cutting-edge fields of science and technology. The CCP has already started to implement policies that will accelerate this transition, such as the country's "11th Five Year Plan," which emphasized the creation of an "innovative state." In July 2018, China surpassed North America in attracting venture capital (VC) funding and now accounts for 47 percent of the world's total VC funding.[104]

Moderating Effects of Environmental Turbulence." Sustainability 9, no. 1 (2017): 142. https://doi.org/10.3390/su9010142.

104 Yang, Yingzhi. "China's Start-Ups Attract Almost Half of World's Venture Capital Investments." South China Morning Post, July 5, 2018. https://www.scmp.com/tech/article/2153798/china-surpasses-north-america-at-tracting-venture-capital-funding-first-time.

THE FOURTH INDUSTRIAL REVOLUTION

Since the mid-eighteenth century, three industrial revolutions have occurred throughout human history.

- The Steam Age (1760–1840) was created by the First Industrial Revolution, marking the transition from an agrarian to an industrial society.
- The Electrical Age (1840–1950) was the rise of heavy industries that produced electricity, steel, railways, chemicals, automobiles, and more. As petroleum became a new source of energy, land and air travel became more prevalent. Countries began to have a greater level of international exchange as the global economy was formed.
- The Information Age (1950-now) came about after WWII, characterized by the use of automation, computers, and telecommunications. These innovations have caused the exchange of information and resources to be more rapid around the world. Similar to the past two revolutions, the degree of human development has reached unprecedented heights.
- The Connected Age (now-future) today, we are in the midst of another revolution. Through deeper scientific, technological, and industrial transformation, we arrive at the Fourth Industrial Revolution. The Fourth Revolution is based on AI, big data, 5G the Internet of Things, and other important technologies. Large-scale breakthroughs, coupled with key drivers such as genetic engineering, quantum computing, and fusion technology, will drive a large number of new industries, transforming—again—the world's productivity.

Every industrial revolution is characterized by new disruptive innovations, bringing about the democratization of information and great leaps of productivity and subsequent living standards. Important innovations have fundamentally altered the trajectory of human development.

In his book *The Fourth Industrial Revolution*, Klaus Schwab, founder and executive chairman of the World Economic Forum, posits that the world is currently at an inflection of economic growth, where the productivity offered by digital technologies will manifest with "full force" in the Fourth Industrial Revolution. Emerging technologies will diffuse much faster than previous ones, and people around the world will have access to never-before-seen digital power.

Increasing digitization will empower more people around the globe and, consequently, also change the way governments relate to their citizens and how superpowers relate to each other and smaller countries. According to Schwab, this upcoming disruption will put pressure on existing "political, economic, and social models," requiring that they become part of a larger "distributed power system that requires more collaborative forms of interaction to succeed."[105]

Further, the Fourth Industrial Revolution will cause a monumental impact on the global economy, influencing all macro-variables such as GDP, investment, consumption, employment, trade, inflation, and so on. How will countries

---

105 Schwab, Klaus. The Fourth Industrial Revolution. Great Britain: Portfolio, 2017.

reconcile with this newfound integration of digital technologies in everyday life and in governance? And how does the Fourth Industrial Revolution play a part in the bilateral relationship between the United States and China?

- Artificial Intelligence: the ability for computer systems to perform tasks that require human intelligence, such as visual perception, speech recognition, decision-making, and translation between languages. As AI becomes more advanced, the integration of this technology in industry will have profound impacts on productivity.[106]
- 5G: A fifth-generation telecommunications technology, capable of much higher capacity, higher speeds (up to 100 times), and lower latency compared to the current fourth-generation technology. Consequently, 5G will not only connect people but also machines, objects, and devices, delivering a new level of connectivity never before experienced by society.[107]
- Big Data: The use of extremely large data sets, analyzed computationally to reveal patterns, trends, and associations, especially relating to human behavior and interactions.[108]

---

106 "Artificial Intelligence: Definition of Artificial Intelligence by Lexico." Lexico Dictionaries | English. Lexico Dictionaries, n.d. https://www.lexico.com/en/definition/artificial_intelligence.

107 "What Is 5G?: Everything You Need to Know About 5G." Qualcomm, December 15, 2019. https://www.qualcomm.com/invention/5g/what-is-5g.

108 "Big Data: Definition of Big Data by Lexico." Lexico Dictionaries | English. Lexico Dictionaries, n.d. https://www.lexico.com/en/definition/big_data.

Throughout each revolution, the competitive status of countries around the world changes. Some countries have emerged and become dominant players in the world economy. During the First Industrial Revolution, Britain became the world's factory with technologies such as the steam engine. In the Second Industrial Revolution, the United States—relying on mass production methods—became the world's industrial and technological hegemon. And, in the Third Industrial Revolution, Japan, relying on lean production methods, rose in industries such as automobile production and home appliances.

During the past 150 years, China has experienced the First, Second, and Third Industrial Revolutions. It currently has the world's most complete industrial system, producing from the lowest ends of products to some of the highest ends. During previous revolutions, the country was only at the low end of the international economy and trade, only achieving low value-added production. Now, in the information age, it is slowly catching up, becoming the world's largest producer, consumer, and exporter of ICT (information and communications technology) equipment.

As the world stands at the threshold of the Fourth Industrial Revolution, China now, for the first time, has the opportunity to stand at the same starting line as countries such as the United States and Japan, as well as the European Union. In the Fourth Industrial Revolution, China and the United States foreseeably must have an arduous contest, especially in the field of digital-centric science and technology. The competition between China and the United States will certainly be a long-term process.

The Fourth Industrial Revolution will center around digital transformation. Technologies such as AI, 5G, and the Internet of Things will greatly increase productivity. Between China and the United States, which country can better grasp the fruits of the Fourth Industrial Revolution? The outcome will reshape not only the future of the bilateral relationship between the two countries but also the global economic structure and competitive landscape.

THE FOUR NEW INVENTIONS OF CHINA

The lives of Chinese citizens are becoming more connected with technological innovations. Just as the country prides itself on its four great inventions of ancient China—paper-making, printing, gunpowder, and the compass—netizens have coined the new term of the "Four New Inventions of China." These four new great inventions are changing the way people live.

In the summer of 2019, one of my American friends visited China. After traveling to Beijing, Shanghai, Shenzhen, and Chengdu, he reflected that everything he experienced was a fresh new encounter. A phrase that stuck with me is when he revealed that "China is the future of America." In terms of transportation infrastructure, skyscrapers, and the diversity of available goods, one can consider China a highly advanced country while the United States remains in development.

- High-speed rail: High-speed rail technology originated in Japan and Europe. However, today, China's high-speed rail network is the world's number one in traffic. It has not only become the first choice for many Chinese people to travel but also promoted economic development throughout the country. The length of the Chinese high-speed rail is expected to exceed 45,000 kilometers by 2030, long enough to wrap around the Earth's equator.

- E-Commerce: With the advent of the mobile Internet era, China has now become the world's largest online retail market with more than 800 million Internet users and more than 200 million online transactions per day. China took only five or six years to reach the world's largest e-commerce country from a society without personal credit. Express mail and delivery services are everywhere. From ordering a refrigerator to receiving a foot massage, anyone can order it at home with one click.

- Mobile Payments: Most Chinese people living in cities have forgotten what a wallet looks like, as most services such as booking accommodation, paying for grocery shopping, and the smartphone replace many other services. China has become the first cashless society with the integration of WeChat Pay and Alipay.

- Dockless Bike Sharing: The phenomenon of dockless bike-sharing first originated in China. In just two years, from 2017 to 2018, colorful bicycles quickly occupied China's streets—especially in subway stations and public gathering points. Shared bikes provide the fastest and cheapest way to travel within 500 meters to two kilometers. Mobike, OFO, and other bicycles have become indispensable living appliances in dozens of large and medium-sized cities in China every day, with more than 1 to 2 billion registered users.

A jungle of dock-less sharing bikes. *(https://www.economist.com/ business/2017/11/25/chinas-bicycle-sharing-giants-are-still-trying-to-make-money)*

UNEQUAL TREATIES

During one chilly autumn day, I sat down with Professor Melanie Manion at a cafe located at the heart of Duke University's gorgeous gothic campus. The topic of discussion was the trade war between the United States and China, which had just started to appear in the front pages of news at the time. Manion dedicated her life to studying China and has conducted extensive research on censorship in China. We were discussing the implications of the US-China trade war.

One sticking point in the US-China tensions is China's technological ambition, which threatens to displace the traditional industrial might of the United States. The Chinese tech sector has grown tremendously in the past twenty years. Seemingly out of nowhere, Chinese tech startups grew into tech titans, controlling the vast majority of Chinese user data and digital experiences that the population interacts with on a day-to-day basis.

One reason why the Chinese tech sector grew so fast concerns venture capital investment. The amount of venture capital spending in China is almost equal to the expenditure in the United States, allowing these young companies to scale up at an incredibly fast pace. Furthermore, another reason is the Chinese entrepreneurial culture. Similar to Silicon Valley, entrepreneurs in China are innovating rapidly, moving swiftly to grow the next business and contribute to the size of the country's tech sector.[109] In 2018, Chinese companies received more than $30.9 billion in venture funding, surpassing for the first time money earned by their US counterparts in the first year.[110]

According to Edward Tse, author of *China's Disrupters*, what lies at the core of China's entrepreneurial spirit is "pride, ambition, and a shared cultural heritage."[111] Tse suggests that Chinese entrepreneurs see themselves as playing a significant

---

109 Fannin, Rebecca. "What's Pushing China's Tech Sector So Far Ahead?" Knowledge@Wharton, October 9, 2019. https://knowledge.wharton. upenn.edu/article/whats-pushing-chinas-tech-sector-so-far-ahead/.

110 Choe, William, Jason Rabbitt-Tomita, Alex Zhang, and Vivian Tsoi. "Why Has Foreign Venture Capital Investment into China Soared in 2018?" Lexology, December 13, 2018. https://www.lexology.com/library/detail. aspx?g=6d4a1b26-d777-455c-a329-53456905f02d.

111 Tse, Edward. Chinas Disruptors: How Alibaba, Xiaomi, Tencent and Other Companies Are Changing the Rules of Business. London: Portfolio Penguin, 2016.

role in the achievement of national prosperity. Seeing their country once again "achieve the kind of national greatness it has enjoyed for much of its history" is a crucial motivator for the Chinese people. This shared cultural memory and ambition bind Chinese entrepreneurs together.[112]

Manion parallels the technological ambition of China to the development of Japan in the late twentieth century. In the 1970s, Japan coined the term "mechatronics" by combining the words of "mechanics" and "electronics," breaking through the boundaries of existing technology and creating new innovations in the electronics field.[113]

"When I was a child, 'Made in Japan' stood for really low-tech, poor-quality things. Now, think about what 'Made in Japan' means! Made in China 2025 is similar to this. ...If Japan can succeed, think about if China can succeed."

China has repeatedly emphasized "self-reliance," aiming to increase the proportion of domestically constructed components used in its high-tech industry to 70 percent by 2025.[114] The government is using everything in its power to provide substantial financial support to critical enterprises. One of

112 Ibid.

113 Paxton, K. Bradley. "Japans Growing Technological Capability: Implications for the US Economy." Journal of International Business Studies 24, no. 4 (1993): 815–17. https://doi.org/10.1057/jibs.1993.57.

114 Mcbride, James, and Andrew Chatzky. "Is 'Made in China 2025' a Threat to Global Trade?" Council on Foreign Relations. Council on Foreign Relations, May 13, 2019. https://www.cfr.org/backgrounder/made-china-2025-threat-global-trade.

THE WORLD'S 20 LARGEST TECH GIANTS
The most significant internet companies only hail from the U.S. or China

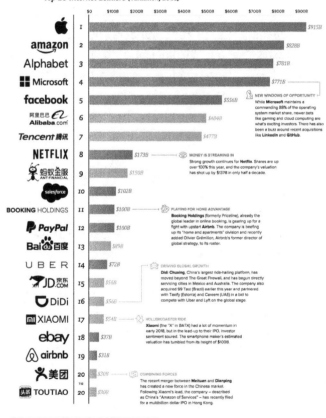

The world's largest technology companies. *(https://biv.com/article/2018/07/infographic-worlds-20-largest-tech-giants)*

the industries that benefits from the Made in China 2025 project is the development of early-stage technology startups in the country.[115] The government has combined hundreds of billions in venture capital funds for companies in addition to tax incentives, grants, and rental subsidies. In December 2018, the Chinese government claimed that it had gained a total of $1.8 trillion in funding to achieve its goal of Made in China 2025.[116]

Manion believes that China appears threatening to the United States due to its ideological differences and the fact that it is already an economic juggernaut. Indeed, the country's latent industrial prowess is just coming to show with the emergence of its startup and technology sectors, serving a market more significant than 1 billion people.

"If we think that Japan after WWII held promise to shake up the world, now just think about China!"

Rather than focusing on the imbalance of trade between the two countries, the US government should instead analyze the technological rise of China. To Manion, many factors influence the trade deficit, such as "how much money the Chinese save and how much the Americans spend," and this

115   Yang, Yuan. "China Fuels Boom in Domestic Tech Start-Ups." Subscribe to read | Financial Times. Financial Times, October 22, 2017. https://www.ft.com/content/b63ee746-afc6-11e7-aab9-abaa44b1e130.

116   Feng, Emily. "China's State-Owned Venture Capital Funds Battle to Make an Impact." Subscribe to read | Financial Times. Financial Times, December 23, 2018. https://www.ft.com/content/4fa2caaa-f9f0-11e8-af46-2022a0b02a6c.

issue is merely trivial, a natural outcome of the international trade regime.

The better focus of the trade war, in Manion's view, is the structure of the trade relationship. Specifically, the United States should focus on the particular parts of the contract that China introduces when it accepts foreign investment from Western companies. Currently, agreements force companies to hand over their technologies to China, which is a very unusual structure. With the Made in China 2025 project, governments around the world fear that China will continue to impose these "unfair" contracts with Western technology companies in its effort to incorporate Western technologies into the country's production.

However, the Chinese market is too enticing for many companies. Often, gaining a market foothold in China is a question of survival for Western companies. On the subject of smartphones, for example, if one does not sell to China, one is out of the picture globally. Therefore, for foreign firms, the Chinese market is too good to ignore, causing them to be coerced into unfair agreements with the Chinese government.

"It is a bit of a prisoner's dilemma — every firm wants its foot in the door. It will see other firms competing with it to also get into China, they hand over the technology."

The agreements entered between the Chinese government and foreign tech companies can be considered the "unequal treaties" of our time, harkening back to the series of treaties signed by the Qing dynasty after military attacks by foreign powers. The West's lust for the Qing's resources spurred them to infringe on the country to obtain its resources. Now, the situation is reversed as Western businesses acquiesce to the demands of China, handing over key technologies. As part of Made in China 2025, China, through its market power of sheer numbers, can impose these unequal contracts on Western businesses.

Manion, however, also argues that one should not blame China: "The issue is, every country wants to succeed, and you can't conflate problems with trade with China's industrial plan to succeed." One can't criticize China for wanting to take over the world in whole industries. Some of the problems with the trade war are that they are based on a perspective that is so anti-China from their very stance—based on the idea that China can't be at an equal stance compared to its Western counterparts.

"There is no other option for China and the US other than peaceful coexistence."

CHINA'S ALTERNATE DIGITAL UNIVERSE OF CENSORSHIP

A group of protesters in the city of Urumqi in Xinjiang gathered to speak against the Chinese authorities. They had prepared a list of grievances on ethnic discrimination and unfair treatment, as well as the inability of the state to protect the local Uyghur population.[117] This event would later be known

---

117 Ryono, Angel, and Matthew Galway. "Xinjiang under China: Reflections on the Multiple Dimensions of the 2009 Urumqi Uprising." Asian Ethnicity

as the 2009 Urumqi Uprising. Ever since the Chinese Han dynasty, when ethnically Han Chinese established governance in what is known now as Xinjiang, ethnic tensions have always festered between the aboriginal Uyghur people and the Han. Human rights issues in Xinjiang are still at the forefront of the news. Now, the state's utilization of technology has facilitated the ease of government control to further stymie ethnic tensions. We will explore some of China's use of technology in digital censorship.

The Chinese authorities had found that the protesters were using Facebook as a tool to organize movements. Swiftly, the CCP began its censoring of Facebook and many other Western online outlets, in addition to blocking access to the Internet in the province. Only ten months after the social unrest did Internet reconnect; however, Facebook (along with other websites, such as Google and Twitter) has remained blocked even today.[118]

China's digital world involves an ideological flavor not found in other countries, opposing the laissez-faire freedom commonly accepted as the norm in Western countries. The Chinese government was the one that originally enacted reforms for economic opening, allowing Chinese technology businesses to flourish. The Chinese government also passed various policies to use technology as a means of controlling the populace.

16, no. 2 (2014): 235–55. https://doi.org/10.1080/14631369.2014.906062.

118   Wong, Edward. "After Long Ban, Western China Is Back Online." The New York Times. The New York Times, May 14, 2010. https://www.nytimes.com/2010/05/15/world/asia/15china.html.

The following is a story on the surveillance state that is China, originally published in *Wired Magazine*:

It was 2011, and she was living in Hotan, an oasis town in Xinjiang, in northwest China. The 30-year-old, Nurjamal Atawula, loved to take pictures of her children and exchange strings of emoji with her husband while he was out. In 2013, Atawula downloaded WeChat, the Chinese social messaging app. Not long after, rumors circulated among her friends: The government could track your location through your phone. At first, she didn't believe them.

In early 2016, police started making routine checks on Atawula's home. Her husband was regularly called to the police station. The police informed him they were suspicious of his WeChat activity. Atawula's children began to cower in fear at the sight of a police officer. The harassment and fear finally reached the point that the family decided to move to Turkey. Atawula's husband, worried that Atawula would be arrested, sent her ahead while he stayed in Xinjiang and waited for the children's passports.

"The day I left, my husband was arrested," Atawula said. When she arrived in Turkey in June 2016, her phone stopped working—and by the time she had it repaired, all her friends and relatives had deleted her from their WeChat accounts. They feared that the government would punish them for communicating with her.

She was alone in Istanbul and her digital connection with life in Xinjiang was over. Apart from a snatched Skype call with her mother for 11 and a half minutes at the end of December

2016, communication with her relatives has been completely cut. "Sometimes I feel like the days I was with my family are just my dreams, as if I have been lonely all my life—ever since I was born," she said.

Atawula now lives alone in Zeytinburnu, a working-class neighborhood in Istanbul. It's home to Turkey's largest population of Uyghurs, the mostly Muslim ethnic minority native to Xinjiang, a vast, resource-rich land of deserts and mountains along China's ancient Silk Road trade route. Atawula is one of around 34,000 Uyghurs in Turkey. She is unable to contact any of her relatives—via phone, WeChat, or any other app. "I feel very sad when I see other people video chatting with their families," she says. "I think, why can't we even hear the voice of our children?"

For Uyghurs in Xinjiang, any kind of contact from a non-Chinese phone number, though not officially illegal, can result in instant arrest. Most Uyghurs in Turkey have been deleted by their families on social media. And many wouldn't dare try to make contact, for fear Chinese authorities would punish their relatives. It's just one of the ways President Xi Jinping's government maintains a tightly controlled net of surveillance over the Uyghurs in China, and it has a ripple effect on Uyghurs living all over the world.

The world of digital censorship in China is highly effective, improving for the CCP its ability to govern citizens. Using an elaborate system of censorship, the government can stop all dangerous online activity. With a massive workforce working to censor the Internet and the increasing optimization of artificial intelligence, Beijing can censor information on the

Internet at a blinding pace.[119] This efficiency is indicative of China's surveillance power and its ability to identify social unrest. As better technologies for tracking and manipulating data become integrated into China's censorship system, officials will become more efficient at stopping any online behavior that undermines the state domestically and (to some extent) abroad.

Consequent to the Internet censorship caused by the Urumqi Uprising, Chinese entrepreneurs have cultivated a homegrown set of Internet services to replace the mainstream services of the West, such as Facebook, Google, and Uber. To some extent, these homegrown services have even begun to outpace the West in terms of sophistication. For instance, WeChat—the popular online messenger platform with over 1 billion users at the time of this writing—is providing Chinese citizens with an abundance of conveniences.[120] In addition to sending messages, WeChat is empowering Chinese citizens, especially rural residents, with the ability to send money (in the form of "red packets"), shop online, top-up phones, pay utility bills, order taxis, and takeaways, and more—all in the same application.

---

119   King, Gary, Jennifer Pan, and Margaret E. Roberts. "How Censorship in China Allows Government Criticism but Silences Collective Expression." American Political Science Review 107, no. 2 (2013): 326–43. https://doi.org/10.1017/s0003055413000014.

120   Statista Research Department. "WeChat: Number of Users 2019." Statista, November 2019. https://www.statista.com/statistics/255778/number-of-active-wechat-messenger-accounts/.

As a result of this homegrown digital universe, the Chinese state is empowered with a greater ability to control information on the Internet. Take, for example, the famous Chinese search engine Baidu, on which the state can remove "vulgar" content and search results from the Internet. Companies like Baidu will hire large teams of censors to respond to the requests made by the government. Its censors would commonly preemptively suppress sensitive topics around critical dates such as June 4 (the anniversary of the Tiananmen Incident) or in response to politically sensitive events.

Through the use of surveillance over the massive amounts of data collected from tech companies in China, the government can respond to civil strife at an alarming rate, perpetuating state ideology. Information is restrained by the government, and civilians not only are getting fed government-regulated information, but they also self-censor their activities online, thereby further creating the echo chamber of official state ideology. In a country like China, with a population of 1.4 billion people, technology has improved the efficiency of governance by leaps and bounds.

In the year 2020, the state is set to roll out a national reputation system called the social credit system, in place of a nonexistent credit system similar to what the United States has. It is a big data-enabled tool for monitoring, rating, and steering of the behavior of market participants in China.[121] At the

121 Meissner, Mirjam. "CHINA'S SOCIAL CREDIT SYSTEM." Merics China Monitor. Merics China Monitor, May 17, 2017. https://www.merics.org/sites/default/files/2017-09/China Monitor_39_SOCS_EN.pdf.

time of this writing, the state has already begun to slowly phase in the infrastructure necessary for this new institution.

The social credit system is an incredibly powerful tool for the CCP to cultivate correct behavior in citizens. According to Princeton professor of East Asian studies Perry Link (2002), the "highest priority of the top leadership of the Communist Party remains ...its grip on power"—that is, regime survival. Consequently, it would make sense for the party to use all resources in its toolbox to ensure survival, preempting instability (Hvistendahl 2017). When viewed in a moral vacuum, the CCP, by gaining data from companies like Baidu, becomes highly effective in dictating the ideological inclinations of its population of 1.4 billion people. This power leads to the better suppression of dissident opinions and popular movements.

By merely tweaking an algorithm in the social credit system, the CCP can send ripples through the ways people act and think. Effectively, this method of invisible governance allows the government to spend fewer resources on physical forms of governance, such as policing. With only a vague understanding of the rules and algorithms behind China's governance, citizens, most of whom are digitally connected, will be wary of their behavior in fear of damaging their credit score. In this technologically integrated society, citizens will have difficulty escaping digital authoritarianism. This situation thus gives the CCP an easy way to catalyze the concept of self-policing.

Importantly, however, the social credit system may perpetuate inequality. Influenced by the biases of programmers and unforeseen feedback loops, this system may become a weapon of math destruction. The lives of innocent citizens may be sent into a downward spiral simply because they had the misfortune of being in a specific minority demographic.[122] Therefore, the government must be transparent. As Rana (2015) mentioned, data is powerful, and China has already taken action to publicize government data. The perpetuation of inequality can perhaps be mitigated with greater transparency; however, this may lead to the reduction of the efficacy of digital authoritarianism, as individuals start to game the system. With these considerations in mind, the reaction of Chinese citizens once the social credit system officially rolls out in 2020 will be interesting, as will whether it creates any unforeseen social phenomena.

For the United States, a country founded upon the principles of civil liberty and equality, the state of Chinese technology and governance appears Orwellian. In the United States, free debate is encouraged, and individuals can discuss sensitive topics. To some extent, this radically different state of affairs sets up the Western world to distrust the Chinese system. In the West, sensitive issues such as the Xinjiang, the June 6 Incident, and Hong Kong/Taiwan issues are fair game. However, in China, to protect the state against devolution forces, the government uses technology to control public discourse. This state of affairs is indicative of the different styles of governance between China and the United States. While the United States can fall prey to public discourse and public sentiment, politics in China are highly centralized, and everyday citizens stand on the sidelines.

---

122 ONeil, Cathy. Weapons of Math Destruction: How Big Data Increases
       Inequality and Threatens Democracy. Great Britain: Penguin Books, 2017.

We can see an information gap between Chinese and American citizens. Due to censorship, the Chinese people know less about the outside world, and because of complicated restrictions by the government as well as self-censorship, the outside world knows less about the real state of affairs inside China. This lack of mutual understanding can make it so that conflict arises between the two parties. One common misconception that the West holds regarding China is that censorship in China is nonselective. As mentioned by King et al. (2013), censors in China do not wholesale remove negative information. Instead, critiques by individual people are tolerated. An individual can speak out against the state as an individual. Still, the matter becomes more problematic when these views are spread to other people, arousing group action and widespread unrest. Dissent is allowed and, in fact, encouraged at the fringe level. These individual grievances will enable the government to know the true feelings of its populace so that it can take relevant action to address societal issues.

However, when these grievances are spread to a group, and this group is willing to take collective action against it (such as the run-up to Facebook's ban in 2009 for facilitating public dissent), the Chinese government is ruthless in censorship. Hence, the Chinese party-state remains resilient, using individual grievances as a form of information collection but taking intense action against societal dissent.

CHAPTER 4

CHINESE TECHNOLOGY: Weapons of "Math" Destruction

We are now living in a completely digitalized world and a completely globalized world, so we have to find some new mechanisms and values to deal with this post-digitalized and post-globalized world.

—KLAUS SCHWAB

CONSUMER TECHNOLOGY

In August 2018, Venezuelan President Nicolas Maduro gives a speech in front of a group of soldiers in Caracas. Mid-speech, Maduro and his wife gaze up at the sky and wince as the sound of an explosion rings out throughout the parade. Lines of troops start to disperse from the area. The media reports that two drones laden with explosives had been set off during the ceremony. Seven soldiers are injured.[123]

This event would be the first of its kind where assailants attempted to kill a head of state with a commercially available drone. It signifies an age where physical warfare is increasingly replaced by machines and smart autonomous delivery vehicles. To the assailants, the use of drones is a relatively inexpensive way to attack a target without risking life. The availability of effective commercially available drones has become a way for terrorists to fashion a poor man's smart bomb.[124]

Maduro's attackers used a DJI Matrice 600, a high-end drone offered by Shenzhen-based manufacturer Dajiang Innovations (DJI). This drone can be acquired by anyone with as little as $5,000. Cheaper versions of drones from DJI could be bought for as low as $1,000.[125] As opposed to military-grade surveillance and combat drones that can cost millions of dollars, the increasing prevalence of consumer-grade drones and their constant improvement is democratizing warfare. Now, nonstate actors can inflict widespread damage and fear not through expensive military-grade weapons but by spending a

123 "Venezuela 'Drone Attack': Six Arrests Made." BBC News. BBC, August 5, 2018. https://www.bbc.com/news/world-latin-america-45077057.

124 Luft, Gal. "The Palestinian H-Bomb: Terror's Winning Strategy." Warfare in the Middle East since 1945, 2017, 475–80. https://doi.org/10.4324/9781315234304-20.

125 "DJI - The World Leader in Camera Drones/Quadcopters for Aerial Photography." DJI Official, n.d. https://www.dji.com/.

few thousand dollars. Indeed, terrorists are now empowered to arm themselves with an air force.[126]

Consumer technologies are becoming more relevant in global affairs. The development of technology is inspiring new uses for people, granting individuals new powers. Now, anyone armed with a computer or drone can inflict significant damage throughout the world.

CHINA'S DRONES

China is the world leader in drones, and DJI is leading the charge in the industry. As of 2018, DJI has a 74 percent market share in the consumer drone market, and its growth shows no signs of stopping.[127] DJI is also the industry leader in filing drone patents.[128] As a result of its industry prominence and Chinese identity, DJI has recently been the target of US pressure. Along with Huawei and ZTE, these three private enterprises have been the target of American attacks in the broader context of bilateral tensions between the United States and China. Coincidentally, these three companies were all once located on the same street in Shenzhen.

---

126 Sims, Alyssa. "The Rising Drone Threat from Terrorists." Georgetown Journal of International Affairs 19, no. 1 (2018): 97–107. https://doi.org/10.1353/gia.2018.0012.

127 French, Sally. "DJI Market Share: Here's Exactly How Rapidly It Has Grown in Just a Few Years." The Drone Girl, September 18, 2018. http://thedronegirl.com/2018/09/18/dji-market-share/.

128 Coulter, Martin. "Walmart Outpaces Amazon in Drone Patent Race." Financial Times. Financial Times, June 16, 2019. https://www.ft.com/content/7cd22fb6-8e79-11e9-a24d-b42f641eca37.

DJI, due to the superiority of its industry-leading technology, has received over 300 different "airworthiness releases" from the US Army to be used on multiple missions.[129] However, in August of 2017, an internal memo within the US Army ordered all personnel to discontinue using consumer drones made by the Chinese manufacturer.

"Cease all use, uninstall all DJI applications, remove all batteries/storage media from devices, and secure equipment for follow on direction," reads the memo from Lt. Gen. Joseph H. Anderson, the Army's deputy chief of staff for plans and operations.

Quoting national security concerns, the US Army ordered personnel to discontinue the use of DJI products due to worries of data intercepting by the Chinese government. Americans argued, similar to the Huawei debacle, that the Chinese technology company could be forced to hand over data to the Chinese government when asked. Thus the use of DJI products posed a cybersecurity risk for the United States.

At the core of this challenge for DJI is the difference of regime type between China and the United States. To the United States, China is an authoritarian state that, with its recent economic rise, threatens the primacy of the United States in international affairs. To US policymakers, the use of technology made by an ideological and economic adversary is unsettling.

---

129 Popper, Ben. "US Army Reportedly Asks Units to Stop Using DJI Drones, Citing Cybersecurity Concerns." The Verge. The Verge, August 4, 2017. https://www.theverge.com/2017/8/4/16095244/us-army-stop-using-dji-drones-cybersecurity.

In the anarchic global system characterized by uncertainty, mistrust, and unseen conflict, the barring of Chinese companies by the United States is only a natural move. While companies such as DJI and Huawei can promise that they will never compromise the information of its users, there is no technical challenge in theoretically gathering and using the knowledge of its users for nefarious purposes. The protectionist nature of countries in the field of technology is not only reasonable but also expected. Countries are cautious when it comes to sharing or welcoming new technology as it can be a Trojan horse.

New technologies and tensions represent an age involving a shift toward the scrutiny of consumer-oriented technologies. For example, before Huawei came under the spotlights of international attention during the context of the US-China trade war, this company had already been barred from operating its consumer business group in the United States, the business group responsible for the company's popular handheld devices. Not until later were Huawei's enterprise-face and carrier network-facing businesses barred in the United States, as well. DJI's drone products may be the next target in the ongoing tensions between the two technology powerhouses.

FIFTH-GENERATION TELECOMMUNICATIONS

Chinese telecommunications giant Huawei controls wireless base station equipment sales in more than 180 countries around the world. Already, the company is the world's preeminent researcher in 5G technologies due to its intense research and development investment annually. At the time of this writing in 2019, Huawei's 5G technology prowess is at least two years ahead of its two largest European competitors Ericsson and Nokia. The United States has yet to cultivate a home-grown telecommunications company that can deliver the same 5G capabilities as Huawei, Ericsson, or Nokia.

However, in the essential field of 5G networks, Qualcomm in the United States still plays an important role. Qualcomm dominates some of the 5G patents and core technologies. One could say that there remains a US advantage in the creation of 5G baseband chips due to Qualcomm's technology. Still, the company cannot independently participate in the construction of network equipment and base stations for wireless networks.

Notably, Huawei's founder Ren Zhengfei humorously stated at a public event that Huawei could sell its 5G chips, codes, and production processes to US companies so they could keep up with Huawei, competing in the same race. This act would be the right way for humanity to enter the Fourth Industrial Revolution Era together. Ren also stated that, in terms of 5G, Huawei is confident that it will maintain its lead over its Western rivals.[130]

ARTIFICIAL INTELLIGENCE AND BIG DATA

Kai-Fu Lee, chairman and CEO of Beijing-based Sinovation Ventures, believes that China has an opportunity to surpass the United States in the AI space even though the latter

---

130 "Live: Huawei Founder & CEO Ren Zhengfei Holds Discussion in Shenzhen." CGTN. CGTN, June 16, 2019. https://news.cgtn.com/news/2019-06-15/Live-Huawei-founder-CEO-Ren-Zhengfei-holds-discussion-in-Shenzhen-HyfoBmbcsw/index.html.

already has several advancements in this area. The United States, for example, has ten times as many top experts in AI compared to China, and the country is home to technology giants such as Google, Amazon, and Facebook, which all have significant competitive advantages in artificial intelligence.

In terms of the development of artificial intelligence, technology creation is not the ceiling. Instead, one's ability to obtain a large amount of data is the ceiling. The protection of data privacy in the United States, therefore, becomes an essential constraint on the development of AI. However, in China, because data access is more accessible due to people's disregard for their privacy, Chinese developers enjoy a more exceptional ability to refine their AI capabilities continuously.

In China, data collection is already leaps and bounds ahead of the United States. Already, the country has installed more than 200 million cameras in various cities. One who lives in any large city such as Beijing would be hard-pressed not to run into facial recognition on the streets, as the use of AI in daily life is indeed very prevalent. The country has already successfully integrated facial recognition systems into the public security infrastructure. The "Skynet Project" is a video surveillance system that encompasses surveillance equipment in multiple locations such as traffic hubs and security card bays, using real-time monitoring and information recording of areas using GIS maps, image acquisition, and transmission technologies.[131]

---

131 Tao, Li. "What You Need to Know about Facial Recognition Firm Sense-Nets." South China Morning Post, April 12, 2019. https://www.scmp.com/tech/science-research/article/3005733/what-you-need-know-about-sense-nets-facial-recognition-firm.

The popular social messaging app WeChat, for example, is a key tool for data collection. Already, the app has 900 million users registered in China and across the world. Compared to the technology of Silicon Valley, information collected by WeChat is far richer than that of Google Wallet or Apple Pay.[132] WeChat has already become a kind of "digital Swiss Army knife for modern life," enabling a variety of activities without ever leaving the app. A user can message friends, pay groceries, book doctors' appointments, file taxes, unlock bikes, and buy plane tickets, just to name a few. In the span of two years, WeChat was able to go from a no-name app to a powerhouse application—sort of a remote control for life in China.

Kai-Fu Lee asserts that, in the era of artificial intelligence, data is the new oil. And China is the new OPEC (Organization of the Petroleum Exporting Countries) in this modern age.[133] From search software to social platforms to smart city and home applications of hardware, data collection portals are everywhere. These portals collected vast amounts of data directly from users in China. Thus, China can far surpass the United States in the acquisition, processing, and use of big data—training its artificial intelligence algorithms to process more and more complex tasks. The neglect of citizens' privacy and the lack of government constraints in its protection seem to be promoting the country's AI technology, pushing it forward to become the world's leader in artificial intelligence.

---

132 Lee, Kai-Fu. AI Superpowers: China, Silicon Valley, and the New World Order. Boston: Houghton Mifflin Harcourt, 2018.

133 Ibid.

ADVANCED SEMICONDUCTORS

In April 2018, the United States announced a restriction on US companies selling parts and software to Chinese telecommunications company ZTE, leaving the world's fourth-largest telecommunications equipment manufacturer on the verge of bankruptcy. The United States banned all sales by American companies to ZTE, after it allegedly made false statements during an investigation into selling equipment to Iran.[134]

After reconciling with the US government, ZTE racked up over $1 billion in fines, a host of executive resignations, and a requirement for US officials to be permanently stationed in the company for compliance checks. The ZTE incident has been seen by the Chinese as an unattractive political move by the United States and a humiliation for the Chinese. Though the ZTE debacle has concluded, the United States has moved on to sanction Chinese telecommunications giant Huawei, an incident widely covered by the media. Huawei, on the cusp of potentially losing its US suppliers, is scrambling to create a stockpile of Chinese-made chips to replace their American counterparts.

The ZTE and Huawei incidents were seminal moments in the US-China technology rivalry. Despite China's large investments in the semiconductor industry, only 16 percent of semiconductor products used in China are manufactured

---

134 Delaney, Robert. "US Slaps China Telecoms Firm ZTE with 7-Year Ban for Sanctions Breach." South China Morning Post, April 17, 2018. https://www.scmp.com/business/companies/article/2142002/us-slaps-zte-seven-year-components-ban-breaching-terms-sanctions.

domestically, with 8 percent of the total semiconductors used produced by Chinese companies. The world's high-end core chips and components are mainly controlled by the United States and Japan. US companies include the likes of Qualcomm, Intel, and IBM, producing equipment such as CPUs, FPGAs, and memory chips—all exported to China.

China's progress in the semiconductor field still requires decades of accumulation of expertise, requiring a generational effort until it can become as advanced as the West. The Chinese government for many years has attempted to cultivate indigenous chip capabilities. However, constructing high-performance semiconductor parts is an extremely complex and expertise-intensive process. The Chinese Ministry of Science and Technology is raising large sums of money to support this process.[135]

Much of the country's official spending has been aimed at allowing its industries to match Western capabilities, not at pushing toward new areas. The country's decision-making rationale is straightforward: unless the country can do the same things as their Western counterparts, they will not be able to move beyond the West's achievements.[136] Many technology companies with large-scale semiconductor business operations have received preferential policies or policies from the government. Huawei's HiSilicon, SMIC (Semiconductor

---

135 Lee, Kai-Fu. AI Superpowers: China, Silicon Valley, and the New World Order. Boston: Houghton Mifflin Harcourt, 2018.

136 Tse, Edward. Chinas Disruptors: How Alibaba, Xiaomi, Tencent and Other Companies Are Changing the Rules of Business. London: Portfolio Penguin, 2016.

Manufacturing International Corporation), Qiqi, and others have reaped the benefits of the government's new push. Furthermore, Taiwan's TSMC (Taiwan Semiconductor Manufacturing Company), the world's largest chip supplier, is also now required to produce in the mainland.

CHAPTER 5

ARTIFICIAL INTELLIGENCE: What is Artificial Intelligence?

———

Success in creating AI would be the biggest event in human history. Unfortunately, it might also be the last, unless we learn how to avoid the risks.

—STEPHEN HAWKING

A GAME OF GO

For millennia, humans have played games with each other, exploring the limits of human thought and strategy. During the digital era, more and more individuals are starting to play games with machines, with the first computer game Spacewar invented in 1962 by the Massachusetts Institute of Technology. This two-player game involved sparring spaceships that fire photon torpedoes at one another. Each player maneuvers a spacecraft and scores by hitting their opponent in the game.

Seemingly a simple concept, this game runs on a computer the size of a large car![137]

Today, individuals are playing far more sophisticated games with computers. No longer do they require two human players, as computers can now artificially simulate the actions of humans with stunning accuracy. With the increase in machines' computational power and the development of artificial intelligence, technology is becoming much better than ever before at simulating human behavior. Machines are winning so much so that they are inspiring doubts about the future of humanity.

In 2017, Google's AlphaGo artificial intelligence is pitted against the world's best Go player, Ke Jie. Go is one of the world's oldest board games, invented more than 2,000 years ago in ancient China, where it has been called *weiqi*.[138] On a nineteen-by-nineteen board filled with black and white stone pieces, this game has so many possible moves that a computer with merely preprogrammed rules will struggle to decipher it. After the first two moves of chess, 400 subsequent steps exist; however, Go has 130,000 possibilities. Players of this game need not only knowledge of the rules and strategies but also an almost Zen-like state of mind to navigate its dizzying complexity.

---

137   "A History of the Computer Game." Jesper Juul, n.d. https://www.jesperjuul.net/thesis/2-historyofthecomputergame.html.

138   Strittmatter, Kai, and Ruth Martin. We Have Been Harmonised: Life in Chinas Surveillance State. Exeter: Old Street Publishing Ltd., 2019.

Chinese Go player Ke Jie. *(https://www.cbc.ca/news/technology/goo-gle-ai-wins-go-chinese-champion-1.4130991)*

During the game, Ke Jie uncharacteristically slumps in his seat, puzzling over his game against the AI adversary. As one of the best Go players in the world, he is usually teeming with cocky confidence; today, however, he sits in the arena confused, staring at the board. The room is dead silent. This match is a showdown of man versus machine, with Ke Jie representing the very brightest of what humanity has to offer. But he is systematically dismantled by the computer opponent opposite to him.[139]

AlphaGo learned the game through a type of machine learning, where it becomes its teacher. By starting with a network that knows nothing about the game, it plays games against itself, learning and tuning itself. During games, it analyzes situations by breaking the game down to tiny parts and

---

139   Ibid.

visualizing all possible moves. After seventy hours of training, it already can play at a super-human level.[140]

Ke Jie threw everything he had at the artificial intelligence machine—to no avail. Through three marathon matches, each lasting three hours, he was ultimately defeated by Alpha-Go.[141] This victory surprised many. The future is indeed here. Technologies at the heart of AlphaGo are going to transform our world to a degree we have not seen since the original Industrial Revolution.[142]

In China, the victory of the British-made artificial intelligence over the country's young prodigy sparked new discussion within its technology community. This loss was not only the defeat of man by machine but also a triumph for Western technology, its prowess, and its international reach. China must have felt what the United States experienced in October 1957 when its greatest rival, the Soviet Union, launched the first human-made satellite into space. As Lyndon B. Johnson asserted, the future is "not as far off as we thought," and whoever wins the space race would have "total control over the earth, for tyranny or the service of freedom."[143]

140 "AlphaGo Zero: Starting from Scratch." Deepmind, October 18, 2017. https://deepmind.com/blog/article/alphago-zero-starting-scratch.

141 Lee, Kai-Fu. AI Superpowers: China, Silicon Valley, and the New World Order. Boston: Houghton Mifflin Harcourt, 2018.

142 Strittmatter, Kai, and Ruth Martin. We Have Been Harmonised: Life in Chinas Surveillance State. Exeter: Old Street Publishing Ltd., 2019.

143 Ibid.

The launch of the Soviet Union's satellite had a profound impact on the psyche of the American public, creating widespread fears of the superiority of Soviet technology. China, like the United States, underwent a sudden change of tactic, initiating a new financial and strategic effort almost overnight, funneling enormous resources into artificial intelligence. Now, the Chinese public has awakened to the infinite possibilities of AI and the power it has. Xi Jinping has called on his country to become the "world leader" in AI as quickly as possible. Scientists, according to Xi, must trudge heroically "into no man's land," so that China can "occupy the commanding heights" in the area of artificial intelligence.[144]

WHAT IS BIG DATA?

AlphaGo, during its initial training of the game, utilizes a database of 30 million human moves to mimic social play. This process enables it to match the movements of Go experts, after which it continues to play games against itself to reinforce its learning. Effectively, the data that AlphaGo uses during its training can be classified as big data. Big data is the raw information that needs to be cleaned, structured, and integrated before it becomes useful. It is, at its core, vast sets of data with varying structures, allowing programs—often artificial intelligence—to gain new insights through analyzing patterns and trends in the data.[145]

---

144 "Xi Jinping: Promoting the Healthy Development of China's New Generation of Artificial Intelligence." Xinhua Net. Xinhua Net, October 31, 2018. http://www.xinhuanet.com/politics/2018-10/31/c_1123643321.htm.

145 "Big Data vs. Artificial Intelligence." Datamation. Accessed January 11, 2020. https://www.datamation.com/big-data/big-data-vs.-artificial

Big data is large, complex data sets so voluminous that traditional data processing methods cannot manage them. They can be used to gain insights that otherwise cannot be found through smaller sets of data. Imagine CCTV footage, a tweet, a voice message, one's shopping history, a passport scan, a photo of a sandwich, an EKG reading—all of these can form the basis of big data.[146]

Big data is a catchall phrase used to describe these extensive databases of information that can be used to understand, analyze, and forecast trends. It can be used interchangeably with big data analytics, analytics, or deep analytics.[147] A misconception exists that the advances made possible by big data are simply a function of the amount of data gathered. The growth of data without the ability to process it is not useful. Thus, big data is commonly used in discussions of artificial intelligence, as the latter can process vast amounts of information.

Big data involves three core concepts: volume, velocity, and variety.[148] According to this model, challenges in significant data management result from the expansion of all three properties, rather than volume alone.[149]

-intelligence.html.

146 "What Is Big Data?" YouTube. World Economic Forum, n.d. https://
     www.youtube.com/watch?v=eVSfJhssXUA.

147 Ross, Alec. The Industries of the Future. New York: Simon & Schuster
     paperbacks, 2017.

148 "What Is Big Data?" Oracle, n.d. https://www.oracle.com/big-data/guide/
     what-is-big-data.html.

149 Rouse, Margaret. "What Is 3Vs (Volume, Variety and Velocity)? - Defi-
     nition from WhatIs.com." WhatIs.com, n.d. https://whatis.techtarget.

- Volume: The amount of data matters. The bulk of data is vital in providing more critical insights. The size of available data has been growing at an increasing rate; for example, a text file is a few kilobytes, a sound file is a few megabytes, and a full movie may be a few gigabytes. Now, hundreds of millions of smartphones send a variety of data into the cloud, and this set-up did not exist just a few years ago.[150]
- Velocity: Velocity is the rate at which data is received. In the past, companies analyze data in a batch process, which involved taking chunks of data, submitting it to the server, and waiting for the result. However, now data is streamed into the server in real-time.[151]
- Variety: Variety refers to the types of data available. From Excel tables and databases, data structures have become loosened. Now, data can exist in text, photo, audio, video, web, GPS, sensor data, relational data, SMS, PDF, Flash, and myriad more. A structure can no longer be imposed like in the past.[152]

Today, big data has become a kind of capital. Good examples of data as capital are large technology companies. The value that these companies offer stems from their acquisition of an abundance of data, which they continuously analyze

com/definition/3Vs.

150 Soubra, Diya. "The 3Vs That Define Big Data." Data Science Central, July 5, 2012. https://www.datasciencecentral.com/forum/topics/the-3vs-that-define-big-data.

151 Ibid.

152 Ibid.

to improve efficiency and produce new products.[153] With increasing volumes of data becoming cheaper and more accessible, businesses can now more accurately make business decisions.[154]

With the advent of the Internet of Things (IoT), more objects will be connected to the Internet, allowing for the availability of much more data, such as customer usage patterns and product performance. Further, cloud computing has expanded big data possibilities.[155]

During previous industrial revolutions, land or iron could be considered the raw material of the times. During the Fourth Industrial Revolution, data has become the new natural resource. The Internet has become an ocean of chaotic information, but now we have a way to connect this information to draw intelligence from it. Consequently, big data has transitioned from a tool primarily targeted for advertising to a device with profound applications for diverse sectors, addressing social problems.[156]

WHAT IS ARTIFICIAL INTELLIGENCE?

In the context of AlphaGo, big data was used by programmers to allow the machine to gain new insights into the rules and

---

153   "What Is Big Data?" Oracle, n.d. https://www.oracle.com/big-data/guide/what-is-big-data.html.

154   Ibid.

155   Ibid.

156   Ross, Alec. The Industries of the Future. New York: Simon & Schuster paperbacks, 2017.

patterns in games of Go. Artificial intelligence, on the other hand, is all about decision-making. After learning the laws of the game, AlphaGo will need to learn further to respond to all moves—expected and unexpected—during real matches. To return to real-game situations is why AlphaGo needs the help of artificial intelligence.[157] The primary differentiator between big data and artificial intelligence is perhaps that big data is the raw input, while artificial intelligence is the output. AI is the intelligence that results from the processed big data, making the two inherently different.[158]

Artificial intelligence is a form of computer engineering that allows machines to perform human-like cognitive functions. Traditional computer applications also react to data, but programmers have to hand-code these reactions; if the user gives any unexpected information, the app will not be able to respond. AI, on the other hand, is continually changing its behavior to accommodate sudden changes. An AI-enabled device is created to analyze and interpret data and solve problems or address issues based on those interpretations. AI is all about decision-making and learning to make better decisions. Whether it is self-tuning software, self-driving cars, or examining medical samples, AI is doing tasks previously done by humans but faster and with reduced errors.[159]

---

157   Patrizio, Andy. "Big Data vs. Artificial Intelligence." Datamation. Datamation, May 30, 2018. https://www.datamation.com/big-data/big-data-vs.-artificial-intelligence.html.

158   Ibid.

159   Ibid.

Three basic AI concepts exist: machine learning, deep learning, and neural networks. Each approach allows machines to become artificially intelligent, albeit through different methods of learning, each more sophisticated than the next.[160]

- Machine Learning: In machine learning, machines receive an incredible amount of trial examples for specific tasks. As the computer processes these trials, it learns and adapts new strategies to achieve a particular object. One salient example of this process is image recognition. If a machine is to recognize apples and pears, for instance, researchers will feed thousands of images of apples and pears. The device may learn that an apple has a round shape and is red while a pear is oval-shaped and green. When asked to identify individual images of fruits, the machine will know whether each is an apple or a pear.[161]
- Deep Learning: While machine learning limits the machine to solving problems in one area after the human input of data, in-depth knowledge enables computers to solve problems in areas outside of what they have learned in one area. For example, a program that has learned how to distinguish apples from pears might use this learning to seek patterns in complex graphs.
- Neural Networks: Neural networks often enable deep learning, which stimulates cells in the brain. Inspired by our biology, neural net models use math and computer science

---

160 Sciglar, Paul. "What Is Artificial Intelligence? Understanding 3 Basic AI Concepts." Robotics Business Review. Robotics Business Review, April 19, 2018. https://www.roboticsbusinessreview.com/ai/3-basic-ai-concepts-explain-artificial-intelligence/.

161 Ibid.

to mimic processes in the human brain, allowing for more general learning. Instead of being built through interconnected brain cells, artificial neural networks use code.

No technology has captured the public imagination like AI. At a conference at Dartmouth College in 1956, researchers launched the field of AI. Within a decade, popular culture had taken hold of the promises surrounding AI, imagining myriad fantastic and catastrophic results of artificial intelligence's impact on human society.[162] While AI research and implementation have indeed progressed at a blinding speed, we will not be seeing killer robots any time soon. Instead, we will see high unpredictability in the global economy. Economics is busy modeling the potential automated post-work economies, and educators are forecasting the skill sets that will be needed by the workforce of tomorrow.[163] With the rising prevalence of advanced artificial intelligence, we will also see increases in economic growth as industries exploit this new tool in their toolbox.

Artificial intelligence is like a new type of electricity, soon to power all branches of industry, as well as our private lives. The Neolithic Revolution occurred 10,000 years ago, when humans first became settlers, then came the Industrial Revolution. Now, the Information Revolution is upon us. Thanks to artificial intelligence, in the future, only a quarter of the population will be required to produce and provide the sum of total of all goods and services. However, only two nations

162 Schwab, Klaus. Shaping the Future of the Fourth Industrial Revolution. Knopf Doubleday Publishing Group, 2018.

163 Ibid.

are going to profit from the AI revolution, the United States and China. Everywhere else lacks the infrastructure; when it comes to AI, the threshold for entry is too high.[164]

Both the US and Chinese governments regard artificial intelligence as a critical technology of the future, and both governments have issued strategic plans to promote the overall level of AI technology. Both have established relatively complete research and development mechanisms at the national level to coordinate the advance of artificial intelligence. Currently, the United States is at the forefront of research. It has maintained a leading position, while China still has a considerable gap to bridge in terms of basic algorithms and theoretical analysis.

From a global perspective, the leading country in the AI race is the United States. As of June 2017, the total number of artificial intelligence companies reached 2,542—of which 1,078 are from the United States, accounting for 42 percent of the total amount. Following the United States is China, with 592 companies, accounting for 23 percent of the international number of AI companies. The remaining 872 companies are located in Sweden, Singapore, Japan, the United Kingdom, Australia, Israel, India, and a few other countries.

---

164 Strittmatter, Kai, and Ruth Martin. We Have Been Harmonised: Life in Chinas Surveillance State. Exeter: Old Street Publishing Ltd., 2019.

CHAPTER 6

ARTIFICIAL INTELLIGENCE: Artificial Intelligence and US-China Relations

---

I'm increasingly inclined to think that there should be some regulatory oversight, maybe at the national and international level, just to make sure that we don't do something very foolish. I mean with artificial intelligence we're summoning the demon.

—ELON MUSK

AI CHIPS

Imagine having the power of AlphaGo in your pocket. Opportunities for the integration of artificial intelligence are vast, from dishwashers to surveillance cameras and from fitness trackers to home robots. Companies in both the United States and China are trying to make this hypothetical a reality with the development of advanced AI-enabled semiconductors, which can optimize AI processing in devices.

Before exploring the importance of AI-enabled semiconductors, however, we must first understand what they are. A computer chip is a dense cluster of semiconductor material embedded on a small wafer plate.[165] They are the core of all electronic products we interact with, from desktops to laptops to smartphones.[166] High-performance chips are the unsung heroes of computing revolutions, and due to the complexity of manufacturing them, their production is significant economically and politically. Manufacturing advanced chips required decades of accumulation of technical know-how and huge investments of capital. For example, erecting a new factory can cost more than $1 billion, and its products can potentially become obsolete in less than five years.[167] Due to the high inputs required for their creation, the chips market tends toward monopoly.

Each digital era requires different chips. Amid the popularity of desktop computers, manufacturers tended toward maximizing processing speed with little regard for power consumption. Now, because of the prevalence of smartphones, the demand has moved toward more efficient uses of power. Soon, as computer programs become replaced by AI algorithms, the original style of chips will change again. New AI chips are central to everything from facial recognition to

165 "Computer Chip." Encyclopædia Britannica. Encyclopædia Britannica, inc., December 22, 2017. https://www.britannica.com/technology/computer-chip.

166 Lee, Kai-Fu. AI Superpowers: China, Silicon Valley, and the New World Order. Boston: Houghton Mifflin Harcourt, 2018.

167 Turley, James L. The Essential Guide to Semiconductors. Upper Saddle River, NJ: Prentice Hall, 2003.

self-driving cars, optimized to provide better functionality to AI-enabled devices and programs. Google, Microsoft, Intel, Qualcomm, and a number of chip startups are planning to foray into the AI chip.

China has been attempting to catch up to the West in terms of market share and level of semiconductor technology, albeit with limited success.[168] This lack of catch-up is due to two factors: the speed of innovation in the semiconductor industry and the structure of the market. Firstly, changes are frequent in the chip industry, putting latecomers at a disadvantaged position, requiring that they work additionally hard to catch up. Secondly, the market for advanced semiconductors is highly integrated and not segmented, giving few opportunities for newcomers in the low-end market.[169]

Even though the Chinese semiconductor industry has faced many obstacles in its search for a catch-up, promising signs are emerging. Consequent to the explosion of the Chinese market for foreign goods, the country has seen a loosening on restrictions for technology transfers to China. Furthermore, China can expect an increasing flow of human capital with chip-making know-how by working with foreign firms and training its human capital in foreign countries. The consolidation of research and development has also improved the capabilities of domestic firms, supported by cutting-edge

---

168   Rho, Sungho, Keun Lee, and Seong Hee Kim. "Limited Catch-up in China's Semiconductor Industry: A Sectoral Innovation System Perspective." Millennial Asia 6, no. 2 (2015): 147–75. https://doi.org/10.1177/0976399615590514.

169   Ibid.

research in Chinese universities. Consequently, China's position in AI chip skills is expected to rise.[170]

The Chinese Ministry of Science and Technology is giving out vast sums of money for the specific goal of chip construction. The Chinese semiconductor industry sees AI chips as an area where the country has the opportunity to overtake the curve, another example of the pervasive shortcut mentality in the industry. The fact remains that AI chips are a completely new segment with no established leaders, allowing startups to fill the vacuum.[171]

AI chips, instead of relying on existing popular platforms, are young enough to see the establishment of new architectures and ecosystems, created from the ground up. This state of affairs gives Chinese chip companies a seat at the table.[172] In their quest to win the artificial intelligence race, the three big Chinese digital companies—Baidu, Alibaba, and Tencent—are all investing heavily in AI startups. Since 2014, this trio of companies has made thirty-nine equity deals in startups that work on AI chips and software.[173] Chinese startups like Horizon Robotics, Bitmain, and Cambricon Technologies

170   Ibid.

171   Xiang, Nina. Red AI: Victories and Warnings from Chinas Rise in Artificial Intelligence. Place of publication not identified: Nina Xiang, 2019.

172   Ibid.

173   Fannin, Rebecca A. Tech Titans of China: How Chinas Tech Sector Is Challenging the World by Innovating Faster, Working Harder & Going Global. Boston, MA: Nicholas Brealey Publishing, 2019.

are full of investment capital, working on products made for artificial intelligence cases.[174]

AI TALENT AND THE THOUSAND TALENTS PROGRAM

Six weeks before the release of the first iPhone, Steve Jobs is furious. He calls upon his most senior team to discuss the upcoming iPhone—the one about to become a huge success. According to Jobs, this phone needs a glass screen. Pulling the prototype phone with a plastic screen out from his pocket, he shows his team that the plastic screen scratches too quickly, so an unscratchable glass screen is needed. Glass needs to be integrated into the phone before full production starts in about five weeks.

Nobody knows how to make a glass screen.

Immediately, one of the company's high-ranking executives leaves for Shenzhen, China's manufacturing hub, where Apple's partner Foxconn sits ready with 200,000 workers, prepared to assemble the new iPhone. Shenzhen is a region with a vast number of engineering experts and specialized companies that Apple can draw on for support in the construction of the glass screen. The problem is figuring out how to precision-cut and grind the hardened glass for phones and do it in the span of just a few weeks.

Within days of arriving in China, the executive is surprised to find that the Chinese company making the bid has already

---

174 Lee, Kai-Fu. AI Superpowers: China, Silicon Valley, and the New World Order. Boston: Houghton Mifflin Harcourt, 2018.

started arranging a new facility for the project, just in case they won the bid. Chinese engineers have already moved into the facility and are experimenting with the new glass.

Within four weeks, this company that ultimately received the glass bid figures it out. The new glass screens are cut, ground, and shipped out to Foxconn, where, within two days, 10,000 iPhones are coming off the production lines. Altogether, 200,000 Chinese workers are involved in the production of the first iPhone. And they are overseen by 8,700 industrial engineers from China.

From this story, we learn that Chinese manufacturing is incredibly fast and flexible. Figuring out how to redesign iPhone screens required considerable brainpower deployed very quickly, and this feat was possible in China. Such speed would not have happened in the United States. According to the *New York Times*, Apple would have taken nine months to find the same number of engineers that China found. In China, this act was accomplished in about fifteen days.[175] This story is about Chinese brainpower and its influence on global business, with the country's ability to mobilize so much talent so quickly.

The source of China's brainpower comes from its universities, and the country is currently undergoing an educational

---

175 Duhigg, Charles, and Keith Bradsher. "How the US Lost Out on IPhone Work." The New York Times. The New York Times, January 21, 2012. https://www.nytimes.com/2012/01/22/business/apple-america-and-a-squeezed-middle-class.html?_r=2&ref=charlesduhigg&pagewant-ed=all&mtrref=www.businessinsider.com&assetType=REGIWALL.

boom. The number of universities has increased from 1,022 in 2011 to 2,824 in 2014, hosting over 40 million students—constituting the world's largest student population, with one in every five students in the world coming from China.[176] Consequent to the number of schools in the country, the Economic Intelligence Unit predicts that China will have the most significant amount of STEM (science, technology, engineering, and math) graduates in the world in 2030.[177]

What are the implications of China becoming a brainpower behemoth? First, as illustrated by the story, is the country's ability to churn out new and innovative products at a blinding pace. However, more importantly, this new position will help boost the country in the research, development, and application of artificial intelligence.

Humans are ultimately the drivers of the AI revolution. Human hands construct "intelligence" in "artificial intelligence." Hence a nation's strength is built upon the smarts of its cutting-edge human capital in industry and academia. As indicated by the number of papers published in the artificial intelligence fields, the United States currently leads the pack of countries, with US scholars contributing most to the development of AI. The ranking is then followed by Taiwan,

176 Frolovskiy, Dmitriy. "China's Education Boom." The Diplomat. for The Diplomat, December 29, 2017. https://thediplomat.com/2017/12/chinas-education-boom/.

177 "Education to 2030." Yidan Prize. The Economist, 2016. https://eiuperspectives.economist.com/sites/default/files/EIU_Yidan prize forecast_ Education to 2030.pdf.

Poland, Spain, and China, with the latter ranking fifth in the list.[178]

Even though China lags behind the United States by four places in the international ranking, individuals are optimistic about the development of Chinese cultivation of AI talent. The top universities in China have always been excellent. Still, they are much better today than they were twenty-five years ago, and they are on a trajectory to become the biggest and best in the world.[179]

In a document released by the Chinese State Council in 2017, the country affirms that artificial intelligence has become a new focus of international competition, as it is a strategic technology that will lead the future, enhance national competitiveness, and maintain national security. Thus China must plan strategically to become a leader in the development of this new technology.[180] One of the ways of getting ahead of the AI curve is the cultivation and gathering of high-end AI talent.

---

178   Sun, Bo, and Zhixue Dong. "Comparative Study on the Academic Field of Artificial Intelligence in China and Other Countries." Wireless Personal Communications 102, no. 2 (November 2018): 1879–90. https://doi.org/10.1007/s11277-018-5243-2.

179   Church, Kenneth Ward. "Emerging Trends: Artificial Intelligence, China and My New Job at Baidu." Natural Language Engineering 24, no. 4 (November 2018): 641–47. https://doi.org/10.1017/s1351324918000189.

180   "State Council on Issuing Notification of New Generation Artificial Intelligence Development Planning." 国务院关于印发新一代人工智能发展规划的通知（国发2017 35号）_政府信息公开专栏, July 8, 2017. http://www.gov.cn/zhengce/content/2017-07/20/content_5211996.htm.

Tim Cook meeting an iPhone manufacturer in China. *(https://www. cultofmac.com/407687/get-the-foxconn-experience-with-new-tourist-factory/)*

The country is taking the construction of abilities as one of the top priorities of artificial intelligence development. The document released by the State Council has affirmed that the country will engage in several training and talent-sourcing initiatives to the strength of the country's basic research, applied research, and operation and maintenance of artificial intelligence. China will not only develop the domestic talent of industry experts and researchers but also focus on introducing top international skills to the country, ones who can help build the nation's abilities in neurocognition, machine learning, autonomous driving, and intelligent robots.[181]

On the list of initiatives set out by the Chinese government, the Thousand Talents Program is one that stands out. It is

---

181   Ibid.

organized by the Central Committee of the Communist Party of China, supervising the introduction of new human capital into the country, money that can meet the demand for high-end AI development. People who enter the Thousand Talents Program face particularly stringent requirements. Generally, a Ph.D. needs to be obtained overseas by the applicant, who must also meet one of the following conditions:[182]

- Serving as an expert and scholar equivalent to a professorship in a famous foreign university or research institute;
- Professional and technical personnel and senior management personnel in senior positions in internationally renowned enterprises and financial institutions;
- Entrepreneurial talents who have independent intellectual property rights or master core technologies, have independent overseas entrepreneurial experience, and are familiar with relevant industry fields and international rules;
- Other high-level innovation and entrepreneurial talents urgently needed by the country.

In the context of US-China technology competition, China's ambitions in attracting the best talents into the country have been shrouded in controversy. The Thousand Talents Program, especially, has been the victim of US attack, as the country has branded the program a threat to the American research enterprise, citing the possible transfer of US research to be used in Chinese technology and military applications.[183]

---

182 "The Recruitment Program for Innovative Talents (Long Term)." Recruitment Program of Global Experts, n.d. http://www.1000plan.org.cn/en/.

183 Portman, Rob, and Tom Carper. "Threats to the US Research Enterprise: China's Talent Recruitment Plans." United States Senate PERMANENT

RECRUITMENT
PROGRAM OF GLOBAL EXPERTS

Logo of the Thousand Talents Program. *(https://mi.wisc.edu/News.htm)*

"Launched in 2008, the Thousand Talents Plan incentivizes individuals engaged in research and development in the United States to transmit the knowledge and research they gain here to China in exchange for monetary payments. ... China unfairly uses the American research and expertise it obtains for its own economic and military gain."

The United States believes that countries exploit their openness to advance their national interest, with the most aggressive state being China. The Thousand Talents Program incentivizes individuals engaged in research and development in the United States to transmit the knowledge they gain to China in exchange for salaries, research funding, lab space, and other incentives.[184] According to the US government, the stealing of American research, not only endangering

SUBCOMMITTEE ON INVESTIGATIONS. United States Senate PERMANENT SUBCOMMITTEE ON INVESTIGATIONS, n.d. https://www.hsgac.senate.gov/imo/media/doc/2019-11-18 PSI Staff Report - China's Talent Recruitment Plans.pdf.

184 Ibid.

the country's national security, but has also contributed to China's meteoric rise in the past twenty years.

One of the most prominent manifestations of the competition of talent between the two countries is the increasing difficulty Chinese scientists have obtaining US visas. In January 2019, the American Association for the Advancement of Sciences (AAAS) announced the 2018 Newcome Cleveland Award, given to a thirty-four-member team led by professor Pan Jianwei of the University of Science and Technology of China. 2018 was the first time Chinese scientists have achieved this honor in the past ninety years. However, due to issues receiving a visa to the United States, Pan Jianwei was unable to attend the award ceremony. Only the first author of his paper, Professor Yin Juan, was present to receive the award.

The Thousand Talents Program continues to attract the best talent around the world to support China's AI research. The country's technology transfer programs are broad, genuinely rooted, and calculated to support the country's development of artificial intelligence. These practices have been used for decades and provide the country access to foreign technical innovations. Searching the program's name and AI disciplines online, selectees of the Thousand Talents Program were overwhelmingly from the United States, and were typically university professors, with experience in intelligent robotics, blockchain, and applied aspects of AI.[185] Additionally, while the Thousand Talents Program is the commonly

---

185   Hannas, Wm, and Huey-meei Chang. "China's Access to Foreign AI Technology." Center for Security and Emerging Technology. Center for Security and Emerging Technology, September 2019. https://cset.

cited example of China's push to attract human capital, thousands of other such programs are available.[186]

DIGITAL TRANSFORMATION

One of my biggest pet peeves in life is going through airports. The crowds, the lines, and the waiting make for an uncomfortable experience. Unfortunately, with flying being one of the main methods of transnational travel in the United States, trips to the airport are an unavoidable affair. Compared to travel hubs in China, airports in the United States seem old and dilapidated.

Exiting my taxi and stepping inside the Shenzhen Bao'an International Airport, I am transported to another world. Standing under a white, webbed cocoon overarching the main entry area, the building I find myself in is vast and stunningly modern. Located in Asia's technology metropolis of Shenzhen, this airport could be one of the most digitally integrated transport hubs in the world. I spot a large screen in the check-in area, live-streaming the planes outside in crystal-clear 4K video—through a fifth-generation telecommunications connection. Scattered throughout the check-in area are also customer-service and security robots, ready to make the traveling experience smoother and more secure for passengers. At the same time, installed in the ceiling of this airport is the most significant number of security cameras I have seen in one place.

---

georgetown.edu/wp-content/uploads/CSET-Chinas-Access-to-Foreign-AI-Technology-2.pdf.

186 Ibid.

Entering the security check area, I am faced with strange-looking mandatory kiosks that I have not been through at other airports. The machine instructs me to insert my identification document as a screen flashes on. I stare back at myself on the screen as a green box appears around my face, and the glass doors swing open. My face was just scanned into a centralized database that I will use for further security checks, for boarding the plane, and for future flights. No boarding pass is needed when I board the plane. I reveal my face, and the gate swings open for me. In the future, the airport should be able to identify passengers throughout the airport and notify them if they are soon to be too late to board the plane.

In addition to the integration of next-generation facial recognition technology into the airport's passenger facing processes, the Shenzhen airport also has digitally transformed many other aspects of the airport operations. One such example is smart airfield ground lighting, based on artificial intelligence and the Internet of Things. With intelligent airfield ground lighting, the airport can more efficiently conduct flight path planning and expedite the taxiing of planes, reducing the time between the flight landing and passenger unloading by 20 percent.[187]

Above are all examples of how digital transformation is enabling the Shenzhen Airport to become more efficient and

---

187 Zhang, Huai. "How Big Data and AI Will Transform Shenzhen Airport." Huawei. Huawei, December 28, 2018. https://www.huawei.com/en/about-huawei/publications/winwin-magazine/32/shenzhen-airport-digital-platform-and-ai.

provide a better customer experience. These technologies are fast being implemented by engineers at other transportation hubs in China, bringing digitization to more aspects of life. At the heart of it all is the country's push in researching and implementing next-generation technologies like artificial intelligence and big data, transforming various industries. However, before discussing the importance of digital transformation and its implications for the competition between the United States and China, we must first understand what it is.

The phrase "digital transformation" is discussed in almost every keynote, panel discussion, article, or study, advising how business leaders should adapt to the twenty-first century to remain competitive. However, behind the buzz, what exactly is digital transformation? Quite simply, digital transformation is a concept that can be applied to all industries in the private or public sector. It involves two separate theories of digitization and transformation. Digitization refers to the use of technology to convert processes in real life into processes aided with technology. Transformation refers to the use of existing sources of data to create value.

Examples of digital transformation and its "digitization," as well as "transformation," can be found everywhere. Digitization, for example, can be as simple as using digital tools in the workplace, like Microsoft Excel to sort data or one's smartphone to order goods online. In these two examples, digital tools have replaced offline processes like entering written data into a physical database or going to a store to buy products.

Chinese women using mobile apps. *(https://sampi.co/top-10-most-popular-mobile-apps-in-china/)*

Transformation, on the other hand, displays itself in more involved examples. Online marketplaces like Amazon, for example, use existing sources of data—having manipulated, sorted, and analyzed them—and convert them into real value. This value manifests itself in the form of personalized product recommendations that enable Amazon to sell more goods. Throughout the transformation process, technologies such as big data and artificial intelligence are used by implementers to make digital transformation more fruitful in creating productivity. In the Amazon example, customer data is first collected through their shopping preferences into a set of big data, which is then interpreted using artificial intelligence to create value for the company. Other technologies may also be used in this process, such as the cloud—for the storage of the vast amount of user data—or 5G—for the collection of more data, allowing more users to input data into the system.

All in all, digital transformation offers to increase the efficiency of various industries. Digitization is the evolution of nontechnologically integrated processes into processes with technology at the core. Transformation is the manipulation of data through big data and artificial intelligence to generate value. The process to watch within digital transformation is transformation, as it integrates the bleeding-edge technologies that promise to change the way we fundamentally live, work, and experience the world. Artificial intelligence is an integral part of digital transformation, and its development will determine how digital transformation impacts industries.

According to a McKinsey & Company Global Institute report in 2018, artificial intelligence is poised to have a deep and profound influence on the global economy. AI will add $13 trillion to the world's economy, which accounts for an annual contribution to productivity of about 1.2 percent between 2018 and 2030.[188] If fully realized, the impact of AI would compare well with other transformative technologies throughout history, such as the steam engine during the 1800s, robotics during the 1990s, and information technology during the 2000s.

---

188 Bughin, Jacques, Jeongmin Seong, James Manyika, Michael Chui, and Raoul Joshi. "NOTES FROM THE AI FRONTIER MODELING THE IMPACT OF AI ON THE WORLD ECONOMY." McKinsey Global Institute. McKinsey Global Institute, September 2018. https://www.mckinsey.com/~/media/McKinsey/Featured Insights/Artificial Intelligence/Notes from the frontier Modeling the impact of AI on the world economy/MGI-Notes-from-the-AI-frontier-Modeling-the-impact-of-AI-on-the-world-economy-September-2018.ashx.

The two countries best prepared to reap the rewards of digital transformation are the United States and China, which are currently responsible for the majority of AI-related activities.[189] Compared to other countries, the two juggernauts will benefit disproportionately by embracing a broad set of artificial intelligence technologies.[190] They will be at the forefront of introducing productive technologies relating to digital transformation, and the gains will be accelerated by the readiness for AI of all parties, from businesses to consumers.[191]

In the race for the digital transformation of all industries, we will see a "follower" and "laggard" paradigm internationally, as countries and companies risk falling behind in reaping the benefits brought by artificial intelligence. Effectively, the world will become one with "AI-haves" and "AI-have-nots."[192] The United States and China will be at the forefront of digital transformation through the implementation of AI, and the distance between the two countries and the rest of the world will widen as others struggle to secure the rewards of digital transformation. China will likely take more time to feel the

---

189 "Economic Impacts of Artificial Intelligence (AI)." European Parliament. European Parliament, July 2019. http://www.europarl.europa.eu/RegData/etudes/BRIE/2019/637967/EPRS_BRI(2019)637967_EN.pdf.

190 Wladawsky-Berger, Irving. "The Impact of Artificial Intelligence on the World Economy." The Wall Street Journal. Dow Jones & Company, November 26, 2018. https://blogs.wsj.com/cio/2018/11/16/the-impact-of-artificial-intelligence-on-the-world-economy/.

191 "Economic Impacts of Artificial Intelligence (AI)." European Parliament. European Parliament, July 2019.

192 Lee, Kai-Fu. AI Superpowers: China, Silicon Valley, and the New World Order. Boston: Houghton Mifflin Harcourt, 2018.

impact of digital transformation and artificial intelligence effectively. Still, profound changes will eventually occur in the country's vast manufacturing sector, and then steadily move up the value chain into more high-tech-driven manufacturing and commerce areas.[193]

Digital transformation requires four main building blocks: abundant data, tenacious entrepreneurs, well-trained AI scientists, and supportive government policy.[194] And China is making leaps and bounds in each of these areas. In the following sections, we will explore the comparative statuses of each of these areas in China.

ABUNDANT DATA

Digital transformation requires data inputs. "Transformation" refers to the conversion of data inputs into tangible value. China is moving quickly ahead of the rest of the world in the utilization of data and the expansion of new inputs of data.

What does having a large population mean? As the most populous country in the world, China contains an abundance of data. We know that the core of artificial intelligence technology is deep learning, which is inseparable from the "feeding" of big data. For example, training AI to predict certain diseases requires a large enough patient data set, and China's patient data sets are much larger than in other countries.

193 "Economic Impacts of Artificial Intelligence (AI)." European Parliament. European Parliament, July 2019.

194 Lee, Kai-Fu. AI Superpowers: China, Silicon Valley, and the New World Order. Boston: Houghton Mifflin Harcourt, 2018.

According to Lee Kai-Fu, we are moving from the age of expertise to a period of data.[195] Once technical talent reaches a certain threshold, it begins to exhibit diminishing returns. And, beyond this threshold, data is what makes the difference in digital effectiveness. With enough data, the algorithms used by an average engineer can outperform those built by leading experts. Now, China is finding itself sitting atop a pile of this critical resource that is powering the digital era: data. The country is the world's largest producer of digital data, ahead of the United States. China's number of Internet users already surpasses that of the United States and Europe combined and is increasing still every day with the digital transformation of life in rural areas. Similar to the Internet, China will become the largest market for AI applications, with rich application scenarios, the most significant number of users, and active data production entities in the world.

In addition to the quantity of data, China is beating the United States in the quality of data gathered. US companies focus on data mainly concerning one's online behavior, such as searches made, photos uploaded, and videos watched. China, on the other hand, boasts a digital ecosystem that extends into the physical world. Services like public transportation, shared bicycles, mobile payments, facial recognition, and more are collecting data from citizens' physical world. Both the public and private sectors will know where and how citizens make purchases, travel, pay their bills, eat, and more. The country's physically grounded digital infrastructure and lack of privacy concerns mean that companies

---

195 Ibid.

can collect a massive amount of data, giving China an edge over Silicon Valley.

China is also increasing the diversity of data inputs. With millions of security cameras distributed across Chinese cities like Beijing and Shanghai equipped with facial recognition technology, the government deals with massive amounts of new information on the lives of Chinese citizens. Entrepreneurs are also inventing new ways to digitally transform citizens' lives, increasing efficiency and introducing a higher number of data inputs for the use of big data. The emergence of fifth-generation telecommunications technology will aid in this venture, helping entrepreneurs envision how more excellent connectivity leads to a world where everything is connected.

TENACIOUS ENTREPRENEURS

In Edward Tse's book *China's Disruptors*, he describes the recent explosion in Chinese entrepreneurship as a "breaching of the dam" after the four-decade-long blockade on innovation and intellectual growth that Mao Zedong created in China during his reign.[196] Now, China has hundreds of thousands of entrepreneurs, all eager to make their mark on the country's intensely competitive but lucrative markets.

Still, the economic impact of artificial intelligence depends on whether sufficient investment exists to fund new companies

---

196 Tse, Edward. *China's Disruptors: How Alibaba, Xiaomi, Tencent and Other Companies Are Changing the Rules of Business.* London: Portfolio Penguin, 2016.

and research. Since the emergence of the first artificial intelligence venture capital investment in the United States in 1999, global AI has accelerated its development. Within eighteen years, a total of 191.4 billion yuan have been invested in AI venture capital.

Investment in artificial intelligence is increasing and is concentrated in the United States and China. Tech giants like Google and Baidu spent an estimated $30 billion on AI in 2016. The United States still has more AI startups than China, but China is making considerable headway in striking equity deals in the AI sphere. In 2013, the United States accounted for 77 percent of such transactions, but that share fell to 50 percent in 2017.

WELL-TRAINED AI SCIENTISTS

In the digital age, the number of artificial intelligence researchers will be more important than their quality. Economic strength won't come just from a handful of elite scientists. Instead, it will originate from troops of well-trained engineers who collaborate with business leaders to turn their discoveries into transformative companies.[197]

Within China, just such an army is being trained. While the United States dominates when it comes to superstar researchers, Chinese companies have filled their ranks with the kind of well-trained engineers who will power the country's era of AI development. This feat has been rendered possible by

197 Lee, Kai-Fu. AI Superpowers: China, Silicon Valley, and the New World Order. Boston: Houghton Mifflin Harcourt, 2018.

combining incredibly hungry and tenacious Chinese programmers with an explosion in access to cutting-edge global research via the Internet. Chinese students of AI are no longer straining in the dark to read outdated textbooks. Instead, they're taking advantage of AI research's open culture to absorb knowledge from the source. A study conducted by the Allen Institute for Artificial Intelligence shows that the number of most-cited 50 percent, 10 percent, and 1 percent of Chinese papers about artificial intelligence is set to surpass the number of top-cited US papers.[198]

SUPPORTIVE GOVERNMENT POLICY

The Chinese government is highly prioritizing digital transformation, including its promotion, for example, in the country's "13th Five-Year Plan" (between 2016 and 2020). China has stated that it aims to create a domestic artificial intelligence market of 1 trillion renminbi ($150 billion) by 2020 and become a world-leading AI center by 2030. The government has always been encouraging of efforts to integrate next-generation technologies into the country's governance as well as to support the development of the private sector.

The private sector is also pushing slowly for AI. China's three digital giants, collectively known as the BAT (Baidu, Alibaba, and Tencent) have joined a "national team" to develop

---

198   Daly, Ciarán, and Ciarán Daly. "China To Overtake US In AI Within 5 Years." The World's Number One Portal for Artificial Intelligence in Business, March 15, 2019. https://aibusiness.com/china-overtake-u-s-ai-within-5-years/.

AI in areas such as autonomous vehicles, smart cities, and medical imaging.[199]

DIGITAL TRANSFORMATION AND THE ECONOMY

While the US-China trade war may ultimately see an end, we will perhaps never know the end of the technological competition between the two countries. The research, development, and mass implementation of new technologies from either side have the potential to catalyze broad economic gains. Compared to other countries, the two technology giants will benefit disproportionately from embracing new technologies.

In the above section, we explored China's leadership in digital transformation, especially in the research and implementation of artificial intelligence. From the abundance of high-quality data available to the supportive policies of the government, China is charging ahead with artificial intelligence in the digital era. What are the implications of these advantages for the competition between the United States and China?

---

199   Bughin, Jacques, Jeongmin Seong, James Manyika, Michael Chui, and Raoul Joshi. "NOTES FROM THE AI FRONTIER MODELING THE IMPACT OF AI ON THE WORLD ECONOMY." McKinsey Global Institute. McKinsey Global Institute, September 2018. https://www.mckinsey.com/~/media/McKinsey/Featured Insights/Artificial Intelligence/Notes from the frontier Modeling the impact of AI on the world economy/MGI-Notes-from-the-AI-frontier-Modeling-the-impact-of-AI-on-the-world-economy-September-2018.ashx.

The big technology companies of the United States. *(https://medium.com/@parismarx/kicking-big-tech-9e4050a08767)*

Because the core technologies of digital transformation are in the hands of giant companies, the layout of giant companies in the industry is unmatched by startups.[200] Technological competition between the United States and China is mainly wrestling between the advantages of the giants.

In the United States currently, Apple, Amazon, Alphabet [Google], Microsoft, and Facebook are the technology giants. They are investing more and more resources to seize various markets in relation to artificial intelligence, big data, and so forth. In China, domestic Internet leaders "BAT" are also actively adopting various technologies to their own advantages. Huawei and ZTE are also leaders in the Chinese telecommunications space, funneling vast amounts of resources annually into the development of fifth-generation communications technologies. These giants, in addition to spending money on research, are also recruiting high-end talent and setting up laboratories to cultivate it. They continue to

---

200 Ibid.

compete through the mergers and acquisitions of various companies as well.

In the United States as of 2019, the total revenues of the country's technology giants combined (Apple, Amazon, Alphabet, Microsoft, and Facebook) generate more than the country of Saudi Arabia: they make $800 billion dollars every year.[201] The five companies are also the most valuable companies in the world, with the most market capitalization. In first place, Apple is worth nearly $1 trillion in the stock market.[202]

In China, the influence of the country's big technology companies has far less impact on the economy than the giants in the United States. Within the BAT companies, only a total of $120 billion was generated in 2019, making the economic impact of Chinese technology companies far less.

ARTIFICIAL INTELLIGENCE GOVERNANCE

Artificial intelligence governance is the idea that a legal framework should surround this new technology, ensuring that it is well researched and implemented with helping humanity in mind. The intersection of ethics and technology is where people attempt to answer questions surrounding the safety of AI, which sectors it's appropriate to be used in,

---

201 Desjardins, Jeff. "How the Tech Giants Make Their Billions." Visual Capitalist, April 9, 2019. https://www.visualcapitalist.com/how-tech-giants-make-billions/.

202 Amadeo, Kimberly. "3 Types of Market Cap." The Balance. The Balance, June 25, 2019. https://www.thebalance.com/market-capitalization-3305826.

what legal and institutional structures need to be involved, and who can control and access personal data.

Machines have been observed to racially profile and engage in unhelpful feedback loops, affecting those more marginalized in society.[203] Thus the governance of AI becomes a necessity. AI governance will determine how to handle situations in which AI-based decisions are unjust or contradict human rights.[204]

If either the United States or China wishes to have more significant international influence in the future, it must implement effective artificial intelligence governance, establishing clear ethical guidelines for the development and application of AI. Aspects of management will also concern how to prevent collected data from being leaked or abused, or how to ensure that AI is transparent and reliable enough to help humans make decisions, avoiding prejudice or discrimination.

Only with these ethical guidelines can either US or Chinese AI companies establish the necessary trust in their platforms in the international arena, winning the cooperation of their users. In June 2019, for example, China issued the first principles of artificial intelligence governance, including eight that account for the respect for privacy, security, control, and shared responsibility.

---

203 ONeil, Cathy. Weapons of Math Destruction: How Big Data Increases Inequality and Threatens Democracy. Great Britain: Penguin Books, 2017.

204 Rouse, Margaret. "What Is AI Governance? - Definition from WhatIs. com." SearchEnterpriseAI, November 2018. https://searchenterpriseai. techtarget.com/definition/AI-governance.

WEAKNESSES OF CHINESE AI

One advantage that China has over the United States is in quantity. The country not only has a higher number of engineers and a larger educated workforce, ready to digitally transform the country, but also the population and technological integration for vast amounts of high-quality data. In certain respects, however, China has not yet caught up to the United States.

The US Data, Technology, and Public Policy Interdisciplinary Think Tank released a comparative report on the strength of AI development in the United States, Europe, and China, which shows that China is ranked second in terms of overall strength, while the United States is listed first.

The first area in which China needs to make improvements is its institutions' ability to contribute to AI's fundamental theory and technological research. If the state does not have a breakthrough in algorithmic research soon, it will hit the ceiling. While the country has surpassed the world average in the citation rate of its papers, its weakness lies in its backwardness in the tools used to build the core technology of artificial intelligence. Furthermore, on the hardware side, most of the advanced artificial intelligence microprocessors are currently developed by US companies, such as Nvidia, Intel, Apple, Google, and AMD. If China does not want to be constrained by other countries in terms of technological standards and hardware, it must work harder to cultivate home-grown research and development.

At present, AI's talent in China is not exactly satisfactory. Although the country has a large number of AI researchers and engineers, ranking the second in the world in terms of numbers, China lacks high-end elite researchers. Its top AI talent—that is, the number of high-yield, high-cited researchers in the paper—is less than one-fifth of that of the United States, ranking only sixth in the world. Now, Chinese institutions are trying to persuade high-performance researchers to return to China. Furthermore, China's education system has increased training, attempting to cultivate new talents. In 2018, thirty-five universities in China were awarded artificial intelligence undergraduate programs. Top universities such as Tsinghua University have established several AI research and talent training centers to train upcoming AI professionals.

CHAPTER 7

ARTIFICIAL INTELLIGENCE: China's Digital Authoritarianism

———

China and the US are two societies with very different attitudes toward opinion and criticism. In China, I am constantly under surveillance. Even my slightest, most innocuous move can—and often is—censored by Chinese authorities.

—AI WEIWEI

CHINA, THE HIGH-TECH SURVEILLANCE STATE

A dragonfly's eye contains 28,000 facets, each a little eye. This endowment gives them a 360-degree view of the world around them and the ability to pick up images six times faster than humans, seeing the world at a blinding speed.

Consequently, dragonflies are able to respond to dangerous situations incredibly fast.[205]

The Chinese state is like a dragonfly, empowered with the ability to respond to dangerous circumstances rapidly. With its digital surveillance apparatus, the government has the unprecedented power to peer into the lives of Chinese citizens.[206] Indeed, scholars have begun to describe the regime as a "digital authoritarian state."[207] The country not only employs millions of people in charge of digital surveillance but has also strengthened its resolve to integrate artificial intelligence and big data analytics into its surveillance efforts. In doing so, the country receives important feedback and insights that allow it to prevent social crises threatening to disrupt the system.[208] The state's digital reach has already permeated fields such as education, transportation, medical care, pensions, environmental protection, urban operations, and judicial services.[209]

Pessimists like to argue that despite individuals' increasing ability to access fresh information on the Internet, the Chinese regime has not fundamentally changed. The CCP remains firmly in control and beyond accountability, having

---

205 Strittmatter, Kai, and Ruth Martin. We Have Been Harmonised: Life in Chinas Surveillance State. Exeter: Old Street Publishing Ltd., 2019.

206 Ibid.

207 Qiang, Xiao. "President XIs Surveillance State." Journal of Democracy 30, no. 1 (2019): 53–67. https://doi.org/10.1353/jod.2019.0004.

208 Strittmatter, Kai, and Ruth Martin. We Have Been Harmonised: Life in Chinas Surveillance State. Exeter: Old Street Publishing Ltd., 2019.

209 Ibid.

developed an "unparalleled system of digital censorship."[210] People are monitored more and more. Actions like taking a bus, purchasing groceries, paying bills, interacting with friends, shopping online, and many more can be incorporated in a massive database accessible by the government. The CCP has partnered with the private sector to construct a "social credit system" that aims to allow the government greater powers of compelling or deterring people's actions in society.[211]

Kai Strittmatter, a Chinese scholar, asserts that the Chinese digital surveillance system works like a panopticon prison.[212] One only needs to know that they are being monitored and will start to monitor themselves. With an all-seeing eye always gazing into the lives of citizens, the state does not need to force the populace into acquiescence, as citizens will automatically self-censor.[213] Perry Link describes this state of affairs as the "anaconda in the chandelier," which gives the state the ability to compel "scholars to lie low, businessmen to pull punches, and lawyers to mince words."[214] Indeed, with the blurring of lines between individuals'

210 Diamond, Larry. "Liberation Technology." Journal of Democracy 21, no. 3 (2010): 69–83. https://doi.org/10.1353/jod.0.0190.

211 Qiang, Xiao. "President XIs Surveillance State." Journal of Democracy 30, no. 1 (2019): 53–67. https://doi.org/10.1353/jod.2019.0004.

212 Strittmatter, Kai, and Ruth Martin. We Have Been Harmonised: Life in Chinas Surveillance State. Exeter: Old Street Publishing Ltd., 2019.

213 Ibid.

214 Link, Perry. "China: The Anaconda in the Chandelier." ChinaFile, April 11, 2002. http://www.chinafile.com/library/nyrb-china-archive/china-anaconda-chandelier.

Facial and object recognition technology integrated into cctv camera footage. *(https://www.teslarati.com/china-surveillance-ai-start-up-4-5b-valuation/)*

real and digital identities, the anaconda, feeding off the data of Chinese citizens, has grown even bigger and more menacing.[215]

The Chinese government originally created reforms for opening up the economy during the 1980s, allowing for the diffusion of fresh and innovative ideas throughout the country. However, this burgeoning of new ideas prompted the Chinese Communist Party (CCP) to take a hands-on approach to its surveillance and censorship efforts to better manage the country. Digital surveillance in China, consequently, is becoming increasingly prevalent.

---

215 Hvistendahl, Mara. "In China, a Three-Digit Score Could Dictate Your Place in Society." Wired. Conde Nast, December 5, 2018. https://www.wired.com/story/age-of-social-credit/.

In the past, the Chinese state has shown what it's capable of when something has been identified as politically desirable. Take, for example, the rapid creation of the largest high-speed train network in the world. Also, the CCP has clearly fixed on artificial intelligence as the key to its own survival and the perfection of its rule.[216]

The party foresees a wide range of uses for AI. Whether in education, public health, or infrastructure, the aim is for new technologies to solve problems and increase productivity. At the same time, the CCP wants to use artificial intelligence to provide central planners with a feedback and steering mechanism, with which it can predict and prevent any potential economic and social crises that might threaten the system. AI promises to make the dream of all authoritarian rulers come true: control and surveillance of the entire population.

NEW ISSUES FOR THE STATE
While China's technological abilities have grown at a stunning pace, problems still exist for central planners. Today's landscape of technology and media is rapidly evolving, changing the way people receive information and communicate with each other. What is the relationship between this technological development and censorship in China?

Censorship has grown complicated with the development of technology and social media. The government now needs

---

216 Strittmatter, Kai, and Ruth Martin. We Have Been Harmonised: Life in Chinas Surveillance State. Exeter: Old Street Publishing Ltd., 2019.

to focus on several factors that were not present in the past, when the Chinese government only needed to exercise control over the dissemination of information through a central source. Now, it not only needs to keep the source of information but also to oversee how data is transmitted between individuals.

Margaret Roberts, the author of *Censored: Distraction and Diversion Inside China's Great Firewall*, offers a few considerations that the Chinese government needs to think about when censoring information.[217] I have identified a few that are especially pertinent to the development of technology—factors that did not exist one or two decades ago:

- Due to the growth of new ways of communication, especially social media, the CCP now needs to worry about how information is transmitted between people. It now has to consider the democratization and disaggregation of information, which is prevalent on the Internet.
- The CCP now needs to concern itself with possible collective action brought about by social media, related to the "dictator's dilemma," as mentioned by Roberts (2018).
- The CCP now needs to worry about the amplification of sensitive issues on the Internet. Due to the development of technology, everyone now is a detective and journalist.
- The CCP also needs to consider the relationship between free speech, technology, and the economy. As Margaret Roberts mentioned with the "dictator's dilemma," we can

---

217   Roberts, Margaret E. Censored: Distraction and Diversion Inside Chinas Great Firewall. Princeton University Press, 2018.

observe a relationship between censorship and economic development.

- The CCP also needs to worry about foreign forces using technology to infiltrate the minds of Chinese citizens.[218]

As one can see, the rise of technology has produced a whole host of new concerns for the Chinese government, making policymaking in censorship more difficult and complicated than ever. Through new forms of media and information-sharing, the tide has turned against centralized information disseminated by the government. How will the CCP reconcile with this new age of democratic information?

THE SOCIAL CREDIT SYSTEM

In 2018, US Vice President Mike Pence visited the Hudson Institute, a Washington, D.C. think tank. There, he began accusing the CCP of interfering in US politics and of directing Chinese businesses to "steal American intellectual property by any means necessary." Pence then turned his attention to the country's human rights abuses, starting not with the persecution of religious minorities but with a Chinese government initiative: the social credit system.

"By 2020, China's rulers aim to implement an Orwellian system premised on controlling virtually every facet of human life— the so-called 'social credit score,'" Pence said. "In the words of that program's official blueprint, it will 'allow the trustworthy to roam everywhere under heaven while making it hard for the discredited to take a single step.'"

---

218 Ibid.

The vice-president's words echo a steady stream of Western media reports published over the past few years that paint the country's social credit system as a dystopian nightmare. They often assert that the Chinese government is using futuristic algorithms to compile people's WeChat connections, shopping histories, location data, and so on into a single score dictating their rights and freedoms in society. Furthermore, the Chinese government is repeatedly condemned for having access to millions of facial-recognition-ready surveillance cameras, spying on the moves of all citizens, and potentially docking social credit points for misbehavior like jaywalking.

The social credit system is China's method of dealing with the societal uncertainties involved with the democratization of information on the Internet. Pundits of this system have described it as "Orwellian," indicative of an "Information Technology-backed authoritarianism."[219] However, is the integration of technology into governance as draconian as it seems?

The dystopian description of China's social credit system is mainly attributed to the lack of privacy that individuals experience under this system of digital governance. Yet, other than a lack of privacy, what real harm is it causing Chinese citizens? Firstly, the impetus behind the social credit system isn't new. The CCP has always sought to "keep tabs

219 Meissner, Mirjam, Rogier Creemers, Pamela Kyle Crossley, Peter Mattis, and Samantha Hoffman. "Is Big Data Increasing Beijing's Capacity for Control?" ChinaFile, August 12, 2016. http://www.chinafile.com/conversation/Is-Big-Data-Increasing-Beijing-Capacity-Control?.

on citizens." Through various nondigital measures, the CCP already has enough information on citizens using which dissidents can be targeted. The addition of a digital system, then, only adds marginal value to the Chinese surveillance apparatus.

Secondly, the social credit system only goes to show the ingenuity of the Chinese government in coming up with pragmatic solutions to pressing issues. China currently does not have a credit system like the United States does; and, in the age of technology, why not include other variables that can increase the flexibility and range of the social credit?

Indeed, in the age of artificial intelligence and big data, the integration of new technologies would be a time-proof way to ensure harmonious societal workings for decades to come. Just as the launch of Sputnik was a pivotal moment in US-Soviet relations, the successful launch of the social credit system could be a source of soft power and prestige for China. The social credit system could indeed be a "Sputnik moment," for other countries, as they realize the efficacy of China's digital authoritarianism.

The social credit system is an incredibly powerful tool for the CCP to cultivate correct behaviors in citizens. According to Perry Link, the "highest priority of the top leadership of the Communist Party remains ... its grip on power."[220] Thus,

---

220 Link, Perry. "China: The Anaconda in the Chandelier." ChinaFile, April 11, 2002. http://www.chinafile.com/library/nyrb-china-archive/china-anaconda-chandelier.

Chinese women show the scores of their Zhima Credit of Alibaba's Ant Financial. *(https://www.thenation.com/article/china-social-credit-system/)*

from a realist point of view, the party's use of all resources in its toolbox to ensure survival and "preempt instability" makes sense.[221] When viewed in a moral vacuum, the CCP, by gaining big data from companies like Alibaba, becomes highly effective in dictating the ideological inclinations of its population of 1.4 billion. This control leads to better suppression of dissident opinions and devolution forces.

Furthermore, technology has increased the efficiency of the CCP's control. By simply tweaking an algorithm in the social credit system, the CCP can send ripples through the ways people act and think. Effectively, this method of

---

221 Hvistendahl, Mara. "In China, a Three-Digit Score Could Dictate Your Place in Society." Wired. Conde Nast, December 5, 2018. https://www. wired.com/story/age-of-social-credit/.

invisible governance allows the government to spend less money on physical forms of governance such as policing. Living off the grid is simply too difficult in China, with cities like Beijing already covered with closed-circuit television cameras.[222] Thus, in this technologically integrated society, citizens will have difficulty escaping digital authoritarianism. This situation gives the CCP an easy way to catalyze the concept of self-policing that Perry Link discussed.[223] With only a vague understanding of the rules and algorithms behind China's governance, citizens, most of whom are digitally connected, will be wary of their own behavior in fear of damaging their credit score. While Larry Diamond described this as "Orwellian," this highly efficient system could potentially transform China into a more principled and rule-based society.[224]

Importantly, however, the social credit system may perpetuate inequality. Influenced by biases of programmers and unforeseen feedback loops, this system may become a weapon of "math destruction." The lives of innocent citizens may be sent into a downward spiral simply because they had the misfortune of being in a specific minority demographic. Therefore, the government must be transparent.

---

222 Diamond, Larry. "Liberation Technology." Journal of Democracy 21, no. 3 (2010): 69–83. https://doi.org/10.1353/jod.0.0190.

223 Link, Perry. "China: The Anaconda in the Chandelier." ChinaFile, April 11, 2002. http://www.chinafile.com/library/nyrb-china-archive/china-anaconda-chandelier.

224 Diamond, Larry. "Liberation Technology." Journal of Democracy 21, no. 3 (2010): 69–83. https://doi.org/10.1353/jod.0.0190.

Data is powerful, and China has already taken action to publicize government data. The perpetuation of inequality can perhaps be mitigated by greater transparency. However, this solution may reduce the efficacy of digital authoritarianism, as individuals start to game the system. With these considerations in mind, we will have to wait to see the reaction of Chinese citizens once the social credit system officially rolls out in 2020 and whether it will create any unforeseen social phenomena.

HOW THE CCP DEALS WITH ILLICIT INFORMATION

Through my research, I have categorized three methods that the CCP employs to deal with illicit information being disseminated in society: prevention, suspension, and strengthening.

PREVENTION

The CCP must first prevent netizen provocateurs from releasing sensitive or provocative information online, either sensitive political information or calls for collective action. Hence it is currently developing technologies to "accurately sense, forecast, and provide early warning of major situations" for the state.[225] The CCP will be able to observe psychological changes in the populace in a timely matter, increasing the capability of social governance in specific areas and facilitating the state's ability to maintain social stability.[226] For

---

225 Strittmatter, Kai, and Ruth Martin. We Have Been Harmonised: Life in Chinas Surveillance State. Exeter: Old Street Publishing Ltd., 2019.

226 Ibid.

example, the government times its censorship efforts near self-immolation events by Tibetan protesters. The timing of censorship by the government is correlated with the number of people who write about specific events online.[227]

Note, however, that the government does not want to deploy too much effort in preventing the spread of sensitive information online, as vocal individual voices are an important source for the state to gather information, allowing for better governance. Only when it sees a threat of collective action does the state crackdown on its people.[228]

SUSPENSION

Margaret Roberts asserts that censorship in China is "porous," meaning that the CCP utilizes strategic ambiguity in conducting its censorship.[229] One example is the censorship of popular Western social media sites like Facebook and Twitter. These sites are blocked but not banned; individuals with a VPN can still access these sites. Technically, these sites

---

227 King, Gary, Jennifer Pan, and Margaret E. Roberts. "How Censorship in China Allows Government Criticism but Silences Collective Expression." American Political Science Review 107, no. 2 (2013): 326–43. https://doi.org/10.1017/s0003055413000014.

228 Chang, Charles, and Melanie Manion. "Political Self-Censorship in Authoritarian States: The Spatial-Temporal Dimension of Trouble." SSRN Electronic Journal, 2019. https://doi.org/10.2139/ssrn.3497976.

229 King, Gary, Jennifer Pan, and Margaret E. Roberts. "How Censorship in China Allows Government Criticism but Silences Collective Expression." American Political Science Review 107, no. 2 (2013): 326–43. https://doi.org/10.1017/s0003055413000014.

are not prohibited, but the costs of accessing are prohibitive enough to deter the majority of the population. Like many issues in Chinese politics, actors don't exist in a binary environment. Instead, nuances abound. The "porous" nature of censorship in China can be comparable to moving water: always there but changing form.

Another example of the porousness of the CCP censorship apparatus is that it differentiates its digital crackdown on citizens. Two different types of censorship exist. For intellectuals, "fear" is the main tool of censorship, while, for the general public, the CCP employs "friction" and "flooding."[230] The targets of fear-based censorship may be subject to personal attacks in the media, intimidation, police visits, and even arrest.[231]

Scholar David Bamman argues that posts are more likely to be deleted by online censors in areas that are more sensitive, such as Tibet and Xinjiang, suggesting that geographic location is also a factor in the government's use of censorship.[232]

STRENGTHENING

In addition to suspending and preventing actions online, China also seeks to strengthen its surveillance apparatus.

---

230 Ibid.

231 Qiang, Xiao. "President XIs Surveillance State." Journal of Democracy 30, no. 1 (2019): 53–67. https://doi.org/10.1353/jod.2019.0004.

232 Bamman, David, Brendan Oconnor, and Noah Smith. "Censorship and Deletion Practices in Chinese Social Media." First Monday 17, no. 3 (February 2012). https://doi.org/10.5210/fm.v17i3.3943.

With the so-called social credit system, the CCP will be able to keep an eye on information beyond the mere credit scoring system that Western societies have. This system will link together different sets of data from both the public and private sectors.[233] Data instrumentation indicates that the government is attempting to evaluate every actor in China and establish a reward and punishment system. This system will determine whether a subject has access to a variety of activities in China.[234]

Instead of merely removing content on the Internet, the government also bans search terms and shuts down websites.[235] The state now collaborates with the private sector on facial and voice recognition technologies, along with artificial intelligence research, to strengthen its ability to monitor and crack down on unsuitable voices on the Internet.[236]

---

233 Síthigh, Daithí Mac, and Mathias Siems. "The Chinese Social Credit System: A Model for Other Countries?" The Modern Law Review 82, no. 6 (April 2019): 1034–71. https://doi.org/10.1111/1468-2230.12462.

234 Liang, Fan, Vishnupriya Das, Nadiya Kostyuk, and Muzammil M. Hussain. "Constructing a Data-Driven Society: Chinas Social Credit System as a State Surveillance Infrastructure." Policy & Internet 10, no. 4 (February 2018): 415–53. https://doi.org/10.1002/poi3.183.

235 King, Gary, Jennifer Pan, and Margaret E. Roberts. "How Censorship in China Allows Government Criticism but Silences Collective Expression." American Political Science Review 107, no. 2 (2013): 326–43. https://doi.org/10.1017/s0003055413000014.

236 Hvistendahl, Mara. "In China, a Three-Digit Score Could Dictate Your Place in Society." Wired. Conde Nast, December 5, 2018. https://www.wired.com/story/age-of-social-credit/.

In the past, the Chinese state has shown what it is capable of when something has been identified as politically desirable.[237] Take, for example, the creation of the world's largest high-speed train network. Now, as the government directs its attention to the research and development of next-generation technology for surveillance purposes, imagine how much the state surveillance apparatus will be strengthened.[238] Xi Jinping has placed considerable emphasis on the concept of "Internet sovereignty," asserting the primacy of rules made by the national government and the authority of the government to regulate web content and providers.[239]

China's vast surveillance system will also extend outside the digital world. When one steps out the door of their home, actions in the physical world are "swept in the dragnet as the government gathers enormous information through the video cameras placed throughout cities."[240] Rogier Creemers posits that the impetus behind the social credit system isn't new.[241] The CCP has always sought to "keep tabs on citizens." Through various nondigital measures, the CCP already has

237 Strittmatter, Kai, and Ruth Martin. We Have Been Harmonised: Life in Chinas Surveillance State. Exeter: Old Street Publishing Ltd., 2019.

238 Ibid.

239 Qiang, Xiao. "President XIs Surveillance State." Journal of Democracy 30, no. 1 (2019): 53–67. https://doi.org/10.1353/jod.2019.0004.

240 Anna Mitchell, Larry Diamond. "China's Surveillance State Should Scare Everyone." The Atlantic. Atlantic Media Company, February 5, 2018. https://www.theatlantic.com/international/archive/2018/02/china-surveillance/552203/.

241 Meissner, Mirjam, Rogier Creemers, Pamela Kyle Crossley, Peter Mattis, and Samantha Hoffman. "Is Big Data Increasing Beijing's Capacity for

enough information on citizens through which dissidents can be targeted by the state. This data-gathering capability of the CCP allows for the strengthening of the Chinese surveillance apparatus.

FEAR-INDUCED SELF-CENSORSHIP

Chinese netizens self-censor their views online due to fear. Perry Link characterizes this fear not as a "sense of panic," but rather "a dull well-entrenched leeriness that people who deal with the Chinese censorship system usually get used to."[242] This fear is the fear of retribution by the state, which, due to the purposeful vagueness charges, is especially frightening.[243] Netizens, consequently, have reservations about speaking out politically regarding sensitive issues.

For example, this fear can materialize in the form of potentially losing a job or even serving time in prison.[244] As Margaret Roberts also asserts, individuals simply lack a conceptual clarity of what state digital surveillance censorship entails.[245] Hence, self-censorship has become the primary form of government control over netizens on the Internet, and this

Control?" ChinaFile, August 12, 2016. http://www.chinafile.com/conversation/Is-Big-Data-Increasing-Beijing-Capacity-Control?.

242 Link, Perry. "China: The Anaconda in the Chandelier." ChinaFile, April 11, 2002. http://www.chinafile.com/library/nyrb-china-archive/china-anaconda-chandelier.

243 Roberts, Margaret E. Censored: Distraction and Diversion Inside Chinas Great Firewall. Princeton University Press, 2018.

244 Ibid.

245 Ibid.

combination of fear, unknown threats, and arrests persuades ordinary users of the Internet to restrain their speech.

Furthermore, as asserted by Darrel Robinson and Marcus Tannenberg, evidence suggests that individuals become "less forthright" in sharing political opinions due to fear that "their opinions may be known to the public or the authorities."[246] Effectively, this state of affairs means that people, knowing that they are being questioned about sensitive political issues by surveyors or officials, will have a greater propensity to censor themselves.

Zhi-Jin Zhong emphasizes that people's perception of Internet censorship also significantly decreases their willingness to talk about sensitive issues online.[247] For example, certain specific terms are more likely to be deleted by state censors on Chinese microblogging sites.[248] Faced with direct censorship by the state, citizens will become fearful and self-censor.[249]

---

246 Robinson, Darrel, and Marcus Tannenberg. "Self-Censorship of Regime Support in Authoritarian States: Evidence from List Experiments in China." Research & Politics 6, no. 3 (2019): 205316801985644. https://doi.org/10.1177/2053168019856449.

247 Zhong, Zhi-Jin, Tongchen Wang, and Minting Huang. "Does the Great Fire Wall Cause Self-Censorship? The Effects of Perceived Internet Regulation and the Justification of Regulation." Internet Research 27, no. 4 (July 2017): 974–90. https://doi.org/10.1108/intr-07-2016-0204.

248 Bamman, David, Brendan Oconnor, and Noah Smith. "Censorship and Deletion Practices in Chinese Social Media." First Monday 17, no. 3 (February 2012). https://doi.org/10.5210/fm.v17i3.3943.

249 Zhong, Zhi-Jin, Tongchen Wang, and Minting Huang. "Does the Great Fire Wall Cause Self-Censorship? The Effects of Perceived Internet

Charles Chang and Melanie Manion explore the impact of stressful times and places on the self-censorship of Chinese netizens.[250] They show that "citizens do not self-censor their political criticism more from fear of punishment by the state when time and place create political stress." The two scholars have found that after a stressful political event, citizens who find themselves in a stressful place display "clear self-censorship for fear of being linked to punishable collective action."[251] This phenomenon occurs when netizens find themselves experiencing "collective action anxiety," when they find themselves in a stressful place at a stressful time.

Haohan Chen asserts that, in political talk, netizens lie about their political preferences to friends while revealing their true preferences to strangers.[252] This behavior, according to Chen, is due to a "combination of psychological rewards for being truthful and social punishment for expressing a different view."[253] By expressing politically contentious topics to friends under a recognizable online alias, netizens are faced with criticism and ostracism. On the other hand, if a netizen expresses controversial beliefs anonymously to strangers, they feel more emboldened. Therefore, netizens

Regulation and the Justification of Regulation." Internet Research 27, no. 4 (July 2017): 974–90. https://doi.org/10.1108/intr-07-2016-0204.

250 Chang, Charles, and Melanie Manion. "Political Self-Censorship in Authoritarian States: The Spatial-Temporal Dimension of Trouble." SSRN Electronic Journal, 2019. https://doi.org/10.2139/ssrn.3497976.

251 Ibid.

252 Chen, Haohan. "Lies to Friends, Truths to Strangers," October 2019.

253 Ibid.

act with more self-censorship while interacting with friends and act with less restraint in front of strangers.

Information suspension cultivates fear in Chinese netizens. One of the most important tools in the CCP's surveillance toolbox is the ambiguity of suspension that it can deal out to individuals. Perry Link characterizes this ambiguity as the "anaconda in the chandelier."[254] In blocking sensitive information online, the government is purposefully vague so that people will be more fearful and consequently withhold information from the Internet. According to Rachel Stern and Jonathan Hassid, power is "most effective when it is least observable.[255] Indeed, due to the ambiguity of government punishments, netizens may very well be in the "wrong place at the wrong time" as collective action anxiety is heightened in an environment where suspension is unpredictable and sometimes violent.[256]

The Chinese government designs its surveillance and information suspension apparatus for utility maximization. By suppressing specific types of information and allowing others, the CCP creates a system in which useful information is

254 Link, Perry. "China: The Anaconda in the Chandelier." ChinaFile, April 11, 2002. http://www.chinafile.com/library/nyrb-china-archive/china-anaconda-chandelier.

255 Stern, Rachel E., and Jonathan Hassid. "Amplifying Silence." Comparative Political Studies 45, no. 10 (2012): 1230–54. https://doi.org/10.1177/0010414011434295.

256 Chang, Charles, and Melanie Manion. "Political Self-Censorship in Authoritarian States: The Spatial-Temporal Dimension of Trouble." SSRN Electronic Journal, 2019. https://doi.org/10.2139/ssrn.3497976.

available while destabilizing information is filtered out. The government keeps the "anaconda in the chandelier" unpredictable, thereby lowering the costs of surveillance.[257]

Another perspective concerns the nationalistic rhetoric radiating from Beijing since the rise of Xi Jinping.[258] Now, Chinese netizens have to be careful about expressing their views online because they could get inadvertently bitten by the anaconda.

In my previous analysis, I touched upon the concept of peer ostracization, as asserted by Haohan Chen.[259] The government suspension of information also inspires fear in netizens' associations with their friends and social circles, leading to possible ostracism within friend groups. Netizens—now more than ever—need to exercise prudence in communicating with their friends, possibly suppressing their real opinions. This phenomenon is especially salient in politically sensitive localities such as Xinjiang and Tibet, where online posts are more likely to be deleted by government censors.[260]

In Xinjiang, through the government's attempts to suspend information, the CCP has created a political culture of

---

257 Link, Perry. "China: The Anaconda in the Chandelier." ChinaFile, April 11, 2002. http://www.chinafile.com/library/nyrb-china-archive/china-anaconda-chandelier.

258 ECONOMY, ELIZABETH C. THIRD REVOLUTION: Xi Jinping and the New Chinese State. S.l.: OXFORD UNIV PRESS US, 2019.

259 Chen, Haohan. "Lies to Friends, Truths to Strangers," October 2019.

260 Bamman, David, Brendan Oconnor, and Noah Smith. "Censorship and Deletion Practices in Chinese Social Media." First Monday 17, no. 3 (February 2012). https://doi.org/10.5210/fm.v17i3.3943.

fear-induced paralysis. Netizens must self-censor their true political opinions lest they are rounded up by the government and sent to a reeducation camp.[261] This fear causes friends and family members to police one another and possibly disassociate as a whole.

In this society where social interactions are shrouded in an atmosphere of fear, individuals fear that friends and family can expose critical information about them, handing it off to the government. Hence people would rather stay quiet about their political beliefs. Indeed, as asserted by Darrel Robinson and Marcus Tannenberg, evidence suggests that individuals become "less forthright" on sharing political opinions due to a fear that "their opinions may be known to the public or the authorities."[262]

According to Bruce Dickson, trust in China is highest within families and lowest with strangers. If the Chinese suspension program has rendered the opposite true, this shift reveals to what extent government coercion is effective.[263]

---

261 Thum, Rian. "China's Mass Internment Camps Have No Clear End in Sight." Foreign Policy, August 22, 2018. https://foreignpolicy.com/2018/08/22/chinas-mass-internment-camps-have-no-clear-end-in-sight/.

262 Robinson, Darrel, and Marcus Tannenberg. "Self-Censorship of Regime Support in Authoritarian States: Evidence from List Experiments in China." Research & Politics 6, no. 3 (2019): 205316801985644. https://doi.org/10.1177/2053168019856449.

263 Dickson, Bruce J. "Who Wants to Be a Communist? Career Incentives and Mobilized Loyalty in China." The China Quarterly 217 (May 2013): 42–68. https://doi.org/10.1017/s0305741013001434.

The main feature behind strengthening is the government's creation of the social credit system. The state's wish to expand its surveillance network will strike fear in people who may find themselves more likely having the wrong characteristics at the wrong time, or individuals may find themselves ostracized by peers.

The government has teamed up with the private sector to obtain information on citizens' social media usage.[264] By doing so, the state adds more variables that could possibly be analyzed in its social credit system, causing citizens to become more fearful and unsure of what are acceptable actions and what is prohibited on the Internet.

For example, as seen right now, those facing debts with the banks face a number of social restrictions, such as the inability to purchase train and airplane tickets. With the integration of the social credit system, restrictions will extend to life outside of personal finance, as one may face social restrictions based on their political views.[265] Netizens may find that their online browsing habits, online shopping habits, and more will come under the scrutiny of the CCP. Consequently, they will have a greater propensity to self-censor, in restraining not just rhetoric but also the actions they take in the digital world.

---

264 Qiang, Xiao. "President Xi's Surveillance State." Journal of Democracy 30, no. 1 (2019): 53–67. https://doi.org/10.1353/jod.2019.0004.

265 Meissner, Mirjam, Rogier Creemers, Pamela Kyle Crossley, Peter Mattis, and Samantha Hoffman. "Is Big Data Increasing Beijing's Capacity for Control?" ChinaFile, August 12, 2016. http://www.chinafile.com/conversation/Is-Big-Data-Increasing-Beijing-Capacity-Control?.

The same fear could be observed within social groups. As the government incorporates more data—including individuals' social circles—in the social credit system, associating with the wrong types of people might serve as an impetus for individuals to become flagged by the government. We are already seeing this play out in Xinjiang, as Uyghurs with "dubious" connections are more likely to be put in reeducation camps.[266] Therefore, we could reasonably imagine that individuals will begin to self-censor in their online circles—even ending relationships—as a result of the strengthening of the Chinese surveillance state.

BUT TECHNOLOGY AND SOCIAL MEDIA ARE NOT UNDERMINING THE CHINESE STATE

The CCP has an elaborate system of censorship, impeding all dangerous online activity. Gary King and his team of researchers were able to show the speed at which the government removes information. This efficiency is indicative of China's surveillance power and its ability to identify social unrest.[267] As better technologies for tracking and manipulating data become integrated into China's censorship system, officials will become more effective at stopping any online

---

266 Thum, Rian. "China's Mass Internment Camps Have No Clear End in Sight." Foreign Policy, August 22, 2018. https://foreignpolicy.com/2018/08/22/chinas-mass-internment-camps-have-no-clear-end-in-sight/.

267 King, Gary, Jennifer Pan, and Margaret E. Roberts. "How Censorship in China Allows Government Criticism but Silences Collective Expression." American Political Science Review 107, no. 2 (2013): 326–43. https://doi.org/10.1017/s0003055413000014.

Top Chinese social networking apps. *(https://www.sekkeistudio.com/blog/top-social-media-platforms-in-china-2020/)*

behavior that undermines the state domestically and (to some extent) abroad.

Furthermore, we should keep in mind that the CCP is receptive to information. As mentioned by King, the censors do not wholesale remove negative information. In fact, the state has a certain tolerance for critiques by individuals. This attitude indicates how China distinguishes between individual and group grievances.[268] Individuals are harmless, and their opinions can be harnessed for the government to better understand and respond to societal issues, increasing the resilience of the Chinese party-state.

Most importantly, Chinese netizens may, in fact, not care much about the country's lack of freedom of speech. Though Larry Diamond discusses the effectiveness of "liberation

---

268 Ibid.

technology" in places such as Malaysia or the Middle East, the same may not apply in the Chinese context.[269] Keeping in mind the concepts of "self-censorship" and the "anaconda in the chandelier," citizens may simply not want to associate themselves with trouble as they are powerless as individuals.[270] Though the Chinese people may be aware of censorship, they may not be compelled to act as long as the CCP maintains its performance legitimacy. Diamond mentions the concerns of intellectuals in Chinese society; this group only makes up a small percentage of the population, and they may not overcome this attitude of ambivalence among other citizens.[271]

The international arena is in a state of anarchy, and states default to self-help behavior. For authoritarian governments, self-help could be characterized by control over domestic information so as to minimize foreign influence. In some instances, censorship may be good for citizens, as it maintains social order and hierarchy, and China is one such example. Here, citizens are aware of the balance between

---

269 Anna Mitchell, Larry Diamond. "China's Surveillance State Should Scare Everyone." The Atlantic. Atlantic Media Company, February 5, 2018. https://www.theatlantic.com/international/archive/2018/02/china-surveillance/552203/.

270 Link, Perry. "China: The Anaconda in the Chandelier." ChinaFile, April 11, 2002. http://www.chinafile.com/library/nyrb-china-archive/china-anaconda-chandelier.

271 Anna Mitchell, Larry Diamond. "China's Surveillance State Should Scare Everyone." The Atlantic. Atlantic Media Company, February 5, 2018. https://www.theatlantic.com/international/archive/2018/02/china-surveillance/552203/.

freedom and livelihood. The CCP remains a driver of economic growth, and the fracturing of the party-state could bring about catastrophic economic effects.

CHAPTER 8

5G TELECOMMUNICATIONS: What is 5G Telecommunications?

Just as we have what used to be supercomputers in our pockets, our homes now require the telecommunications infrastructure of a small city.

—STEVEN LEVY

UNDERSTANDING 5G

What is all the hype surrounding 5G? 5G telecommunications will bring us many benefits, and indeed it is a fresh "generation" of technology, built on a completely new foundation of technology that incremental improvements upon the current 4G LTE model cannot bring us. This new wave of technology is a paradigm shift in the way data travels between electronic devices. To better understand how this new technology will impact our lives, we need a basic understanding of how this technology works. In short, three key engineering considerations apply to 5G, affecting its efficacy in different applications:

- Increased Speeds
- Lower Latency
- Decreased Energy and Cost

INCREASED SPEEDS

Perhaps the most important of the three features is the increased mobile data traffic rate. Within the realm of increased data rate are three metrics that engineers use to measure the speed and reliability of networks: aggregate data rate, edge rate, and peak rate.

Aggregate data rate refers to the total amount of data the network can serve, characterized in bits per unit area. With the advent of 5G, the aggregate data rate is believed to soon be 1,000 times that of 4G technology.

The edge rate involves the worst data speeds a user can receive when getting the weakest signal. 5G also vastly outperforms 4G in this area. In the worst-case scenario connection, 5G connections will continue to deliver speeds between 100MB/s to 1GB/s, which is at least a hundred times faster than the edge rate of 4G of 1MB/s. To paint you a picture, even in the case of the worst signal connection, you would still be able to download a two-hour HD movie in less than thirty seconds!

Last is the peak rate of data transfer, which refers to the theoretical maximum speed of data download. Often peak rate is

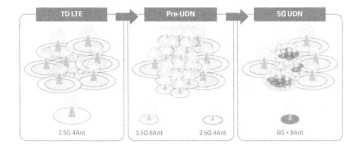

Extreme densification of telecommunications nodes. *(https://
www.zte.com.cn/china/about/magazine/zte-technologies/2016/11/
cn_1215/461216)*

used in a marketing term and rarely can a user actually achieve
such speeds. The peak rate of 5G is likely in the tens of GB/s.

Increased data transfer has many implications for us, like
faster video streaming, downloads, and access to the cloud.
Most importantly, increased data transfer will enable the
creation of the Internet of Things (IoT). IoT will connect
all our daily objects to the Internet, such as our electronic
devices, furniture, appliances, transportation, and more.
This increased connectivity will digitally transform our lives,
creating an enormous amount of data. It will also offer many
conveniences in our lives.

Another important result of increased connectivity is the
offloading of computational power into the cloud. With
increased data speeds, we may see a decreased need for physical processing units in our devices. Electronics, through
5G, may simply send information to be processed to a cloud,
where it will be processed by a supercomputer. Consequently,

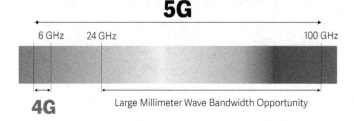

Millimeter wave bandwidth spectrum. *(https://www.androidauthority.com/what-is-5g-mmwave-933631/)*

the supercomputer will return the processed information through the 5G network.

LOWER LATENCY

The second consideration for the implementation of 5G is the topic of latency. Latency, in telecommunications lingo, is simply the time a bit of data takes to travel between two places. For example, if I were to send a message to my friend on Facebook over the Internet, the time that it takes between when I click "send" and when they see the message pop up on their screen is the latency. At the point of this writing, the latency of 5G technology is fifteen milliseconds, which does not dramatically differ from the latency of the previous generation. It is enough for daily uses like video-streaming and gaming; however, for 5G to have greater societal impact, its latency must be reduced to that of one millisecond, enabling its use in highly precise automation such as driverless cars, remote surgery, and public safety uses. Right now, latency remains one of the main bottlenecks to the widespread adoption of 5G in next-generation uses of technology.

DECREASED ENERGY AND COST

The last important engineering aspect of 5G is its cost and energy of operation. As the bandwidth of 5G technologies is considerably higher compared to current 4G technologies, the energy cost per bit of information will also decrease. Furthermore, it is said that mmWave Spectrum technology and the high frequency required for 5G solutions will enable cost-saving opportunities for carriers compared to 4G solutions.

ACHIEVING 5G SPEEDS

5G has the potential to be 1,000 times faster than its 4G LTE predecessor, but how can we achieve such awesome speeds? We must completely reconceptualize the design of networks. The first technique for increased speed is the "extreme densification" of telecommunications nodes. Put simply, instead of cell towers carrying antennae that can cover areas with many square kilometers, telecom stations will be miniaturized to fulfill areas as small as only hundreds and even tens of meters. By increasing the number of connection nodes, the same spectrum of connection can be reused in different geographic areas, allowing for less competition between users for single resources. With ultra-dense 5G networks (UDD), instead of cell towers in cities, you may find numerous small base stations scattered throughout your life—in homes, offices, and even coffee shops.

The second piece of technology required for the adoption of 5G is the use of Millimeter Wave, otherwise known as mmWave. Currently, to transfer information across space, traditional technology largely makes use of the lower

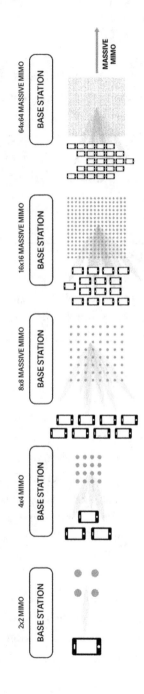

Massive MIMO. (https://uk.mathworks.com/discovery/massive-mimo.html)

frequencies in a slim area usually between several hundred MHz to a few GHz. As time has passed, however, these lower frequencies have become too crowded with information, with the increasing prevalence of telecommunications use and smartphone usage, rendering the traditional spectral band (sometimes known as the "beachfront spectrum") occupied, especially during times of high use. Currently, the mmWave Spectrum lies idle because this part of the spectrum poses myriad technological challenges. Due to its high frequency, for example, it has difficulty penetrating objects such as buildings, and even rain and atmospheric conditions can absorb signal; furthermore, higher frequencies are susceptible to noise and high equipment costs. Now, thanks to the development of technology and the lowering of equipment costs, some of these technical issues can be surmounted by companies.

To combat the issue of low range, blockage, and absorption, a technical solution is to completely reimagine the concept of the telecom cell. If we visualize telecom equipment as a source of light, the traditional thinking is that cell towers are large lightbulbs in the city, spreading light over a vast area, with the only limiting factor the distance. Now, however, researchers have reimagined the 5G cell to be that of a flashlight, where, to combat the downfalls of high-frequency mmWave, the cell equipment leverages large arrays and narrow beams of directed energy from base stations, like shining a flashlight on our phones. This new approach changes the traditional design of base stations and telecom cells. One extra technical challenge that still does not have a viable solution to create this web of directed energy base stations is how the hardware will be able to create the link acquisitions to our cell phones. Because information is received in a directed, focused manner, how can we solve the issue of moving targets? This issue requires researchers to come up with new and novel ways of imagining base station networks.

The third 5G-enabling technology is massive MIMO. MIMO stands for "multiple input multiple output" and is in fact in use today in Wi-Fi and 4G LTE technologies. In a nutshell, MIMO refers to the use of multiple antennas in a base station to transmit information simultaneously over the same radio channel. Currently, MIMO networks can use up to four antennae, but 5G massive MIMO features tens to hundreds of antennas. The result is that multiple connections will be made using the antennae, all using the same band of spectrum, drastically increasing the amount of information able to be transmitted.[272]

5G DRONES

Currently, drones are controlled via Wi-Fi technology within a range of approximately two kilometers. However, when drones connect to the network of a telecom operator, the control distance will not be inhibited by geography. Massive MIMO of 5G networks will provide better coverage for low-altitude airspace than existing networks, and a low latency, as well as higher bandwidth, will allow for more

---

272   Mundy, Jon, and Kevin Thomas. "What Is Massive MIMO Technology?" 5G.co.uk – UK's Premier 5G Resource, n.d. https://5g.co.uk/guides/what-is-massive-mimo-technology/.

accurate control of drones and the transmission of information back to the user in high frame rates and resolutions.

Connected drones can be used in a wide variety of scenarios in the public safety field, for example. When receiving a fire alarm, a telephone operator can remotely dispatch drones to fire sites in addition to sending firefighters. Drones can transmit videos of fire sites to the monitoring center in real-time, and then the teams can communicate and organize as required. In addition, similar cases can be used for the police, firefighters, and medical care personnel to respond more efficiently to disasters. Combined with the benefit of artificial intelligence and facial recognition technology, 5G allows governments to be as responsive as ever.

5G VIRTUAL REALITY

Two types of virtual reality are currently available in the market: VR based on smartphones and VR based on wired connections. Both, at the stage of this writing, provide mediocre experiences and do not have widespread use by consumers. VR based on wired connections also poses prohibitive costs for consumers and requires them to have powerful computers to operate the technology.

In the future, Cloud VR can combine the mobility of smartphones and high-performance PC. It will reduce costs by means of cloud rendering, offloading the processing required for virtual reality to be processed in the cloud and then sent back to the end-user. The requirement for this new type of VR is mobile networks that can satisfy high bandwidth requirements and low latencies. At the current stage of technological development, 4G is unable to provide such performance. In the age of 5G, this kind of performance will be possible.

5G SELF-DRIVING AUTOMOBILES

5G-enabled automobiles will benefit passengers, drivers, and vehicles. Passengers will be able to enjoy high-speed mobile Internet services in vehicles. Drivers, through increased speeds of data transmission, can receive relevant information such as navigation, music, and video. The most important benefits in 5G-enabled automobiles go to the vehicle itself. Four scenarios exist for the 5G-enabled automobile: automated driving, vehicle platooning, improved traffic efficiency, and remote driving.

- Automated Driving: Systems equipped on some vehicles combine information from sensors, radars, and cameras to replace human drivers to some extent. However, these systems have major limitations. Cars with automated driving systems cannot operate safely in all weather conditions. Radars, for example, may fail to properly assess conditions on the road at night, during heavy rain, and in fog. 5G communication is a solution. 5G-enabled cars communicate with nearby vehicles, roads, and infrastructure to obtain a greater volume of information regarding the surroundings, making decisions from aggregate information rather than inputs from a single vehicle.
- Vehicle Platooning: A popular scenario of 5G in automobiles is vehicle platooning. A platoon is a group of vehicles that can travel closely together safely at high speed. Each vehicle communicates with the others in the platoon. 5G will enable this technology by optimizing the

platooning scheme to a specific destination. Platooning involves certain effects, especially in long-distance freight services. Not only does it reduce the operating costs of hiring additional drivers, but it also lowers fuel consumption.

- Improved Traffic Efficiency: In the future, smart transportation management systems can calculate, analyze, and process massive data. Through 5G, they will receive information, as well as deliver safety suggestions and instructions to vehicles. Furthermore, they could implement real-time intelligence scheduling of vehicle routes based on collected data, including vehicle location and road conditions. The result is significantly improved travel efficiency.

- Remote Driving: Remote driving technology allows users to remotely connect to and control vehicles at any location via 5G networks. In this way, unmanned vehicles can work in harsh and dangerous areas, helping enterprises improve efficiency and reduce costs. Japan has already released government guidance documents concerning remote driving, which define a standard working scheme for automated driving with video surveillance by the driver in the front vehicle and the operator in the control center.

5G USES IN DIFFERENT COUNTRIES

The uses of 5G are different across the world, in various countries and regions. This technology gives the impression of being able to provide a large bandwidth and a fiber-like experience. However, the actual uses of this technology will depend on the locality they are deployed in. For example, the

United States has 50 to 60 million families, many of which are subscribed to broadband networks. Considering the high costs of deploying optical fibers in the United States across homes and cities, the use of 5G connection will be able to mitigate all the costs of a broadband network, delivering connection to homes wirelessly and with the same efficacy as a traditional broadband network.

In Korea, on the other hand, due to high urban density and the increasing penetration rate of fiber, the country has no strong demand for 5G to be used in the same way as in the United States. For example, in Korea, greater use of 5G can be put into the area of the Internet of Vehicles. SK Telecom in Korea owns T map, Korea's largest electronic map platform. The future of unmanned driving will rely heavily on high-precision maps. And the connectivity offered by 5G will allow SK Telecom to further develop its Internet of Vehicles business rather than home Internet services.

CHAPTER 9

5G TELECOMMUNICATIONS: 5G Telecommunications and US-China Relations

_____

Secure 5G networks will absolutely be a vital link to America's prosperity and national security in the twenty-first century.

—DONALD TRUMP

THE BATTLE OF BARCELONA

A battle between US officials and China's Huawei is playing out in the city of Barcelona in Spain. Hailing from Washington, D.C., an American delegation has been sent to the city's grand event, the Mobile World Congress. Attracting over 100,000 professionals from the telecommunications industry, this event is the biggest of its kind and one of the largest annual events for the Chinese telecom giant Huawei.

Mobile World Congress 2017. *(https://medium.com/forward-media-global/the-big-show-at-mobile-world-congress-2017-is-the-show-you-cant-see-af10a293ee6c)*

Present at the Mobile Congress are representatives from the Departments of Defense, Commerce, and State—all coordinating a huge lobbying push on the United States' European allies. They hope to convince the participants of the Congress to dismiss Huawei's leading 5G communications technology due to security concerns.

Dubbed the "Battle of Barcelona," Huawei is not giving up without a fight in this showdown. The company has stated that the US attack is politically motivated and that no evidence suggests that the company spied or conducted cyberattacks on behalf of the Chinese government. The company also asserts that spying on people would destroy customers' trust and consequently ruin the business. Anticipating pushback from the largest economy in the world, Huawei has markedly stepped up its rhetoric, using a more aggressive tone. Its founder has accepted a series of media interviews, saying that the United States will not be able to crush Huawei. At the Mobile World Congress, the company has also booked out a huge stand to unveil its new generation of mobile phones in its usual glitzy fashion.

The US government has been leveraging all its political and diplomatic influence to pressure Huawei, using every tool at its disposal—including both judicial and administrative powers, as well as a host of other unscrupulous means—to disrupt the business operations of Huawei and its partners:

- Instructing law enforcement to threaten, menace, coerce, entice, and incite both current and former Huawei employees to turn against the company.
- Unlawfully searching, detaining, and even arresting Huawei employees and Huawei partners.
- Attempting entrapment: pretending to be Huawei employees to establish legal pretense for unfounded accusations against the company.
- Launching cyberattacks to infiltrate Huawei's intranet and internal information systems.
- Sending FBI agents to the homes of Huawei employees and pressuring them to collect information on the company.
- Mobilizing and conspiring with companies that work with or have a business conflict with Huawei, to bring unsubstantiated accusations against the company.
- Launching investigations based on false media reports that target the company.
- Digging up old civil cases that have already been settled and selectively launching criminal investigations or

filing criminal charges against Huawei based on claims of technology theft.
- Obstructing normal business activities and technical communications through intimidation, denying visas, detaining shipment, etc.

The fact remains that none of Huawei's core technology has been the subject of any criminal case brought against the company, and none of the accusations levied by the US government have been supported with sufficient evidence.

The challenge for Huawei, however, is that its business operations may rest in the hands of public opinion and international politics. The fate of the company lies in the future status of US-China relations, international public opinion, and trends in 5G development. The question remains whether countries will fall into diametrically opposing camps reminiscent of the Cold War, as the standards of 5G continue becoming standardized and implemented across the world.

The development of 5G will be a point of major contention between the United States and China. Currently, Huawei—a Chinese company—holds the largest number of patents pertaining to 5G. The United States does not have a home-grown telecommunications company capable of developing the technology needed for 5G, and the country continues to rely on inferior European counterparts Nokia and Ericsson. 5G promises major economic gains in all industries, enabling the collection of a greater quantity of data throughout society and speeding up the implementation of artificial intelligence. China's massive population, forward-thinking central government, and prowess in 5G may give the country a boost in its race with the United States—a good reason for the United States to remain wary.

ERAS OF CHANGE

A good analogy for the development and influence of 5G on society would be the urban growth that US cities have experienced over the past two centuries. Just as modes of transport fundamentally shaped the design of US cities over the years, 5G has the power to catalyze paradigm shifts in the way humans interact with each other and with the world.

The urban landscape of nineteenth-century America was drastically different than the urban metropolises of today like New York, San Francisco, and Los Angeles. The "walking city" of the time featured highly compact cities, characterized by an intermingling of residences and workplaces. It was a world without commuting, without traffic, and everyone walked to work. They would go to open markets for buying and selling goods and hang out at parade grounds for special occasions. Other than horseback travel, few other ways allowed people to traverse the city.

However, during the "streetcar era" between 1880 and 1920, the urban landscape of the United States changed once again, as industrialization began to pick up speed in US cities. Low-fare electric streetcars replaced the horsecar, offering public transportation to a wide ridership. Light rail tracks radiated out from the center of the city, and urban growth concentrated on these lines of transportation. Amid this change in transportation technology, the lives of American citizens also began to change. Cities became larger as people could now live farther away from their place of work, migrants entered cities, and they had a greater separation between where they worked and where they lived.

However, American life changed again forever after the introduction of the automobile in the twentieth century. Cities became even larger, and urban sprawl grew. The US middle class could now live farther away from the city center, where the cost of living was high. They now escaped inner-city congestion and pollution by living in the suburbs. Ever since, the US urban landscape changed forever, as cities are designed around cars. A web of highways traverse the country, creating large cities like Los Angeles or Houston, where pedestrians have become endangered species.

This historical progression is analogous to how widespread implementation of technology advances can influence the way we live forever. As technologies become more advanced, we humans have adapted our lives around it, by designing different cities, choosing how to spend our time, and deciding how we live our lives. Due to the introduction of the automobile, American cities today are urban sprawls connected by highways, with the car as the major form of transportation.

The same phenomenon is true in the tech world. Humans have changed the way they live based on the changing development of tech in the world. One is unable to escape this trend and is pulled along with the societal changes. People take the Internet for granted these days; having a fast, instantaneous 4G connection to the Internet in our pocket is the norm in our lives and in our work. Soon 5G will become the standard in our lives, not only offering us far greater connection speeds in our smartphones but also powering the intelligence of everyday objects we interact with, as part of the Internet of Things.

The definition of soft power is "a persuasive approach to international relations, typically involving the use of economic or cultural influence," which is generally used in the realm of international relations. However, the same concept of soft power can apply in the area of technology. Certain disruptive technologies have the ability to change how we live our lives, and a great amount of power comes to the creator of this norm-changing technology.

Take the smartphone, for example. Apple, which has recently been crowned the most valuable publicly traded company in the world, built its success on its defining innovation of the original iPhone. After the creation of the first iPhone, a rising tide in smartphones swept over the world, and today almost everyone owns an iPhone. As the original creator of the iPhone, Apple holds unprecedented power.[273] Essentially, whoever sets the trend gets to rule.

Humans took millions of years of continuous thinking and innovation to discover electricity in 1879. And in the one hundred years since then, humans have discovered nuclear power, space flight, the Internet, and artificial intelligence.

---

273   Feiner, Lauren. "Apple Is Once Again the Most Valuable Public Company in the World." CNBC. CNBC, February 6, 2019. https://www.cnbc.com/2019/02/06/apple-is-once-again-the-most-valuable-public-company-in-the-world.html.

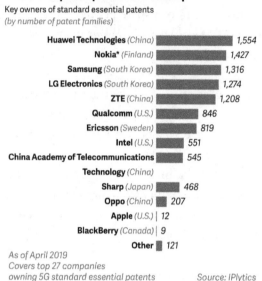

Huawei tops 5G patent ownership

Key owners of standard essential patents
(by number of patent families)

Huawei Technologies *(China)*	1,554
Nokia* *(Finland)*	1,427
Samsung *(South Korea)*	1,316
LG Electronics *(South Korea)*	1,274
ZTE *(China)*	1,208
Qualcomm *(U.S.)*	846
Ericsson *(Sweden)*	819
Intel *(U.S.)*	551
China Academy of Telecommunications Technology *(China)*	545
Sharp *(Japan)*	468
Oppo *(China)*	207
Apple *(U.S.)*	12
BlackBerry *(Canada)*	9
Other	121

As of April 2019
Covers top 27 companies
owning 5G standard essential patents   Source: IPlytics

Distribution of 5G technology patents across companies. *(https:// asia.nikkei.com/Spotlight/Cover-Story/Fears-of-digital-iron-curtain-spread-as-US-and-China-dig-in)*

Today, humans are sending robots to explore other planets and growing organisms in space! Indeed, the speed of technological growth has been dizzying, and the fact that you who are reading this book were born in this era of tremendous change is a miracle. Humans now have the responsibility of tearing through this opening and carving out a brighter future for all mankind. Now, change is becoming the norm as new disruptive technological norms are set to continue rewriting the rules of this world.

5G is one of the big technologies poised to change the way that we live again, as part of an era of interconnectedness some have described as the Fourth Industrial Revolution. Due to the vastly increased wireless bandwidth that will be made widely available with the deployment of 5G telecommunications technology, many things will become available. From self-driving cars to remote surgery to the Internet of Things, we will experience wide-ranging social impacts in every aspect of our lives. Our digital landscape will change, as will the way we navigate the world with technology.

In addition to the increasing interconnectedness that will be brought on by 5G connections, facets of our lives and societies will become far more productive. As tools and methods become more technologically integrated, we will have greater room for automation and the offloading of data storage and processing power. Imagine a phone that only relies on an Internet connection to a centralized supercomputer able to produce calculations at amazing speeds. Then, the devices that we use every day simply become a conduit of information between a more efficient centralized command and our sensory systems. Furthermore, in industries like manufacturing and energy, the increased connectivity and low latency of 5G connectivity allows for greater automation of these productive industries.

Thus 5G becomes an issue of hard power for a country. A country with a widely adopted 5G network will experience many societal changes and increased efficiency throughout its industries. 5G bandwidth is also the linchpin for other new fields of growth, such as big data and artificial intelligence. Effectively, whoever has 5G has the power to rule the world, as it speeds up the growth of a country, thereby magnifying the size of its coffers. Technological change is powerful, from

A Huawei Technologies 5G base station deployed by China Mobile in Henan province in central China. *(https://www.scmp.com/tech/gear/article/2188723/huawei-goes-legal-warpath-twin-north-american-lawsuits)*

the soft power of changing tech standards to the hard power of national productivity brought on by changes, increasing a country's international competitiveness.

The vanguard of 5G research, development, and integration will come from the private sector—namely, the roles of telecommunications equipment manufacturers and regional telecom carriers to fulfill massive 5G integration. As of now, Huawei is the undisputed leader in 5G technologies research and development, holding the most "standard essential patents," amounting to 1,500 patents followed by Nokia, Samsung, and LG.[274]

---

274 Ip, Adrian. "Huawei May Have Largest 5G Patent Portfolio—Starting to Flex IPR Muscle." Wccftech. Wccftech, July 1, 2019. https://wccftech.com/huawei-has-largest-5g-patent-portfolio-starting-to-flex-ipr-muscle/.

Having funneled billions of dollars into research and development, Huawei has amassed a war chest of patents, in what some have called a form of basic "weapons of economic warfare." The company has a total portfolio of active patents and published applications of over 100,000, many in areas essential to the development and implementation of 5G.[275]

Just as Qualcomm was a leader in the 2G and 3G fields with its innovations in GSM and CDMA and the number of industry-defining patents that this company holds, Huawei is set to become its contemporary in the 5G age, defining the standards of technology that can have implications for its technological soft power. Seeing the wide-ranging effects of new generation interconnectivity, Huawei, in 2019, opened up a fifth business group in the company that will be responsible for self-driving automobiles, in addition to its four other traditional business groups (Carrier Network, Enterprise, Consumer, Cloud). In fact, the company is currently working with German car manufacturer Audi to test technology that would power self-driving cars to be sold in China.[276]

Due to the soft power and hard power ramifications of 5G, technology is becoming ever more a matter of politics.

---

275 "Huawei Has 56,492 Patents—and It's Not Afraid to Use Them." South China Morning Post. Bloomberg, June 14, 2019. https://www.scmp.com/news/china/article/3014625/weapons-economic-warfare-huawei-has-56492-patents-and-its-not-afraid-use.

276 O'Kane, Sean. "Audi Taps Huawei to Help Power Self-Driving Cars in China." The Verge. The Verge, October 12, 2018. https://www.theverge.com/2018/10/12/17967320/audi-huawei-self-driving-cars-china.

Fittingly, ZTE and Huawei, both Chinese companies in the telecommunications field, have become targets of US sanctions as part of the larger picture of the technological competition between the two largest global economics. Standards of technology like 5G may not have any free-riders, and, in fact, can be controlled by few individuals and countries. To reap the benefits of new technologies or risk being left behind, industries and countries will need to follow the footsteps of the pioneer in this field. The forerunner has a lot to gain in terms of setting the standards of something like 5G. And, unfortunately for the United States, which has traditionally held a large monopoly on cutting-edge technology development, China is catching up.

TELECOMMUNICATION STANDARDS BEFORE 5G

Standards of technology are at the heart of the success of the telecommunications industry. These standards have evolved in an increasingly social world, spurred on by academic research conducted by researchers and designers whose decisions affect system architecture down to the smallest details.[277]

Throughout different eras of the past, based on different political environments, technology has developed differently, and factionalization has historically plagued the telecommunications industry. During the 2G era, wireless communications networks were divided into the GSM (Global System

---

277 Taleb, Tarik, Rolf Winter, Tuncer Baykas, and Farooq Bari. "Telecommunications Standards." IEEE Communications Magazine 51, no. 3 (2013): 78–79. https://doi.org/10.1109/mcom.2013.6476869.

for Mobile Communication) and CDMA (Code Division Multiple Access) standards. The vast majority of the world has utilized the GSM standard, which features the use of SIM cards in phones. However, the United States and Russia, in the 2G era, adhered to the CDMA standard, which featured the use of phones tied to the carrier's networks.[278] The GSM and CDMA standards show that the world is split in two in terms of technology use. This division continued on to the 3G era.

During the time of 3G telecommunications, the world was divided into three factions: WCDMA, CDMA2000, and TD-SCDMA, which are used by Europe, the United States, and China respectively. These three standards were used by different mobile carriers in these countries. Some phones were not designed to work in all ecosystems and were thus tied to a specific geographic location. After the rise of digital circuits and wireless technologies in the 1990s, the United States believed it could promote the use of US-developed CDMA and WIMAX technologies. However, the standard of CDMA was developed too inaccessible by Qualcomm, and telecommunications operators around the world would not support it. The United States also actively promoted the application of WIMAX technology but failed.

From the ashes of US efforts in creating its own widely used telecommunications protocol came the 3GPP organization, which stands for the 3rd Generation Partnership Project. This international standards organization is responsible for

---

278 Hill, Simon. "CDMA vs. GSM: What's the Difference?" Digital Trends. Digital Trends, December 5, 2019. https://www.digitaltrends.com/mobile/cdma-vs-gsm-differences-explained/.

developing many mobile protocols used today. Through a partnership of US, Japanese, European, Indian, South Korean, and Chinese organizations, the 3GPP aims to determine the general policy and strategy of the organizations' developments.

Through the 3GPP, European and Chinese researchers came together to create international communications protocols, allowing Chinese researchers to learn and prompting the rise of Chinese equipment manufacturers such as Huawei and ZTE. The failure of the United States in unilaterally developing its standards led to the 3GPP, enabling international collaboration on telecommunications standards. This development helped support Chinese industry.

THE RACE FOR 5G ADOPTION

A one-size-fits-all standard of 5G communications has not been finalized by researchers yet, meaning that the perfect 5G standard currently does not exist. Presently, two camps exist in the 5G standards development, represented by Huawei in China and Qualcomm in the United States. Tensions and anxieties are high. The competition between the two factions is exacerbated by political and economic tensions between the United States and China, as well as the media coverage on the importance of 5G.

In late 2019, companies, faced with market competition, are beginning to implement what they see as a suitable standard of 5G telecommunications, showing signs that the world is moving to different standards in different geographic localities. In the future, a sort of digital "iron curtain" may appear, as different parts of the world start to utilize different standards of 5G communications, with Huawei representing China and Qualcomm representing the United States and its allies.

China is putting massive amounts of resources into the development of standards, protocols, and ecosystems for next-generation technologies. Knowing that it will face difficulty and ire from the United States in directly competing in more fundamental technologies such as chip creation and computer operating systems, the country is focusing on the standards of the future. 5G is a ripe ground for new ecosystems to appear, ones that may be created by China. Consequently, the Chinese government is using money to buy time in its 5G competition against the United States and the West, setting off a tsunami of 5G development and adoption.

On June 6, 2019, the Chinese Ministry of Industry and Information Technology issued the first batch of 5G licenses, giving them to China Mobile, China Unicom, China Telecom, and China Radio and Television. It plans to finish large-scale commercialization of 5G technologies in 2020, allowing the masses to access 5G connections. Unlike the United States, China's unique style of authoritarian governance allows it to carry out public projects at a blinding pace, putting the power of the government behind commercial endeavors. In the 2G to 4G era, China built seven million base stations, and it plans to upgrade currently existing base stations into 5G-enabled ones.

Due to the technical constraints of 5G telecommunications, the number of base stations must increase to cover the same area as 4G connections. Sometimes, the technology will require five times as many base stations compared to 4G, increasing the time and costs for construction. In 2019, China has already begun to take the lead, having constructed 400,000 5G base stations in the country, ten times as many as the United States.

Two reasons account for why the United States is currently lagging behind China in the adoption of 5G base stations. A recent report created by the Department of Defense asserts that one reason is due to the US military's occupation of certain band frequencies.[279] The reservation of certain telecommunications frequencies for the military pushes 5G telecom operators to use a more limited frequency, which has a weaker penetration rate. Hence a greater number of 5G base stations are required to cover an area in the United States as compared to China, increasing the costs of construction. Furthermore, the United States currently does not have a home-grown telecommunications equipment manufacturer like China's Huawei. The country must rely on Europe's Ericsson or Nokia to fulfill the entire 5G industrial chain.

BANNING CHINESE 5G

In August 2018, Trump authorized a bill banning the US government's use of Huawei and ZTE technology as part of the broader Defense Authorization Act. US allies, including Australia, New Zealand, Japan, and the United Kingdom have also followed suit, with some making public their

---

279 "THE 5G ECOSYSTEM: RISKS & OPPORTUNITIES FOR DoD." Defense. gov. Defense and Innovation Board, April 2019. https://media.defense. gov/2019/Apr/03/2002109302/-1/-1/0/DIB_5G_STUDY_04.03.19.PDF.

policy of banning Huawei from future 5G networks, and some expressing concern over the use of Huawei's equipment in telecommunications networks. Slowly, the roll-out of new telecommunications networks is becoming a proxy of US-China competition, as the United States continues to punish Chinese manufacturers as well as push other governments to minimize Chinese influence in their countries.

What are the international political implications of 5G development and implementation, and why is the United States pressuring its allies? The answer lies in the geo-economics of 5G. The implementation of 5G is a zero-sum economic game—as viewed by the United States and China. Rather than viewing it as a win-win situation where technological advances are shared for mutual gain, the geo-economics perspective asserts that widespread 5G implementation will shift the balance between the world's two most advanced economies. 5G will lead to massive digitization of society, transforming industry and data analytics. Widespread implementation empowers both producers and consumers to become more efficient.

Moreover, 5G implementation by either the United States or China will empower the two countries to replicate similar models in other countries, creating political clout in the form of geopolitical, economic, and technological influence. Through its lead in the cultivation of 5G technologies and standards, China, for instance, can influence its periphery states, endowing them with superior Chinese technology in exchange for political or economic leverage. Thus 5G has the potential to redraw the lines between Chinese and American camps, especially in Northeast, Southeast, and South Asia.

Due to the political and economic ramifications of 5G network proliferation, the United States has a fundamental deep distrust toward any concrete Chinese practices, which has precipitated a concern that the United States is susceptible to Chinese cyber espionage, or even subject to the disruption of critical cyber infrastructure that may paralyze the nation. The 5G issue is thus a conduit through which US fears of Chinese hegemony are materializing, and the outcome of 5G could become an important proxy to assess the state of the US-China bilateral relationship—or the depth of how icy it could get.

Concerns over cybersecurity have driven states to coalesce around US leadership and policy on the future of 5G networks. Indeed, the countries that have publicly adopted the US position on 5G and Huawei are either its allies or close partners. It is only a matter of time before both the United States and China separately gather allies to take a position on the issue of incorporating Huawei's technology into 5G networks.

States that have heretofore been sitting on the fence and unwilling to commit to either Chinese or American policy on the matter could be forced to take a stand under intense diplomatic pressure. This scenario would specifically apply to states like South Korea, the Philippines, Thailand, and Vietnam—countries that are ostensibly strong US military allies or close partners but which also fall within Beijing's political influences due to their proximity to the middle kingdom. Through the 5G issue, both superpowers will likely take stock of and develop a clearer picture of where each country—Asian or otherwise—stands on the broader US-China geopolitical chessboard.

CHAPTER 10

HUAWEI:
Its Prolific Rise

Huawei's vision is to bring digital to every person, home and organization for a fully connected, intelligent world.

—HUAWEI.COM

CHINA'S OWN GSM

Within Building One of the Shenzhen High-Tech Industrial Park, an office is trashed with rows of desks, cobwebs of wires, and scattered computer parts. There, young engineers are buried in their books, in what constitutes a fertile ground of youth, dreams, and ambition. Here is the heart of China's burgeoning tech hubs, and young people have rushed here to grasp life-changing opportunities. The young people in this office make up the research and development team in charge of inventing China's first GSM telecommunications protocol.

The year is 1996 and telecommunications technology has just evolved from a first-generation (1G) to a second-generation (2G) GSM protocol. In the West, giants such as Ericsson, Nokia, and Motorola have already developed 2G systems ready for commercial use. In China, an ecosystem has not yet been invented, and businesses are rushing in to come up with the country's domestic solution.

The climate in the southern city of Shenzhen is hot and humid. The young engineers and researchers strip down to their vests to continue working, occasionally splashing cool water onto their faces to remain energized. Each night, they share bowls of instant noodles and retire to their futons underneath their desks in the office, only to wake up again the next day to continue working. Such is the condition and relentless ambition at Huawei Technologies during its early days, before it becomes the telecommunications giant it is known as today.

This lifestyle was not imposed upon these young men. Similar to the dorm-room entrepreneurs of US colleges and Silicon Valley, these young men are fueled by a youthful energy and an optimistic outlook for the future. The romanticism of struggling with their fellow engineers, living and working together, is a big draw for these young men. This DNA of collective struggle and communal lifestyle lives on within Huawei to this day, as the company expands operations across the globe to the least-traveled-to and most hostile places in the world.

With hard work, the Huawei research and development team finally creates China's first-ever domestically made

The Huawei booth at Mobile World Congress 2017. *(https://www. telecomlead.com/wp-content/uploads/2017/02/Huawei-booth-at-MWC-2017.jpg)*

2G telecommunications ecosystem. In 1997, the company finally produces the 2G GSM system. And, at the country's International ICT Exhibition and Conference in Beijing, the team unveils its work, hanging up a banner proudly with the slogan "China's own GSM," in front of a backdrop of the five-starred red national flag. At the exposition, telecom operators over the country and senior government officials congratulate Huawei for this outstanding achievement.

FRENCH AESTHETICS

Today, Huawei has become an international giant, having expanded its operations all over the world. Not only does it continue to be the number-one seller of telecommunications equipment but it has also branched out to sell consumer products like laptops and smartphones.

Situated between the Louvre and the Musée D'Orsay is Huawei's Aesthetics Research Center. In this fashionable part of Paris, this new research center is radically different from the spartan and industrial office buildings that housed the company's early research and development team in the seventies. With a view of the Eiffel Tower in the distance, this new office is modern and elegant, putting even the museums to shame. Here, design experts from some of the world's most prolific fashion brands are collaborating to energize the company's public image for the world.

The company is no longer producing technical solutions for the Chinese domestic market. Now, it services the entire world. Relentless in its pursuit of innovation, the company has continued to invest heavily in research and development. It houses researchers in centers around the world, devoting a substantial portion of its annual revenue into R&D. As a testament to the company's focus on continuous innovation, almost half of the company's employees are researchers and developers, working on the next innovative breakthrough.

Due to the company's rise, it fittingly needs to present a more confident version of itself to the world. The team in Paris is tasked with designing its new visual identity. The "New Huawei" needs to embody an identity that is, according to prominent creative figure Jacques Séguéla, elegant, fluent, and human—with an oriental flavor. This new identity will add a human touch to technology, improving the experience for users and adding a unique character to the Huawei brand. The team in Paris has set forth to discover new natural and real materials to incorporate into its designs, as well as research different approaches to colors and styles that will better personify the soul of the brand.

As the company becomes increasingly consumer-facing due to the growth of its handset business, Huawei needs to present a better image of itself to the world. Consequently, the Paris team is tasked with designing the company's presentation booth at the 2016 Mobile World Congress in Barcelona (MWC). The MWC is the world's most significant trade show for the telecommunications industry, and the team is going all out to design the company's massive exhibit.

After entering a twenty-seven-meter-wide entrance, visitors are transported to a different world, with a clear blue sky above them and glass floor paneling beneath them. They will enter the digital world created by Huawei, immersing themselves in the white display islets and the demonstrations meticulously prepared by the design team and the technical staff behind the scenes. Huawei's three-day appearance at MWC required almost a year of preparation by the design team in Paris and teams in China. Despite being the smallest Huawei research group, the Aesthetics Research Center in France certainly made monumental shifts in how Huawei is perceived around the world.

WHAT IS HUAWEI?

During the early days of the company—a time when glitzy expo appearances and Parisian design teams did not exist, but rather futons, instant ramen, and men in tank-tops—the company's rise to prominence would have been unheard of. Today, Huawei has become the preeminent telecommunications company, with operations all over the world. It is the only telecoms equipment vendor that still spans consumer, enterprise, and service provider markets.[280] Its competitors in the West have all experienced divestments as well as mergers and acquisitions while Huawei remains the same company it was when it was founded.

The founder of Huawei, Ren Zhengfei, once mused that the "most basic goal of an enterprise is to survive, and to survive sustainably." Not only did his company survive amid the harshly competitive Chinese markets where hundreds of similar companies existed, but Huawei thrived.[281]

The image of realist international relations can also be applied in the business sphere. Just as Thomas Hobbes' brutish anarchic world is characterized by mistrust and competition, leading to individual self-help actions, companies need to fight to remain relevant in today's globalized world. They must out-survive their competitors, always improving, adapting to industry disruptions, and continuously serving their customers.

"Survival is our most basic goal and we must have markets to survive. If there are no markets, we cannot achieve

---

280 Bilderbeek, Pim. "How Apple, Cisco and Huawei Disrupted the Telecom Equipment Market." The METISfiles, April 15, 2015. https://www.themetisfiles.com/2015/04/how-apple-cisco-and-huawei-disrupted-the-telecom-equipment-market/.

281 Huang, Weiwei, Zhifeng Yin, Ke Lv, Saixiong Hu, Guodong Tong, Hongbin Gong, and Chunbo Wu. Dedication the Huawei Philosophy of Human Resource Management. London: LID Publishing, 2016.

economics of scale. If there are no economics of scale, costs cannot be low. If we have neither low costs nor high quality, it will be hard for us to compete and our company will definitely decline."

During the time of this writing, Huawei currently receives the vast majority of its revenue from three different business groups: the Consumer Business Group (CBG), Carrier Business Group (CBG), and Enterprise Business Group (EBG). Each business group corresponds to a different type of customer, from the average consumer on the street to telecom network operators to large corporations.

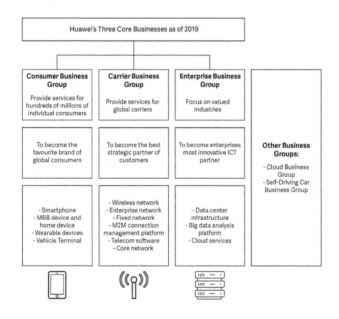

Huawei's Three Core Businesses Groups as of 2019. *(Dennis Wang 2019)*

From its humble beginnings, the company mainly served telecom operators. In the United States, these companies are the likes of AT&T and Verizon, providing operators with equipment (like base stations and antennas) and technical solutions. However, Huawei, in recent years, has begun to receive more revenue from its consumer business group, driven largely by the popularity of Huawei handheld smartphones.

China's progress and institutional reforms were critical to the company's success, because Huawei would not have pulled itself up on its own accord if the business environment was not right. On the other hand, Huawei has also made great contributions to China's development—contributions that are no less significant than those of many state-owned enterprises. Over the past two decades, it has paid over CNY 300 billion in taxes and both, directly and indirectly, created millions of jobs. Together, Chinese telecom companies like Huawei, ZTE, Datang, and Great Dragon have saved the country trillions on infrastructure development.

Just as an executive at a well-known Western telecom company once said, with its cost-effectiveness and disruptive technological innovation, Huawei has helped provide billions of people in the world with low-cost, high-quality information technology and services, which is valuable beyond measure. In China especially, where the information sector has evolved into a core strategic industry, the value of Huawei's contribution can't be denied.

Despite its contribution, given the many resources that have been bestowed on state-owned enterprises and all the incentives that Huawei's foreign-invested counterparts have also enjoyed, Ren Zhengfei continues to wonder why the government hasn't provided his company with a bit more support.

HUAWEI'S FOUNDER REN ZHENGFEI

I am on a usual post-dinner walk with my colleague throughout the local neighborhoods in the Moroccan city of Casablanca. Despite it being in the middle of the summer, the air is cool and one can feel the subtle sea breeze against their skin. Walking through the silent neighborhood, streaks of brilliant orange and purple appear above us as the sun sets on the horizon. Not a single sound can be heard except the distant barking of stray dogs.

This is one of our usual recreational activities: walking to clear our minds and get some fresh air. Unfortunately, employees at Huawei work until very late, and the office has a serious atmosphere, similar to many companies in East Asia. Walking outside is a pleasant break from the office environment.

As I walk, I strike up a conversation with my colleague beside me. I've always been interested and curious about the culture of the company and the centrality of its founder Ren Zhengfei, so I really want to talk to a more senior employee about it. Within the company, the name Ren commands respect, almost worship. To me, it seems almost reminiscent of China's Mao era, where the masses touted Mao's ideology as the absolute truth. Can it be another type of corporate brainwashing?

"Before coming to Morocco, I worked in South Africa. I saw people working extremely hard, even harder than us, but not earning so much money. It was Ren and Huawei that he started that have given us this platform for a better life."

Sure, you can find many tech company founders out there, and these people are all filthy rich! I still don't understand the obsession with Huawei's founder.

I continued prodding my friend for answers. "Yes, we are lucky to end up in such a fast-growing company, but don't you think Ren is brainwashing us into his cult of personality?"

"Well, Ren is a great man. Mao was also a great man," he responds.

I do a double-take. In the West, Mao is often demonized as a tyrannical figure who killed millions of people. Some compare him to the Soviet Union's Stalin who ruled with an iron fist or even Hitler in Nazi Germany. Mao's disastrous economic policies ultimately forced millions of citizens to starve.

"Because of Huawei's technologies and Ren's leadership, I am working less hard than those people I saw in the slums of South Africa, but earning thirty to forty times more than them," my friend explains.

What he asserts is indeed true. Huawei employees earn disproportionately more than their Chinese counterparts. Employees are treated very well, earning money equivalent to US companies such as Google or Facebook and enjoying a high level of prestige for being a Huawei employee. Huawei, as a company, blossomed right when the country was experiencing rapid economic growth after having joined the World Trade Organization. People like my colleague grew up during this time of unbounded ambition and opportunity—something that previous generations did not experience.

Everything is beginning to make sense. In the eyes of the Chinese people, Mao—although still contentious—is the founding father of modern China, the man who declared that "the Chinese people have stood up again" after a century of Western incursion. Under the Communist Party that Mao helped cultivate, the country has experienced such rapid economic gains.

"A book about Huawei is a book about its founder. Ren Zhengfei has made a difference that many will never appreciate in building what is likely the most successful private business to come out of post-Mao China. Ren is a humble man with humble beginnings, he is a proud Chinese, a former People's Liberation Army (PLA) soldier, but unlike how the Western press would portray Ren, he is not a career military officer and was not a high-ranking 'general' as some in the West have wrongly represented him as."

Ren, like the Chinese Communist Party, relies on performance legitimacy to survive in the hearts and minds of the company. Ren continues to maintain his cult of personality as long as Huawei continues to steamroll the telecommunications market, just as CCP remains legitimate in China thanks to the country's continuing economic growth. At the same time, without a doubt, Ren is also an incredibly shrewd and hardworking businessman. He transformed his small startup in Shenzhen into the largest telecommunications equipment maker in the world, defeating traditional European competitors like Nokia and Ericsson. Ren and Huawei have also contributed greatly to the country's economic rise. As the most internationalized Chinese company in the world, Huawei has brought tremendous economic growth to the country.

The cult of Ren is quite real and genuine. Huawei's employees respect him for his farsightedness and focus on building the company's core competencies and culture. The company has a culture of continuous investment into R&D, spending 14 percent of its annual revenues in R&D,[282] hence it is not only able to overtake its Chinese competitors but also shine in the international telecommunications market. Ren also saw the potential threat of US political pressure years in advance, having set out to build Huawei's own operating system five years before the United States announced its embargo on the company. Furthermore, while other Chinese companies diversified into lucrative fields such as real estate, Ren did not deviate from the company's mission, continuing to focus on developing the best telecommunications products in the market and cultivating the company's unique culture.

---

282 "Huawei's R&D Investment in 2018 Exceeds $15 Billion." Huawei's R&D investment in 2018 exceeds $15 billion - Chinadaily.com.cn, September 4, 2019. https://www.chinadaily.com.cn/a/201904/09/WS5ca-c0859a3104842260b5265.html.

HUAWEI'S FOOT SOLDIERS

Huawei prides itself on being fundamentally Chinese, and the corporate culture reflects this attitude. Resilience and hard work are prized—qualities that reflect traditional Chinese heritage. Almost every day at work, Chinese employees would work overtime, leaving after other nationalities have already left. Characteristically, under every desk are mattresses and pillows. Not infrequently, the entire office takes a nap after lunch or power naps during different times of the day to remain efficient.

During my time at Huawei Morocco, seeing colleagues working over 90 hours a week and coming in on the weekends was not uncommon. Furthermore, complementing the traits of resilience and hard work is the expectation that employees put the group ahead of their own interests, whether for the company or the client.

Another piece of evidence reflecting the company's Chinese heritage is the use of slogan and rhetoric in Huawei to promote company culture, creating a structure that is very hierarchical in nature. Posters and banners promoting company values and missions are plastered throughout the office, in addition to the many books for the taking that discuss the company's culture and mission.

Doing a Google search online, one can find many videos and pictures of what might appear to be eccentric company events. They are created to fire up company spirit and ambition. Below is a picture of a swearing-in ceremony of the company's consumer products business group in 2019. Below is a sample of the swearing-in ceremony.

终端铁军	*The irony army of the Consumer business group*
王者之师	*Master of kings!*
勇往直前	*Move forward!*
势不可挡	*We are Unstoppable!*
胜利 胜利 胜利	*Victory, Victory, Victory!*
三年一千	*$100B revenue in three years.*
五年一千五	*$150B revenue in three years.*
铁军出击	*Iron army attack!*
力争第一	*Strive for number one!*
我们的目标	*Our goal:*
胜利 胜利 胜利	*Victory, Victory, Victory!*

Huawei Consumer Business Group swearing in ceremony. *(https://www.youtube.com/watch?v=hZxXeW4iiF0)*

This event occurred during a time that the company founder Ren Zhengfei described as 战时, which translates into "a time of war," a time when the United States was mounting its pressure against the Chinese telecommunications company. In Chinese fashion, the company is firing up the spirits of its employees by using a combination of corporate culture and Chinese nationalism. Events like the above would likely not occur in a Western company, where the center of gravity tends toward the individual rather than the group.

Indeed, Huawei retains a hierarchical structure that is almost military-like. Its founder, Ren, before creating Huawei, served as a communications engineer for the Chinese People's Liberation Army (PLA). He has carried parts of PLA culture into Huawei.

During the company's underdog days, Huawei's strategy can be characterized by Mao Zedong's famous military doctrine of "people's war," a form of guerrilla warfare that stresses battle in the countryside against an adversary. As such, the company operated in the fringes of the international markets, like in many Sub-Saharan countries. By going to impoverished nations and providing local carriers with effective equipment at a very low cost (backed by China's manufacturing capacity), Huawei was able to gain a foothold in many emerging markets.

Ren also employs the concept of self-criticism, another Maoist doctrine. Self-criticism involves the need for CCP cadres and intellectuals to scrutinize themselves, discovering flaws so that they can improve. The company's human resource management culture requires that employees be open and accepting of self-criticism as well as criticism from others—to improve their performance. The concept of self-criticism reflects Huawei's unique business management style and particularly its founder's roots in the Chinese PLA.

In his prominent book *Principles*, American investor Ray Dalio, founder of the largest hedge fund in the world, Bridgewater Associates, outlines his principles for company management. One of the ideas he asserts is the concept of "radical transparency," which breaks down communication barriers between employees. This transparency allows individuals to understand what their strong and weak points are, allowing them to become more productive. This "radical transparency" translates into a set of company "baseball cards," where each employee has a profile (like a baseball card) that includes their strong and weak points—all stored in a central database.

Huawei operates in a similar framework of radical transparency. Within the company database, employees are able to look at profiles (or baseball cards) of all their colleagues throughout the world. In a specially designed internal phone app, employees can view their own rank within the company, as well as their peers' ranks. Additionally, staffers can look at all the previous experiences of their peers, including promotions and demotions.

This system reflects the radical transparency promoted by Dalio, a structure where each employee has a digital baseball card profile. In his usual fashion, Ren describes this system as an innovation within the human resources department, comparing it to the likes of a military, which he also describes as the "most effective team in the world." To him, one characteristic of the military is that "their ranks are completely public, and are displayed on their shoulders."

Due to the large size of the company, as well as the entrenched nature of business processes, groups, and modules, every employee in Huawei is highly replaceable. This culture of replaceability fosters a sense of insecurity and stress for its employees, spurring them to work harder. While the salary is incredibly attractive, demotions are common, as if the company is composed of layers of generals, commanders, foot soldiers, and special forces.

In Ren's speeches, he has often made analogies comparing Huawei employees to roles in the military. He has even likened his employees to atoms in a nuclear bomb, believing that when put in the suitable harsh environments, they can set off a chain reaction of energy. These comparisons may, again, be representative of his past in the Chinese army. Just as some of the top corporate leaders in the United States have military backgrounds, military culture may indeed be conducive to good corporate governance.

"To say that Huawei's success is rooted in its management philosophy is no exaggeration. Ren Zhengfei once said, 'Without any special background or resources, we can rely on no one but ourselves; each bit of progress is in our own hands, and no one else's.' He went on to note that the company's systems and culture are powerful forces—perhaps the mysterious power behind Huawei's success."

Huawei employees are like foot soldiers. Often, they are positioned abroad in some of the most hostile and inhospitable countries in the world. In all of Huawei's offices around the world, the core team of employees comprises of Chinese expatriates, where locals work through an inferior contract or at the lower levels of the company. Even though sending out domestic Chinese foot soldiers to international locations incurs higher costs for the company, often the cultural difference between local workers and Huawei is too great to justify hiring locally. The expatriates of Huawei have grown to call each other "brothers" and "comrades" for their collective struggle. Indeed, when one works and lives with their fellow employees for every hour of the day—often in an inhospitable country—a sense of brotherhood often naturally develops between these foot soldiers.

Huawei expatriates often sacrifice their family for their work. This group frequently consists of men who still have families in China but are working abroad. In some cases, the wives and children of Huawei employees travel with the men to different parts of the world. The children of these Huawei foot soldiers often enroll in local international schools, where they study with the children of foreign diplomats.

Due to the company's international reach and its emphasis on collective struggle, stories of Huawei employees working in war zones are not uncommon. Huawei has operations in countries like Syria, Yemen, Libya, and North Korea, and you will definitely find a team of Huawei foot soldiers on the ground in these places.

HUAWEI LIFESTYLE

Many of the employees I talked to expressed that the company's culture is quite unique, and that as a result, great success within the company often does not necessarily translate to success outside of the company. Huawei employees are incredibly collegial, embodying both Chinese and Western elements. Fundamentally, Huawei is a Chinese company, but it has struggled and worked hard to learn from industry leaders to create internal transformation.

The collegial culture at Huawei does not just mean collaboration in the workplace. Work at Huawei truly requires unique people. Employment at the company feels like life on a college campus. From group overtime at the office to messy and spartan dorm rooms to weekend drinking, Huawei employees treat each other like brothers. The classic look of the company is a Chinese man with glasses in his late thirties to mid-forties, who majored in engineering at a Chinese university.

In the many rep offices of Huawei around the world, Huawei employees work, eat, and live together. Often accompanying the employees are Huawei chefs who cook three meals a day for staffers, increasing morale by providing them with tasty Chinese food that reminds them of home. As for accommodation, the employees live together in dorm-type suites assigned by the company. For the Huawei expatriates who do not have their wives and children with them overseas, the dorm rooms are often spartan, messy, and bare, not so different from those of college students.

Huawei's European-themed campus in China. *(https://www.theat-lantic.com/photo/2019/05/photos-of-huaweis-european-themed-cam-pus-in-china/589342/)*

On weekends, the employees drink, cook, and play sports together. A classic scene is employees in their dorms with their roommates or friends, making hotpot, drinking, and bantering. On the weekend, they go for a swim or play basketball or badminton together.

Jian works at the head Huawei North Africa office, located in Morocco, responsible for overseeing the operations of over twenty countries in the North Africa Region. He currently lives in the company's dormitories in Casablanca with two roommates. On weekends, Jian often prepares hotpot for his roommates or goes out to play badminton with other colleagues. I have personally experienced Jian's famous hotpots, which was definitely a very fun experience. In his dormitory, Jian and his roommates also keep a pet tortoise they lovingly named CaCa, representing the first and last syllables of the city name Casablanca. Jian and his friends take care of the tortoise and play with it, give it food, and put it in a maze they have constructed using Heineken beer bottles.

I had the pleasure of being taken to a friendly weekend game by Jian. Badminton is a Chinese national sport, and many Chinese people enjoy playing it recreationally and competitively. In Casablanca, which has a large Chinese population, the Chinese Consulate organized a friendly badminton competition, an annual competition played by Chinese expatriates in Casablanca. Present were teams from Huawei, ZTE, Bank of China, China State Construction Engineering Corp (CSCEC), and China Railway Construction Corp (CRCC).

One day before the tournament, all participants showed up at the venue to help set up the space. In the dimly lit warehouse-like sports arena, employees from all the companies came together to tape up the badminton lines on the ground, taking a total of five hours. Banners were hoisted up to the top of the arena, as well as the Chinese flag alongside the Moroccan flag. Everyone was like a family: all from different backgrounds but acting like a family in Morocco, taking time out of their weekend to take part in and support this event.

The next day, teams from different Chinese enterprises in Morocco arrived on the scene. Already, some could hear the pitter-patter of rackets and the back-and-forth motion of the shuttlecock. On the sidelines, the families of expatriates sat, preparing fruits, local pastries, and refreshments for everyone. The environment was very merry all around. Team members from different companies wore their sporting clothes; like uniforms, each team wore different clothes, displaying their company affiliation. There was even a DJ at the scene; as the athletes warmed up, one could hear the sound of Bruno Mars and "The Lazy Song" blasting throughout the arena.

The tension was fierce between the teams. One could hear the shouts of encouragement and cheers of team members as they watched their fellow teammates battle on the court. The athletes were totally riveted by the game, which required great focus, speed, and agility. In the hot court without air conditioning, the heat took a toll on the players, and one could see the sweat dripping from their foreheads and arms as they jumped back and forth, synergizing with their doubles partners to win just one more point.

The playing lasted all morning, until lunchtime, when players departed for Chinese restaurants close by or snacked on the food brought by the event volunteers, which consisted of wraps from McDonald's and various fruits brought by one of the employees.

The game continued late into the afternoon and even the evening. Already, the players were exhausted from all of the playing. After the last cheer, the players finally finished, and Huawei was able to sweep all three sections: mixed doubles, men's singles, and women's singles. Jian was able to lead his mixed doubles team into victory. Leading one of the four Huawei doubles teams, he named his team HongMeng (鴻蒙), which is the name of Huawei's new back-up operating system that will ultimately replace the company's dependence on US platforms.

Ultimately, this experience shows the collegial culture of Huawei. Working at the company is very much like being a student in college. People work, eat, live, and play together, often overseas in distant lands, away from their families. From working overtime with all your colleagues to living in the same dormitories to drinking and playing sports during time off, Huawei employees all over the world experience a sense of brotherhood, as well as a tight-knit community that is fertile seed-ground for the cultivation of the firm's unique and fierce corporate culture.

Huawei employees live and breathe the company. In fact, the company recently opened a new campus in Dongguan, China, able to house 25,000 employees and complete with entertainment facilities, restaurants, scenery, employee housing, and a school for the kids of families. The new and eccentric campus is modeled after famous European architecture, complete with imported materials from Europe and a tram from Switzerland to provide transportation within the campus. In this day of corporate feudalism, no wonder employees at Huawei live and breathe the company.

CHAPTER 11

HUAWEI:
The Most International
Company

If you want to win in the twenty-first century, you have to empower others, making sure other people are better than you. Then you will be successful.

—JACK MA

ANGOLA RAILROAD BOY

Bloody fighting erupts in Angola, taking the lives of over 500,000 people. It's the height of the Cold War, and the two world superpowers are vying for influence across the world in places like Sub-Saharan Africa. After twenty-six years of brutal bloodshed, the Angolan Civil War concludes in 2002. Institutions and infrastructure in the country are in a terrible state of disrepair.

Simon is a scrawny kid in college, wearing his signature round glasses and always immersed in his studies. Little does he know that he will be spending the next ten years of his life in Africa. Having graduated from university with a fresh civil engineering degree in hand, Simon started work at the China Railway Group and was sent to Angola. At the time, the living environment for workers like Simon is Spartan. At 9 p.m. every evening, the electricity generator turns off, leaving everything to the dark and humid Angolan night. Employees certainly did not have access to modern luxuries that we enjoy today, like the Internet or Wi-Fi.

Simon and his colleagues are in Angola as part of China's massive foreign direct investments into infrastructure development projects in Africa. The China Railway Group is tasked with rebuilding the crucial but badly damaged Benguela Railway that provides a much-needed window to the world for the Angolan hinterland. Other than his numerous Chinese colleagues, Simon cannot communicate with anyone else.

A Chinese native but confident in his grasp of intermediate English, Simon looks forward to stepping outside the constraints of his university walls, making a name for himself in the world. However, he is shocked that barely anyone speaks English in Angola, where the official language is Portuguese. However, after meeting a Catholic pastor in his local community, he starts learning the local language after the pastor gave him an English-Portuguese manual. Every day, Simon digs into his studies intensively, studying during the night and practicing during the day. Often, he practices his Portuguese by speaking with the local children, and his language improves fast. After half a year, he is able to communicate

The Benguela Railway. *(https://www.railjournal.com/africa/ben-guela-railway-reconstruction-completed/)*

with the locals, discussing ideas in civil construction and playing soccer with them.

Soccer is a growing passion for Simon. In his spare time, he often entertains himself with casual games of soccer with community locals and also other Chinese ex-pats in the country. Through soccer, Simon finds his big career break. The other Chinese ex-pats he plays with are in Angola working for Huawei Technologies, then a rather obscure Chinese company. Under the introduction of his soccer friends, Simon switches from working on the railway project to pivot into sales and business, which he finds more interesting.

By entering the prestigious Huawei firm, Simon thinks it's his big break. Little does he know that Huawei will send him back to Angola to work on the firm's operations there due to his knowledge of Portuguese and of the local environment. Besides the occasional gunfights that occur around his residence, life in Angola is relatively peaceful but very different from the life he once enjoyed as a college student in China five years ago.

Simon's story is like those of many other individuals who found their way working at Huawei. As the most international Chinese technology firm (and rather obscure at the time), Huawei targeted underdeveloped countries like Angola as their prime markets where other more well-known Western telecommunications firms would not go. Offering cheap telecommunications equipment and boosted by the booming Chinese economy, Huawei was able to gain a foothold in countries like Angola.

EMERGENCY

BANG! Simon and his colleagues kick down the door, bursting into his employee's apartment. Clothes cover counters and chairs, dirty ashtrays lie uncleaned, and leftover cans of beer litter the room. In the dusty dormitory, they can barely make out a figure on the floor, illuminated by the light from the incandescent bulb in the hallway radiating inside. The silhouette is not moving.

Two days have passed since he disappeared in Angola while working for Huawei Technologies. There he is, face down on the floor like a rag doll, arms outstretched and head lopsided. Immediately, Simon and his team spring to action, hoisting the employee by his limbs and hauling him off the floor as they head for the local clinic. In the humid Sub-Saharan night, the team bursts into the shanty clinic of the residential complex.

"No. You must leave. He will die soon" is the grim prognosis the doctor gives Simon and his colleagues.

The clock has almost struck twelve, but the only option for the team is to continue searching. Since that night, Simon has not slept for three days straight, instead taking his patient from hospital to hospital in Luanda. None can help, not even the Presidential Hospital, which has the best facilities in the country. As dawn breaks once again, painting streaks of gold and turquoise upon a blue canvas in the sky, Simon despairs. The employee is indeed on the brink of death.

Simon receives a phone call from the Huawei administration, informing him that it has arranged for a charter flight from South Africa with a doctor on board. Practically ready to collapse, Simon feels a rush of newfound hope.

When the doctor arrives, he takes one look at his patient and states, "He is very ill, but I will take him to a hospital in South Africa."

In the 2000s, this camaraderie enabled Huawei to thrive in the most hostile environments around the world. Upon arrival in South Africa, the employee enters an intensive care unit. Only after fifty-six days in a coma, eighty pounds lost, and many liters of donated blood does he finally recover. His colleagues support the blood transfusion throughout while consoling the employee's family.

This team represents the scrappy and audacious spirit of Chinese companies like Huawei, tackling the frontiers of business in the most brutal environments while China grew economically. Still an obscure company at the time, Huawei began its ascent to prominence by targeting underserved frontiers like countries in Southeast Asia, the Middle East, Africa, and Eurasia.

The company leveraged its ability to provide cheap telecommunications solutions backed by a growing Chinese economy to carve footholds in international markets like Angola. Today, it is one of China's preeminent companies, with increasingly global operations and reaches. Not only did the company beat out its early competitors, but in 2018, it also surpassed Apple to become the world's second-largest phone manufacturer in the smartphone market.[283]

FUKUSHIMA

In 2006, when Matsumoto first joined Huawei in Tokyo, the company was still an industry underdog, and not many in the industry knew about its presence. Setting up its Japanese subsidiary office in Tokyo's high-end business district of Otemachi, the new subsidiary was young and fresh but very ambitious. To Matsumoto, leaving his prior telecommunications for Huawei was a new and exciting opportunity, a chance to take on a larger role in a team and to have an impact

---

283 Chan, Edwin. "Huawei Overtakes Apple to Become Second Biggest Smartphone Maker." Bloomberg.com. Bloomberg, May 2, 2019. https://www.bloomberg.com/news/articles/2019-05-03/huawei-again-overtakes-apple-as-global-smartphone-market-tanks.

Great East Japan Earthquake and Tsunami. *(https://www.theatlan-tic.com/photo/2016/03/5-years-since-the-2011-great-east-japan-earthquake/473211/)*

in a new and entrepreneurial atmosphere. And, indeed, he found its corporate culture to be quite different from that of other Japanese companies, and he admired it very much.

Four years later, Japan experienced one of the worst disasters in its recent history. On March 11, 2011, at 2:46 p.m., a magnitude-nine earthquake rocked the nation, followed by a tsunami that wreaked havoc on the country's eastern coast. From the television screen, Matsumoto was shocked to see entire towns submerged and destroyed. Calling his wife who lived in the affected area, Matsumoto was relieved to find that his family was okay.

However, soon after, Japan also experienced one of the world's most significant nuclear disasters, as the Fukushima

Daiichi nuclear power station melted down, leaking radioactive materials into the air. During this time, some of Huawei's local competitors moved south to Osaka, to avoid potential adverse effects of radiation. And, according to Matsumoto, some even chartered planes to relocate employees and their families to Hong Kong. The Huawei staff were terribly anxious and wondered if they should also do the same. On the night of March 15, every employee of the Huawei Japan rep office received an English letter from the office director, detailing that Huawei would commit to its social responsibility by staying with its customers and upholding its customer-centric philosophy. Rather than leaving, the Chinese employees remained vigilant.

EMOBILE was one of Huawei's main Japanese customers at the time, and many of this carrier's base stations in the disaster area had gone offline. Though the carrier did not request help from Huawei, stating that it would be too dangerous for Huawei employees, Huawei continued to push forward with its customer-centric philosophy. Soon after, the Japanese government set up a no-go zone around the area of disasters; however, despite not being able to enter, the Huawei team in Tokyo continued to direct resources toward the area, delivering power supplies, generators, and other equipment to the available base stations outside the zone.

After some time, power was gradually restored to the disaster area, and some base stations had come online. However, EMOBILE still was not able to ameliorate some of its problems in the disaster areas and required solutions to provide mobile communications services to the disaster's refugees. Matsumoto was a member of the elite team that the company had assembled to tackle the customer's requests, attempting to restore communications in the disaster-stricken area.

On the evening of April 5, the team departed for Rikuzentakata as soon as possible to restore communications for the people there. Passing through a town roughly fifty kilometers from the nuclear station, the Geiger counter sounded its alarm, showing them that they were being exposed to radiation levels twenty times higher than that of Tokyo. However, so as not to feel anxious because of the reoccurring alarms, they raised the possible maximum permissible radiation level on the device so it would not ring anymore.

The air was putrid when they arrived at Rikuzentakata, a city that has been hit by both the earthquake and tsunami. Houses had collapsed, vehicles were seriously damaged, and key infrastructure such as railways, highways, and bridges had been cleared out. Atop the hill, icy rain chilled them to the bones as they attempted to repair the base station at hand. Out in the distance, the landscape seemed barren, with all the houses collapsed. Overnight, the homeland to thousands of people had been cleared out, and Matsumoto wondered if they should even bother repairing the tens of base stations affected by the disaster—no one lived out here anymore to use the communications services.

Matsumoto and his team elevated the antenna bracket back into the air and faced the direction of the antenna toward the refugee camp, then connected the equipment to the data center via a satellite. On the first day of their mission, they were able to reconstruct their first mobile base station, and communications were finally restored in the evening. Though their work made for a crude fix, the refugees from the disaster could finally call and communicate with their loved ones.

That evening, the team was awoken by another earthquake. The lights shut off and the emergency lights went on. The quake continued for several minutes until it finally stopped. Windows cracked and the building squeaked with the violent seismic movements. They had no choice but to wait anxiously until the shaking stopped. The team later discovered that they had experienced a magnitude-six earthquake and that the epicenter had been very close to their location.

However, within a week, the team was able to help its customer EMOBILE restore connection back to forty base stations in the disaster-stricken area. They became so engrossed by the process and their mission that they forgot to use their Geiger counter. They simply worked as hard and as efficiently as possible so that the refugees could communicate with their families again. They later found out that they had been working in one of the most dangerous places to restore communications, and that other people from outside the company were shocked that they had done what they did at such a time. Matsumoto felt that, as a local employee, he had the responsibility to support his country during this time of need, and he felt proud of this accomplishment. He and his team proved that Huawei values its customers and that they will stand by their side no matter whatever happens, even during times of disaster. Through blood, sweat, and tears, the team was able to restore communications to the area struck by the disaster.

From my time working at Huawei, I know one of the important tenets of the company's mission can be put into the simple Chinese phrase 以客户为中心, which is a rough translation of "the customer as the core." This phrase, coined by Ren, is known throughout the company. And, in fact, many Chinese books have been written on this concept, offering stories that exemplify it. In a nutshell, at Huawei, employees are expected to show unrelenting support to the customer no matter the circumstance. Self-sacrifice and long-term struggle are expected of every employee to satisfy the requirements of customers and over-deliver on their promises.

In the case of the Fukushima earthquake disaster, the Huawei team and administration displayed this unrelenting dedication to their customer. Despite working in an area that had been hit by one of the worst disasters that the country had seen, the employees continued to push forward to carry out their mission. This no-excuses mentality is what has allowed Huawei to rise from the position of an industry unknown, to an underdog, to ultimately the most powerful firm in the telecommunications industry.

At the time of the company's Huawei Japan rep office inception, EMOBILE was the only customer that the company had, and the company had to work hard to get to the position it's in today. EMOBILE was only a small company compared to the Japanese carrier giants Softbank and NTT Docomo (note that EMOBILE's parent Company YMOBILE was later acquired by Softbank). Huawei, like EMOBILE, was a small player in its telecommunications equipment industry, paling in comparison to European firms like

Ericsson. Only through the struggle of over-delivering for its customers and putting massive amounts of investments to create better and better products was the company finally able to gradually increase its market share of the telecommunications equipment to become the largest vendor in the industry.

During my time working at Huawei in Africa, I learned that Huawei equipment makes up the majority of the equipment of many vendors on the continent. And, in fact, the telecom operators have adapted their systems to the proprietary innovations of Huawei that deliver better performance than its industry counterparts. These carrier network operators switching to other equipment vendors will pose a high cost. This situation puts Huawei in a favorable position at the negotiation table with these carrier network operators. However, due to the culture of the company of prioritizing its customers, Huawei will continue to over-deliver on its promises to its customers, even if it involves going into disaster-stricken areas, radiation zones, war zones, and impoverished nations around the world.

This philosophy has allowed the company to become the most international Chinese company. Today, the company still conducts much of its operations outside of China, sending its Chinese employees to some of the most remote regions of the world. Ren Zhengfei once mused that at his company, employees should not face the company and put their butts out to its customers, as was the case of many Chinese state-owned enterprises. Rather, he will only respect employees who put their faces toward the customers and their butts to the Huawei company itself.

BURKINA FASO

In January 2019, Chinese Foreign Minister Wang Yi paid an official visit to the continent of Africa in what Chinese state television CGTN (China Global Television Network) named as an important step in a "new chapter in China-Africa cooperation."[284] Along the way, Wang had an official visit to the West African country of Burkina Faso. Less than one year ago, Burkina Faso cut ties with the Republic of China, otherwise known as Taiwan. The country reasserted its diplomatic relations with the People's Republic in 2018. The embassy in the capital of Ouagadougou has not been established for a very long time.

In Burkina Faso, the national GDP is still low compared to other countries around the world, and infrastructure is lacking in many parts of the country. However, Huawei already established its presence in the country over ten years ago, and it discovered a deal with the Ministry of Public Security in Burkina Faso. One of the main drivers of the company's enterprise business group is Huawei's surveillance solutions. The deal with the Ministry of Public Security involved Huawei's help in setting up the country's surveillance network system. This project involved the installation of surveillance cameras as well as the fiberoptic and wireless infrastructure needed for the cameras. Huawei was also responsible for helping the Department of Public Security install storage solutions and front-end user interface that allows people in the government to monitor the lives of its citizens.

---

284 "Wang Yi's Africa Visit: A New Chapter in China-Africa Cooperation?" YouTube. CGTN, January 6, 2019. https://www.youtube.com/watch?v=lQHBSu9_jOc.

The Ministry of Public Security is a shabby building devoid of any form of security. After passing my passport to the front desk, I am allowed to enter the building and guided through by one of the employees there. In stark contrast to what we would usually imagine as the stark and dystopian headquarters of a country's surveillance center, the building seems awfully innocuous. However, this ministry was responsible for preventing the likelihood of violent attacks throughout the country and for ensuring the safety of its citizens. Burkina Faso is a country plagued by divides and situated at the front line against jihadism in West Africa. In 2016, Al-Qaeda extremists attacked a hotel frequented by Westerners in the capital, killing thirty. And, in 2018, another group of jihadists stormed the French embassy and other government entities throughout the city with suicide bombers and militants.

The reason for my visit today is not for the installation or maintenance of Huawei equipment. Rather, we recently heard news that a Chinese national had been robbed at a bank in the past. The Chinese embassy in Burkina Faso had put up a notice for the Chinese people in the city to be aware and prudent while running errands at public places such as these. Seeing an opportunity, my team and I go individually to investigate this crime so that we may gather evidence of the efficacy of the Huawei surveillance system. The success of the investigation will serve as proof of the effectiveness of the new surveillance network, justifying the future expansion of the project.

However, after chatting with the officers at the ministry, we learn that no reports have been made at their office of this incident. And, lacking information from the embassy, we are unable to locate the footage of the crime scene. Disappointed, we are led out of the office building. We retrieve our passports back at the front desk and leave.

This deal between Huawei and the Ministry of Public Security is one of the largest projects for the engineering team in Ouagadougou due to the scale of the project. The project has only gone through the first phase of completion, and subsequent phases are still in the talks. At the very beginning, this project was facilitated by the Chinese embassy in Burkina Faso, with financial support to the Ministry of Public Security by the Bank of China. For the newly established Chinese embassy in the country, this infrastructure project shows the country's commitment to its new diplomatic partner, demonstrating that it can offer advantages that aren't available from the country's previous diplomatic partner of Taiwan. Through this project, and subsequent ventures in the country, bilateral relations between the two countries will become warmer, and a norm of cooperation will be formed.

The Ministry of Public Security is receiving a state-of-the-art security solution at a competitive price. In a country riddled with public security concerns and frequent news of ethnic conflict and extremism, the newly installed system is a positive step in the country's self-governance.

Huawei remains of the few telecommunications companies that offer equipment and technical solutions that spans consumer, enterprise, and carrier network businesses. Unlike its Western counterparts like Cisco, Nokia, or Motorola,

Huawei and Coca-Cola Advertisements. *(Unknown)*

Huawei has never divested any parts of its core businesses (for example, the Microsoft acquisition of Nokia's consumer handset business).[285] This deal between the Chinese and Burkanese businesses can set the norm for future collaboration in other government ministries or state-owned businesses. Huawei, on the other hand, like any business, thrives on delivering value to its clients. This project is simply another source of income for the company branch in Africa.

---

285 Bilderbeek, Pim. "How Apple, Cisco and Huawei Disrupted the Telecom Equipment Market." The METISfiles, April 15, 2015. https://www.themetisfiles.com/2015/04/how-apple-cisco-and-huawei-disrupted-the-telecom-equipment-market/.

One may have heard about China's increasing investments in various countries in Sub-Saharan Africa, supporting the growth of infrastructure projects. In addition to telecommunications, the projects include the building of infrastructures such as roads, bridges, dams, ports, railways, and more. Huawei, as the biggest telecommunications equipment manufacturer in the world, is part of the country's industrial clout, which can be converted into political leverage in the international stage as a form of hard power. Through the contribution of capital and expertise, China's government can win over the minds of many governments throughout the world. And, in fact, after the establishment of diplomatic relations between China and Burkina Faso, Eswatini (formerly known as Swaziland) remains the only country that has diplomatic relations with Taiwan. A country's private sector and government, in this case, form a synergistic relationship. The government can help Huawei discover new business opportunities while Huawei, to the government, is an advantage that it can offer to Burkina Faso.

What makes Burkina Faso interesting is that Huawei—unlike the majority of other Chinese companies on the continent—is not a state-owned enterprise. Huawei, since its inception, has always been a private company and is not owned by the state. Why, then, is Huawei collaborating with the Chinese government in Burkina Faso to court this landlocked West African nation? Private businesses can play a part in international politics. True, in Burkina Faso a synergistic relationship exists between Huawei and the Chinese embassy, but are there any other cases where such a relationship can exist?

Huawei Mauritania Office. *(Dennis Wang 2019)*

In January 1979, a world-recognized beverage company based in Atlanta made its debut in the PRC. The opportunities were not just in soft-drink consumption; indeed, Chinese industrialists and policymakers saw this move as an opportunity for the country to industrialize amid the time of economic liberalization under Deng Xiaoping.

To the Chinese, Coca-Cola, once loathed as a symbol of US imperialism, now became a symbol of progressiveness, as Chinese companies rushed to partner with this Western giant to push the country's industrialization, gaining valuable manufacturing equipment in bottling and packaging. Soon, people across the country drank Coca-Cola, and it became a symbol of progressive livelihood.[286]

---

286 Kraus, Charles. "More than Just a Soft Drink: Coca-Cola and China's Early Reform and Opening*." Diplomatic History 43, no. 1 (September 2018): 107–29. https://doi.org/10.1093/dh/dhy060.

The expansion of Coca-Cola to the world's most populous country did not happen in a vacuum. In fact, it happened in the same month of the same year that the United States formally changed its diplomatic recognition of China from Taipei to Beijing, heralding a new age of US-China bilateral relations and increased US economic support for China's burgeoning experimentation of capitalism under Deng. Coca-Cola took these political changes as an opportunity to open up a new lucrative market for its products. In fact, pundits of the company in postwar France have coined the term "cocacolonization," in resistance to the perceived US cultural imperialism that they condemned as brought by the consumption of American products of Coca-Cola throughout Europe.

Huawei, like Coca-Cola, has become entrenched throughout the world. From the plains of the Serengeti to the Peruvian Alps, Huawei equipment supports telecommunications infrastructure everywhere. In addition, Huawei's handheld smartphones can be seen in the hands of people throughout the world.

MAURITANIA
On a weekend evening, I sit on the floor of a dimly lit apartment building with my Huawei colleagues. The sound of prayer can be heard outside the window as the local Muslim population makes their daily prayers.

"HAH, we win!" shouts the colleague to my right as he slams down a pair of jokers on the table: his trump cards.

As we scramble the game cards on the table for another round, I take a bite out of my midnight shawarma snack and a sip of the local avocado juice. At the same time, we are watching the show *The Voice of China* on the small television screen next to us, the Chinese version of America's *The Voice*. Other than playing the latest video games, this communal activity is a typical weekend recreation of the six Chinese Huaweiers in Mauritania.

Outside is the sandy night of Nouakchott, where the locals can be seen sitting in cafes until late in the night and where wild dogs roam the streets. The city of Nouakchott is carved straight out of the Sahara, in a country where three-quarters of the land is covered by the desert. The office building, cafeteria, and dormitory are all located across the street from each other. Going to work involves simply walking for twenty meters to the office. The office is simply an old, rented-out building that used to house a large family, now turned into a makeshift office for the six Chinese staff and a team of around ten local staff. Working in the country of Mauritania with Huawei indeed feels like living in a college dormitory.

In the company's management, Mauritania is considered a "level 6" country, the lowest on the scale of one to six in terms of development. Other level 6 countries include the likes of Syria, Libya, or Yemen, war zones with a significant difference in the quality of life compared to China. However, as with all Huawei offices, a dedicated company cook will be sent over from China. Every day, he will make three delicious Chinese meals sourced from markets all over the city. We even have the luxury of enjoying pork stir-fry, in this Muslim country where pork is not sold.

The cook, with a Chinese accent reminiscent of home, hails from the same province as me: the landlocked province of Anhui. His experiences reflect the company's internationalization; already, he has been abroad for over ten years, stationed throughout the Persian Gulf in countries like Iran, Bahrain, and the United Arab Emirates. Before coming to Huawei as a cook, he also served in the People's Liberation Army.

What brings Huawei to the corners of the globe? Certainly, the push for business and delivering solutions to clients is the main driving force of this phenomenon. However, employees also hold a certain sense of mysticism and romanticism within the company culture of being deployed to a far-flung land. Pundits have criticized Huawei's international operations as motivated by political factors, drawing connections to the so-called Chinese neocolonialism. Can the interests of individual private businesses be conflated with the national ambitions of a country? This question strikes at the heart of much of the debate surrounding Huawei and the common accusations against the company. Whether real political intentions lie behind Huawei's international pervasiveness, one may not know.

CHAPTER 12

HUAWEI:
The Huawei Offensive

There's no way United States can crush us. The world needs Huawei because we are more advanced.

—REN ZHENGFEI

THE US CAMPAIGN

In February 2011, Huawei's new deputy chairman Hu Houkun penned an open letter addressing the US government to clarify the allegations in Western media that heavily criticized Huawei. These accusations included Huawei's alleged close connections to the Chinese military as well as its receiving of government funds. The media argued that the company was a threat to the national security of the United States. In his letter, Hu invited US authorities to conduct formal investigations into any concerns they may have about Huawei.

Unfortunately, the allegation of military ties is nothing new. They are based entirely on the fact that the company's founder Ren once served in the PLA's Engineering Corps in a technical position similar to that of a deputy regimental chief. However, military origins of business leaders are nothing rare among the CEOs of Fortune 500 companies. Many have graduated from the likes of West Point, a school that is not only a military academy but also an incubator for business leaders.

After WWII, the three major US military academies of West Point, the US Naval Academy, and the US Air Force Academy have created over 1,500 CEOs, 2,000 presidents, and 5,000 vice-presidents of Fortune 500 companies. Furthermore, these academies have also created thousands of leaders at small and medium-level enterprises. One should wonder: does this phenomenon signify these companies have ties to the US military?

The allegations against Huawei for having government ties originates from a speech by Cisco's John Chambers at a summit in Europe, where he equated Cisco's unfortunate performance to the US equivalent of $30 billion of financial support that Huawei supposedly receives annually from the Chinese government. Consequently, Huawei sent out another kindly-worded letter and explained that the company has engaged with KPMG—a US global accounting firm—to audit its financial statements. Huawei asked Chambers where this $30 billion came from and where it has been spent.

In 2013, the US House Permanent Select Committee on Intelligence issued a report on Huawei. Other than the question of why a private company has a "Communist Party committee," the other accusations of this report were criticized heavily by major US and U.K. media as being farfetched and feeble, and full of "American imagination." The former party secretary at Huawei, Chen Zhufang, has recalled that when the Huawei Party committee was formed, she went to the US-invested Motorola to learn from their party committee and from their operations. According to a media report, the German joint venture Shanghai Volkswagen has even strongly supported the establishment of a Party Committee within the company. They believed that doing so would enhance employee collaboration and improve labor relations.

Thus, as a Chinese company, why can't Huawei form a party committee? In fact, Huawei's party committee (which is internally referred to as the committee of ethics and compliance overseas) plays a crucial part in governing the morality and social responsibility of leaders within the company.

Since the start of 1993, the world has undergone a range of disruptive changes in the development of technology, which, in such a short period of time, were unprecedented in human history. The United States, by virtue of its innovative culture, has brought mankind into a new era of prosperity. In the past two decades, the country has produced legendary companies with the likes of Google, Microsoft, Cisco, Apple, and Facebook. The country's strength continues to rely on creative disruption and its hundreds of super-corporations—some richer than entire countries.

The United States' core competitiveness comes from its businesses. At the same time, the American people hold a fundamental belief that the law of natural selection will ensure the survival of the fittest in business. Therefore, over the past two decades, a number of US businesses, many giants, have fallen and disappeared amid the tempest of technological change and disruption.

Similar to Cisco and Google, Huawei is a rising company that poked its head above the horizon a mere twenty years ago. It has beat out its domestic competitors and learned from US companies. Throughout this process, it has witnessed the rise and fall of numerous tech juggernauts.

Starting in 2003, when Cisco first filed a lawsuit against Huawei, a number of American companies had also taken their own offenses toward the Chinese company. Simultaneously, the US government and media accused the company of posing a national security threat and engaging in unfair competition. Later, their attempts at suppressing Huawei intensified and the aim was clear: they wanted to banish Huawei from US territory. Behind all the smoke, they were engaging in trade protectionism to defend the market position of US companies.

Long before Donald Trump started his campaign against Huawei, the company had been embroiled in countless troubles in the United States. Starting in 2007, Huawei fell victim to a nonstop onslaught of allegations from Western media. The most typical revolved around the company's supposedly dubious background and sales of equipment to countries that are not friendly with the United States—such as Iraq and Iran—threatening the national security of the United States. One of the most absurd claims came from the *Wall Street*

Journal, asserting that Huawei was assisting the Iranian government with the tracking of dissidents. Consequently, Huawei issued a statement of denial, condemning the report as false, misleading, and patently untrue.

Another example of the US campaign against Huawei in the first decade of the century was the acquisition of 3Com Corporation to Bain Capital. Bain is a global private investment firm and has sought to buy 3Com. As part of the deal, Huawei would acquire a minority stake of 16.34 percent of the company and become a strategic partner of 3Com. Ultimately, however, this deal was resisted by a number of US congresspeople and was denied by the federal government.

In 2010, Huawei made an offer to acquire Motorola's wireless network business at a premium over the transaction's leading contender. Ultimately, though, this bid was denied by the US government once again. In fact, Huawei was the original equipment manufacturer of Motorola's wireless products, in which Huawei's proprietary technologies were already being used by the American telecommunications network.

CISCO VERSUS HUAWEI

2003 was a low point in the company's history but also a turning point. On Jan. 22, 2003, Chinese New Year was just around the corner. Cisco, a global communications equipment giant, caught Huawei off guard with a major lawsuit for intellectual property infringement. The indictment was eighty pages long and covered every type of intellectual property law in existence.

Litigation was to take place in a district court in an eastern district of Texas, which is peculiar. However, upon further investigation, a US lawyer informed Huawei that this specific courthouse is known for quick judgments on intellectual property suits, as well as severe penalties. The people in this part of Texas were fairly conservative and known for their attitude toward foreigners.

Immediately, as with the case in the past, a number of Western—and even Chinese—media outlets started to smear Huawei left and right, painting it as a "robber" and "technology thief," suggesting that the company was in over its head. One of Cisco's senior executives in the Asia-Pacific region, a foreign citizen of Chinese ethnicity, even said in a public statement that "this time we need to make Huawei go bankrupt."

The company had been planning its suit against Huawei for over a year. They started with the US government, then relevant departments in the Chinese government, preparing their team of lawyers and plans for public opinion management and choosing the time and place of the litigation. This endeavor was all painstakingly designed. Huawei was not the least prepared for what it would undergo.

Americans were the ones who had taught Huawei how to follow international rules as well as the many core processes within the company. In the case of the lawsuit, the Americans were also the ones who taught Huawei the art of imitation of how to use an international approach when countering rivals in court.

Cisco logo exhibited during the Mobile World Congress 2019. *(https://www.cnbc.com/2019/05/14/bank-of-america-cisco-big-tech-stock-to-buy-for-low-china-trade-risk.html)*

As the legal processes continued, some recommended that Huawei position itself nationalistically as the "defenders of Chinese enterprises" to win local media and government support. However, the company rejected this approach. Its decision-makers believed that this lawsuit was an international one, and the trial was being held in one of the most conservative US states; thus, besieging the besiegers would only complicate matters. The company would need to bravely answer the charges thrown against it in court because the company's executives believed that only by boldly facing its challenger could they successfully broker peace. If they lost the suit—even though it would be incredibly painful for the company—this debacle would not signify the end of the company. If the executives played the nationalism card in the company's defense—and lost—this debacle would mean the end of Huawei's development in the international market.

The fact of the matter is that, given the global nature of the IT industry, Huawei cannot fully be a "Chinese" company in the first place. From the first day, Huawei was facing world-class competitors, and it had to not only compete with them but also learn from them as well. As a Huawei senior executive put it, Huawei has really come out with the better end of the bargain for the past twenty or so years. After all, existing companies could show Huawei the way forward, such as Alcatel, Ericsson, Nokia, and Cisco. In learning from other companies, Huawei could better manage which direction its products and markets were going in, its management models, and so on. Most importantly, by learning from Western competitors, Huawei learned about international business regulations.

Ren has never been one to shy away from decisions, and he firmly believes that a well-handled crisis is likely to become an important opportunity. At great expense, Huawei hired strong legal counsel in the United States and met Cisco head-on along two tracks: the lawsuit itself and in the media. The dramatic ups and downs and twists and turns were no less thrilling than a war novel. A year later, on July 28, 2004, the dust finally settled on the lawsuit that 3Com's global CEO, Bruce Claflin, called an "entertaining theatrical performance." The suit ended with a mutual settlement: each company left to its own devices and each responsible for its own attorney fees. The outcome saw no apologies, certainly no indemnities, and a ruling that Cisco could never bring the same claims against Huawei in the future.

HOW PEOPLE VIEW HUAWEI

Huawei, depending on who you ask, is either a scrappy telecom company that has climbed its way to the top, with over $100 billion in sales today or a cowboy capitalist that has grown from technology theft and should be blocked from ever installing equipment in the United States. In China, the company is definitely seen by Beijing as the nation's crown jewel of national innovation. In the United States, the Trump team views the company as a giant global espionage device for the Chinese Communist Party.

One of the biggest headaches for Huawei is that it must choose between the two opposing governments, but Huawei has no option other than to stand on the Chinese side. It has been forced to be labeled as "China's Great Innovative Enterprise" and as the country's "most Chinese enterprise" by the Chinese government. This upgrade in rhetoric is completely different from the state of affairs before the trade war between the two countries. Then, through the eyes of the Chinese government, Huawei's position was two to three levels lower than that of many state-run enterprises such as PetroChina, Sinopec, China Mobile, and some major Chinese banks.

For the government, the country's national brands are a source of soft power. China is abundant in hard power—such as its thriving economy and military clout—but severely lacking in soft power. In an age of Sinophobia, especially in many Western countries, Chinese brands such as Huawei improve the country's image, connecting on a very personal level with consumers around the world. This relationship between soft power and Huawei is another reason why it pays for the Chinese government to increase its rhetorical support of the company against foreign pressure.

Huawei has become a bastion of Chinese nationalism and pride. In an age when Xi Jinping is revving up the rhetoric of national rejuvenation, any form of foreign pressure is seen as an attack on the country's unique heritage. Huawei is one of the shining examples of the country's economic reforms at the end of the twentieth century and also one of the largest Chinese research institutions in the world. Naturally, for Chinese citizens, foreign pressure against Huawei can be conflated with an attack on the country. This debacle would play out differently if Huawei were an American company. Due to a different political culture, Americans likely feel less solidarity with private corporations. In fact, they have a high distrust of large US tech corporations.

The company not only outshines the traditional Chinese industry giants of state-run enterprises but also has provided jobs for hundreds of thousands of Chinese people around the world. Walk into any Chinese bookstore and you will find books written about Huawei, discussing the stories of the company's founding, its history, and its unique management practices. Indeed, many top Huawei executives have left the company to work as industry consultants or educators, teaching individuals and companies how to emulate Huawei's legendary success. This practice is representative of the prestige of Huawei in China.

Ultimately, Huawei's position in US-China tensions reflects not only business and politics but also cultural differences between the East and the West. In China, due to citizens' collectivist mentality, people yearn for a symbol of national pride and rejuvenation. As seen from the United States, however, where a different political culture abounds, this phenomenon may appear that Huawei truly has ties to the Chinese government and is supported by the country's taxpayer money.

What compounds Huawei's mystique in the United States are the ideological differences between the United States and China. A remaining artifact of the Cold War, some Americans may still hold the entrenched belief that China is a communist country similar in style to that of the Soviet Union or North Korea. After all, because Huawei is a Chinese company with a Chinese name, it can be viewed by the US public as a representative of Chinese communist ideology. Huawei's case is not helped by the logo of the company being distinctively red.

One needs to understand that in the political debacle between the United States and China, Huawei is a two-sided symbol. It has no other choice than to be branded by governments, the media, and public consensus as inherently political. For China, it is a symbol of nationalism. For the United States and its allies, it is a symbol of the influence of the Chinese government in international affairs. The country has simply no way to remain neutral against the backdrop of political tensions between the two largest economies in the world. After remaining low-key for decades until the media focus on US-China relations and the trade war, the company simply wishes to do its business as usual, continuing to invest in its research, development, and growth. Politicization is ultimately unfruitful for the company, putting it in difficult situations.

During media interviews, Ren has urged the public to reduce their nationalistic zeal amid rising tensions between the United States and China. He cautions consumers against equating buying decisions with patriotism and calls for an end to the criticism of US corporations. He identifies the culprit for Chinese citizens as US politicians themselves rather than US companies for politicizing trivial matters. In other public appearances, Ren has been seen with Apple products, in a clear show of support for US corporations. In other media interviews, Ren has publicly stated that he admires the US company Apple. He calls upon the public to not boycott Apple products in China.

REN AND POLITICS

Huawei's older employees all know one fact: that the company's boss, Ren, is not a fan of politics. Ren will deliberately keep his distance from party officials and Chinese politics. This antipolitical attitude may derive from his personal experience or the experience of his parents. His generation of entrepreneurs has experienced several political upheavals in China, witnessing the plundering of assets, capitalists, and enterprises by the Communist Party of China. Hence Ren keeps a low profile, only focusing on the business itself. He was not seen in the media for twenty years before the start of the US-China trade war, and he is not a fan of participating in ceremonies for various awards presented by the media or by society.

Ren Zhengfei speaks during an interview at Huawei's headquarters in Shenzhen, China. *(https://www.cnbc.com/2019/02/20/huawei-founder-ren-zhengfei-says-he-would-not-aid-chinese-espionage.html)*

As a result of the media attention on the company amid the US-China Huawei incident, Ren has emerged from the shadows, suddenly becoming a national interest overnight. He has taken on an almost legendary image in China, with people asserting that his vision and strategy are beyond that of the top national leaders. Despite his newfound fame, Ren continues to thread a similar political stance, characterized by impartiality and fairness:

- He has not committed any crimes against the Chinese Communist Party.
- When discussing his daughter Meng Wanzhou, who has been put under house arrest in Canada over allegedly breaking US sanctions, Ren never talks about the details of her case. He only praises the laws of the United States and Canada.

- He places great emphasis on the relationship between Huawei and Europe and says he hopes that this relationship will continue.
- Ren repeatedly emphasized that Huawei will not introduce external capital to the company and will not go public. In terms of internal management, he opposes 100 percent democracy.

THE PHOENIX

One common saying within Huawei is that "a bird that cannot be burned to death is a phoenix." This saying represents the company's stoic culture of collective struggle, teaching employees to endure tremendous stress without giving up. Only by escaping fire unscathed can employees become "phoenixes" and soar. Huawei foot soldiers who overcome great struggle are heralded as heroes.

Along a similar line, Huawei as a company is currently enduring the tremendous stress it has been placed under by the United States. The corporation is currently a bird being tested by the flames of international politics. Whether the company will suffer the same fate as ZTE and wither is a possibility entertained by the media. However, when thinking about the life and death of Huawei, one must consider the circumstances the company is in.

At the time of this writing, Huawei continues to dominate the massive Chinese market, both in telecom equipment and smartphone sales. China alone contains over 40 percent of the entire world's 4G base stations, serving its massive population. If Huawei stops distributing telecommunications equipment around the world, it will continue to survive, supplying equipment to a lion's share of the world's market in China alone. In the extreme scenario that Huawei is blocked from the entire global market, it will still remain one of the largest telecommunications companies.

Another consideration in Huawei's survivability is the company's efforts in research and development. Huawei is currently the number-one researcher in 5G technologies, as well as one of the largest smartphone chip manufacturers through its subsidiary HiSilicon. If the company is blocked off international supply chains, it can domestically source and create the required parts to continue makings its products. At the time of this writing, the company is undergoing a successful de-Americanization process in its products, aiming to source zero percent of its equipment from the United States.

Now, as a result of ongoing US attacks, Huawei, as well as a number of other Chinese technology companies, are investing massive amounts of capital into self-reliance efforts. US threats of cutting off China's access to American technology have sparked alarm, and the country is striving to increase its domestic ability to produce core technologies such as chips and operating systems. Huawei, for example, at the time of this writing, will soon announce its Harmony Operating System (HarmonyOS, known in China as Hongmeng), which will end Huawei smartphones' reliance on Google's Android operating system.

In targeting Huawei, the end result is not the death of the company but rather the weakening of US power around the world. China, through major government and private sector initiatives, will soon increase its prowess in the technologies that US companies have traditionally had control over. The country will become another international competitor to the US technology industry, with Chinese operating systems, equipment, and ecosystems. The two countries, housing the most technologically advanced companies, will soon compete with each other for international market share in a form of digital colonialism.

Indeed, as the saying goes, by not getting burned to death in the fire, Huawei and the Chinese technology industry will become a phoenix. The company will continue to remain an important actor in the technological rivalry between the two world powers.

CHAPTER 13

THE FUTURE

——

A new generation of technology represented by artificial intelligence, quantum information, mobile communications, Internet of things and blockchain is accelerating breakthrough applications.

—XI JINPING

In terms of future-oriented technology, our vision may only realistically imagine the next ten to twenty years. Although science fiction writers can fantasize unrestricted about what will happen fifty years later, such speculations do not actually have much practical significance.

In the future, one may see the technological competition between the United States and China in any field imaginable by both countries. Against a powerful adversary, even the smallest advantage for either party will need to be sought. In the fields of cancer detection, gene editing, controlled nuclear fusion, space travel, artificial photosynthesis, anti-aging, brain-computer interface, and other fields, American and Chinese scientists are creating scientific research at a faster pace.

In information communication technology-related areas, such as blockchain, quantum communication, quantum computing, new materials, and more, the United States and China have become fiercer in terms of scientific research investment and industrial policy support.

BLOCKCHAIN

Blockchain is a fashionable world today. If artificial intelligence represents a new type of productivity, then blockchain can be seen as a new type of production. First-generation blockchain technology, as represented by bitcoin, still has many defects, such as extremely high transaction costs and low transaction frequency, rendering it unusable for securities trading or use as a settlement when purchasing commodities. The second-generation blockchain is improved. "Ethereum" is a good example of this progress, a platform allowing people to use blockchain as a platform and solve practical problems. With increasing input from the open-source community and large companies, blockchain technology will soon have large-scale applications in business. This technology can solve many problems encountered in business, especially when it emphasizes the security and convenience of data storage.

The technology competition between China and the United States may occur in any field, to gain any advantage possible. In cancer detection, gene editing, controlled nuclear fusion, space travel, artificial photosynthesis, anti-aging, brain-computer interface, and other fields, scientists from China and the United States have promoted the progress of scientific research at a faster speed. Capital and industry have compared the landing of products and the realization of commercial value in any possible application field. In ICT-related technologies, blockchain, quantum communication, quantum computing, new IT device materials, and other aspects, China and the United States are facing more fierce competition in research investment and industrial policy support. Any progress in these aspects can immediately expose a visible gap between the two.

During a collective learning session of the Central Political Bureau of China, Xi Jinping notably emphasized the importance of blockchain as an important breakthrough. The country must accelerate the research and implementation of blockchain, making it play a greater role in developing a digital economy and creating economic and social development. Like other technologies and industrial sectors, promotion by the Chinese government is a powerful driving force, as government funding floods into areas the party deems important.

At the government level, when it comes to the supervision and compliance of the application of blockchain in the financial industry, DCEP and Libra are two major topics. DCEP stands for Digital Currency Electronic Payment and is a digital currency that will be launched by the Central Bank of China. Libra is a digital currency that is expected to be launched by Facebook. Although the two projects have not yet been successfully implemented, the early prototypes of both have aroused global discussion. Once implemented, the two digital currency projects will certainly affect the direction of the future financial regulatory system.

Digital currency will play an important role in the future of the global economy, and the United States and China are now at a crossroads. The two digital currencies represent a new financial paradigm at odds with the traditional system. The two countries' willingness to adopt these new technologies will affect their increasing digital transformation, with implications for economic growth. Behind these developments is the willingness of the two nations to lead the new financial paradigm with these digital currencies. At the time of this writing, the implementation has not fully matured yet, and the upcoming competition between the United States and China in the digital currency space has yet to be seen.

QUANTUM SCIENCE

One of the most important engines of future information technology development is quantum science. Quantum science enables humans to study and manipulate the physical characteristics of the microworld. Put simply, a quantum is the smallest unit of anything, and quantum science is the study of these particles and their application. We know, for example, that all matter is made up of atoms; what, however, is the smallest component of an atom and how does it react to stimuli? This simple question has led to a field of science exploding into the disciplines of engineering and technology.

"Quantum communication" and "quantum computing" are two branches of quantum science. This field has significant implications for data security.

We deal with data every day, and the security of our data is consequently imperative. So far, no absolute form of information security exists, causing data leakages to occur from time to time. Nowadays, the issues of network security and people's privacy have become one of the hottest topics of the information age. Leaks from Edward Snowden and WikiLeaks have spread new awareness to the topic of data security and privacy. The whole world is looking for new ways to protect data, and quantum communication technology has the key to this problem.

Today, sensitive data is typically encrypted, then sent across fiber-optic cables or other channels with the digital "keys" needed to decode the information. The data and the keys are sent as classical bits—a stream of electrical or optical pulses representing 1's and 0's. And that makes them vulnerable. Smart hackers can read and copy bits in transit without leaving a trace.

Quantum communication, however, takes advantage of the laws of quantum physics to protect data. These laws allow particles to take a special state called "superposition," meaning they can represent multiple combinations of 1 and 0 simultaneously. The particles are known as quantum bits or qubits. The beauty of qubits from a cybersecurity perspective is that if a hacker tries to observe them in transit, their super-fragile quantum state "collapses" to either 1 or 0, meaning a hacker can't tamper with the qubits without leaving behind a telltale sign of the activity.

China understands the strategic importance of quantum technology for further developing its economy and military.

And the United States has allowed China to take the lead in many areas of quantum research. Once quantum technology matures, it will have a profound effect on almost every facet of our lives. China has initiated an aggressive effort in quantum research. Xi Jinping, in 2016, established a national strategy for the country to become technologically self-reliant. Xi funded a multibillion-dollar quantum computing mega-project that is expected to achieve significant quantum breakthroughs by 2030. The country has also committed billions to establish a National Laboratory for Quantum Information Sciences. This center may eventually become a global hub for quantum research and a magnet for future quantum research talent.

As an example of China's continuing efforts in quantum, Pan Jianwei, a professor at the University of Science and Technology of China, recently won the Cleveland Prize for his achievements in quantum communication. Under his leadership, China has become the first country in the world to establish a quantum communication network. Other Chinese researchers have also made continuous progress in the fields of quantum cryptography, communications, and computing.

In September 2018, a newly established US security center of the US Defense and Security Think Tank released a report titled "Quantum Hegemony: China's Ambitions and Challenges to the US Innovation Advantage." The report asserts that China's progress in quantum science may affect the future of international military and strategic balance and may even surpass the advantages of traditional US military technology. It also argues that, while predicting the trajectory of the implementation of quantum technologies is difficult, China may "offset" the key pillars of US military power. As the country transfers its most sensitive military, government, and commercial communications onto quantum networks, US cyberespionage efforts may be able to retrieve information from China.

One thing is very clear in the world of quantum computing: the development of these technologies is another technological highland that will be contested between the United States and China. Quantum computing has implications for national security, and its implementation will affect the efficacy of data encryption, protecting against sensitive information leaks. We are witnessing a battle being fought in research labs by brains instead of guns, and by scientists instead of soldiers. Moreover, the critical ammunition for this battle is research funding. It presents an epic struggle between the world's only superpower and the second-place power intent on replacing America as the world's high-tech leader. Both countries are engaged in a no-holds-barred struggle to develop and deploy the most disruptive quantum warfighting technology in the world. If the United States loses, the long-term effect will be chilling.

NEW MATERIALS

Technological advances drive history. Bronze and iron were so crucial to ancient societies that entire eras have been named after these materials. With the rise of the US steel industry, railroads spread from the Atlantic to the Pacific, veins that carry the blood of the nation. In the modern era, silicon semiconductors facilitated the growth of computer

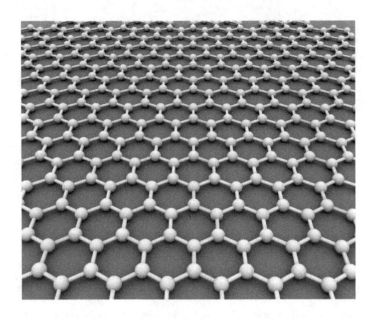

Graphene is an atomic-scale hexagonal lattice made of carbon atoms.
(https://en.wikipedia.org/wiki/Graphene#/media/File:Graphen.jpg)

technologies and the greatest surge in information technology since the creation of the printing press. These materials shaped the development of society and helped determine which countries dominate international politics.

In the past half-century, technological progress has been, to a large extent, dependent on the growth of semiconductor technology. However, with the increasing density of semiconductor-integrated circuits, power consumption has also increased. Most of the energy consumed by integrated circuits is wasted on the creation of heat energy. Energy consumption through heat-creation has become a bottleneck for information technology development. To overcome this issue, new and game-changing technologies need to be created.

Graphene is a new type of material able to be integrated into semiconductor circuits; it is revolutionary in its power-conserving characteristics.

Put simply, graphene is a single, thin layer of graphite—the soft, flaky material used in pencil lead. This material possesses the same atoms as the element carbon but arranged in a different way, enabling unique and useful properties. Graphene is one of the strongest materials in the universe, a hundred times stronger than steel. Furthermore, this material is also flexible, transparent, and highly conductive, making it ideal for a wide range of applications.

In 2004, the University of Manchester physicist Andre Haim and Konstantin Novoselov successfully separated graphene from graphite, proving that this material can exist alone. This team of two won the Nobel Prize in physics in 2010 due to their pioneering work in two-dimensional graphene materials.

Graphene-related research has become one of the most popular areas of materials science research. However, overall, the graphene industry is still in its early stages of industrial breakthrough, and the material cannot yet be fully used in large-scale industries. China's production of graphite ranks first in the world, and it and the United States are also in a competitive state regarding the research, patenting, and industrialization of graphene.

With upcoming technological advances in areas such as next-generation materials, one really could not say what the future holds for the status of the relationship between the

United States and China. What is certain is that China isn't showing signs of slowing down and its technological potential can only put more pressure on the United States.

BIBLIOGRAPHY

———

"State Council on Issuing Notification of New Generation Artificial Intelligence Development Planning." 国务院关于印发新一代人工智能发展规划的通知（国发〔2017〕35号）_政府信息公开专栏, July 8, 2017. http://www.gov.cn/zhengce/content/2017-07/20/content_5211996.htm.

"A History of the Computer Game." Jesper Juul, n.d. https://www.jesperjuul.net/thesis/2-historyofthecomputergame.html.

Allison, Graham T. *Destined for War: Can America and China Escape Thucydides's Trap?* London: Scribe, 2018.

"AlphaGo Zero: Starting from Scratch." Deepmind, October 18, 2017. https://deepmind.com/blog/article/alphago-zero-starting-scratch.

Amadeo, Kimberly. "3 Types of Market Cap." The Balance. The Balance, June 25, 2019. https://www.thebalance.com/market-capitalization-3305826.

Angell, Norman. *The Great Illusion.* New York: G.P. Putnam's Sons, 1910.

Anna Mitchell, Larry Diamond. "China's Surveillance State Should Scare Everyone." The Atlantic. Atlantic Media Company, February 5, 2018. https://www.theatlantic.com/international/archive/2018/02/china-surveillance/552203/.

"Artificial Intelligence: Definition of Artificial Intelligence by Lexico." Lexico Dictionaries | English. Lexico Dictionaries, n.d. https://www.lexico.com/en/definition/artificial_intelligence.

Atwill, David G., and Yurong Y. Atwill. *Sources in Chinese History: Diverse Perspectives from 1644 to the Present*. Upper Saddle River, NJ: Pearson/Prentice Hall, 2010.

Bamman, David, Brendan Oconnor, and Noah Smith. "Censorship and Deletion Practices in Chinese Social Media." *First Monday* 17, no. 3 (February 2012). https://doi.org/10.5210/fm.v17i3.3943.

Batjargal, Bat, and Mannie (Manhong) Liu. "Entrepreneurs' Access to Private Equity in China: The Role of Social Capital." *Organization Science* 15, no. 2 (2004): 159–72. https://doi.org/10.1287/orsc.1030.0044.

"Be Careful What You Wish For." The Economist. The Economist Newspaper, n.d. https://www.economist.com/books-and-arts/2011/10/29/be-careful-what-you-wish-for.

Beveridge, Albert . *MARCH OF THE FLAG: Beginning of Greater America*. Place of publication not identified: FORGOTTEN Books, 2016.

"Big Data vs. Artificial Intelligence." Datamation, n.d. https://www.datamation.com/big-data/big-data-vs.-artificial-intelligence.html.

"Big Data: Definition of Big Data by Lexico." Lexico Dictionaries | English. Lexico Dictionaries, n.d. https://www.lexico.com/en/definition/big_data.

Bilderbeek, Pim. "How Apple, Cisco and Huawei Disrupted the Telecom Equipment Market." The METISfiles, April 15, 2015. https://www.themetisfiles.com/2015/04/how-apple-cisco-and-huawei-disrupted-the-telecom-equipment-market/.

Black, Jeremy. *British Foreign Policy in an Age of Revolutions: 1783-1793.* Cambridge u.a.: Cambridge Univ. Press, 1994.

Bo, Xiang. "China Focus: China Increases Science Education to Boost Innovation." Xinhua, September 1, 2017. http://www.xinhuanet.com/english/2017-09/01/c_136574669.htm.

Borak, Masha. "World's Top Drone Seller DJI Made $2.7 Billion in 2017 · TechNode." TechNode, July 24, 2018. https://technode.com/2018/01/03/worlds-top-drone-seller-dji-made-2-7-billion-2017/.

Boundless. "Boundless World History." Lumen, n.d. https://courses.lumenlearning.com/boundless-worldhistory/chapter/the-congress-of-vienna/.

Boxhill, Ian. *From Unipolar to Multipolar: The Remaking of Global Hegemony.* Kingston, Jamaica: Arawak, 2014.

Bughin, Jacques, Jeongmin Seong, James Manyika, Michael Chui, and Raoul Joshi. "NOTES FROM THE AI FRONTIER MODELING THE IMPACT OF AI ON THE WORLD ECONOMY." McKinsey Global Institute. McKinsey Global Institute, September 2018. https://www.mckinsey.com/~/media/McKinsey/Featured

Insights/Artificial Intelligence/Notes from the frontier Modeling the impact of AI on the world economy/MGI-Notes-from-the-AI-frontier-Modeling-the-impact-of-AI-on-the-world-economy-September-2018.ashx.

Cai, Yongshun. "Power Structure and Regime Resilience: Contentious Politics in China." *British Journal of Political Science* 38, no. 3 (2008): 411–32. https://doi.org/10.1017/s0007123408000215.

Callahan, William A. "Dreaming as a Critical Discourse of National Belonging: China Dream, American Dream and World Dream." *Nations and Nationalism* 23, no. 2 (March 2017): 248–70. https://doi.org/10.1111/nana.12296.

Cgtn. "China Releases List of World Leaders Attending V-Day Parade." CGTN America, September 8, 2015. https://america.cgtn.com/2015/08/25/china-releases-list-of-world-leaders-attending-v-day-parade.

Chai, Winberg, and May-lee Chai. "The Meaning of Xi Jinping's Chinese Dream." *American Journal of Chinese Studies* 20, no. 2 (2013): 95–97.

Chan, Edwin. "Huawei Overtakes Apple to Become Second Biggest Smartphone Maker." Bloomberg.com. Bloomberg, May 2, 2019. https://www.bloomberg.com/news/articles/2019-05-03/huawei-again-overtakes-apple-as-global-smartphone-market-tanks.

Chan, Edwin. "Huawei Overtakes Apple to Become Second Biggest Smartphone Maker." Bloomberg.com. Bloomberg, May 2, 2019. https://www.bloomberg.com/news/articles/2019-05-03/huawei-again-overtakes-apple-as-global-smartphone-market-tanks.

Chang, Charles, and Melanie Manion. "Political Self-Censorship in Authoritarian States: The Spatial-Temporal Dimension of Trouble." *SSRN Electronic Journal*, 2019. https://doi.org/10.2139/ssrn.3497976.

Chang, Weih, and Ian C. Macmillan. "A Review of Entrepreneurial Development in the Peoples Republic of China." *Journal of Business Venturing* 6, no. 6 (1991): 375–79. https://doi.org/10.1016/0883-9026(91)90026-a.

Chen, Haohan. "Lies to Friends, Truths to Strangers," October 2019.

Chiu, Karen. "The Story of Drone Pioneer DJI." Abacus, October 2, 2018. https://www.abacusnews.com/whois-whatis/dji-dominates-world-drones/article/2128689.

Choe, William, Jason Rabbitt-Tomita, Alex Zhang, and Vivian Tsoi. "Why Has Foreign Venture Capital Investment into China Soared in 2018?" Lexology, December 13, 2018. https://www.lexology.com/library/detail.aspx?g=6d4a1b26-d777-455c-a329-53456905f02d.

Chu, Yun-han. *How East Asians View Democracy*. New York: Columbia University Press, 2010.

Church, Kenneth Ward. "Emerging Trends: Artificial Intelligence, China and My New Job at Baidu." *Natural Language Engineering* 24, no. 4 (November 2018): 641–47. https://doi.org/10.1017/s1351324918000189.

"Computer Chip." Encyclopædia Britannica. Encyclopædia Britannica, inc., December 22, 2017. https://www.britannica.com/technology/computer-chip.

Coulter, Martin. "Walmart Outpaces Amazon in Drone Patent Race." Financial Times. Financial Times, June 16, 2019. https://www.ft.com/content/7cd22fb6-8e79-11e9-a24d-b42f641eca37.

Dahl, Robert A. *Democracy and Its Critics.* Johanneshov: MTM, 2019.

Daly, Ciarán, and Ciarán Daly. "China To Overtake US In AI Within 5 Years." The World's Number One Portal for Artificial Intelligence in Business, March 15, 2019. https://aibusiness.com/china-overtake-u-s-ai-within-5-years/.

Delaney, Robert. "US Slaps China Telecoms Firm ZTE with 7-Year Ban for Sanctions Breach ." South China Morning Post, April 17, 2018. https://www.scmp.com/business/companies/article/2142002/us-slaps-zte-seven-year-components-ban-breaching-terms-sanctions.

Desjardins, Jeff. "How the Tech Giants Make Their Billions." Visual Capitalist, April 9, 2019. https://www.visualcapitalist.com/how-tech-giants-make-billions/.

Diamond, Larry. "Liberation Technology." *Journal of Democracy* 21, no. 3 (2010): 69–83. https://doi.org/10.1353/jod.0.0190.

Dickson, Bruce J. "Who Wants to Be a Communist? Career Incentives and Mobilized Loyalty in China." *The China Quarterly* 217 (May 2013): 42–68. https://doi.org/10.1017/s0305741013001434.

"DJI - The World Leader in Camera Drones/Quadcopters for Aerial Photography." DJI Official, n.d. https://www.dji.com/.

Dreyer, June Teufel. "The 'Tianxia Trope': Will China Change the International System?" *Journal of Contemporary China* 24, no. 96 (2015): 1015–31. https://doi.org/10.1080/10670564.2015.1030951.

Duhigg, Charles, and Keith Bradsher. "How the US Lost Out on IPhone Work." The New York Times. The New York Times, January 21, 2012. https://www.nytimes.com/2012/01/22/business/apple-america-and-a-squeezed-middle-class.html?_r=2&ref=charlesduhigg&pagewanted=all&mtrref=www.businessinsider.com&assetType=REGIWALL.

"Economic Impacts of Artificial Intelligence (AI)." European Parliament. European Parliament, July 2019. http://www.europarl.europa.eu/RegData/etudes/BRIE/2019/637967/EPRS_BRI(2019)637967_EN.pdf.

ECONOMY, ELIZABETH C. *THIRD REVOLUTION: Xi Jinping and the New Chinese State.* S.l.: OXFORD UNIV PRESS US, 2019.

"Education to 2030." Yidan Prize. The Economist, 2016. https://eiuperspectives.economist.com/sites/default/files/EIU_Yidan prize forecast_Education to 2030.pdf.

Evans, Richard J, and Harold James. "Debate: Is 2014, like 1914, a Prelude to World War?" The Globe and Mail, June 19, 2017. https://www.theglobeandmail.com/opinion/read-and-vote-is-2014-like-1914-a-prelude-to-world-war/article19325504/.

Fannin, Rebecca. "What's Pushing China's Tech Sector So Far Ahead?" Knowledge@Wharton, October 9, 2019. https://knowledge.wharton.upenn.edu/article/whats-pushing-chinas-tech-sector-so-far-ahead/.

Fannin, Rebecca A. *Tech Titans of China: How Chinas Tech Sector Is Challenging the World by Innovating Faster, Working Harder & Going Global.* Boston, MA: Nicholas Brealey Publishing, 2019.

Feiner, Lauren. "Apple Is Once Again the Most Valuable Public Company in the World." CNBC. CNBC, February 6, 2019. https://www.cnbc.com/2019/02/06/apple-is-once-again-the-most-valuable-public-company-in-the-world.html.

Feng, Emily. "China's State-Owned Venture Capital Funds Battle to Make an Impact." Subscribe to read | Financial Times. Financial Times, December 23, 2018. https://www.ft.com/content/4fa-2caaa-f9f0-11e8-af46-2022a0b02a6c.

"Frank Wang." Yo! Success, August 20, 2016. https://www.yosuccess.com/success-stories/frank-wang-dji-technology/.

French, Sally. "DJI Market Share: Here's Exactly How Rapidly It Has Grown in Just a Few Years." The Drone Girl, September 18, 2018. http://thedronegirl.com/2018/09/18/dji-market-share/.

Frolovskiy, Dmitriy. "China's Education Boom." The Diplomat. for The Diplomat, December 29, 2017. https://thediplomat.com/2017/12/chinas-education-boom/.

Fukuyama, Francis. *The End of History and the Last Man.* London: Penguin, 2012.

Gaddis, John Lewis. "The Long Peace: Elements of Stability in the Postwar International System." *International Security* 10, no. 4 (1986): 99. https://doi.org/10.2307/2538951.

"GDP Ranking, PPP Based." GDP ranking, PPP based (GDP PPP) | Data Catalog, December 23, 2019. https://datacatalog.worldbank. org/dataset/gdp-ranking-ppp-based.

Haber, L. F. *The Poisonous Cloud: Chemical Warfare in WWI.* Oxford: Clarendon Press, 2002.

Hamilton, Alexander, James Madison, and John Jay. *The Federalist Papers.* New York: New American Library, 1962.

Hannas, Wm, and Huey-meei Chang. "China's Access to Foreign AI Technology." Center for Security and Emerging Technology. Center for Security and Emerging Technology, September 2019. https://cset.georgetown.edu/wp-content/uploads/CSET-Chinas-Access-to-Foreign-AI-Technology-2.pdf.

He, Canfei, Jiangyong Lu, and Haifeng Qian. "Entrepreneurship in China." *Small Business Economics* 52, no. 3 (May 2018): 563–72. https://doi.org/10.1007/s11187-017-9972-5.

Hill, Simon. "CDMA vs. GSM: What's the Difference?" Digital Trends. Digital Trends, December 5, 2019. https://www.digitaltrends. com/mobile/cdma-vs-gsm-differences-explained/.

Hobbes, Thomas. *Leviathan.* S.l.: Ancient Wisdom Publication, 2019.

Huang, Weiwei, Zhifeng Yin, Ke Lv, Saixiong Hu, Guodong Tong, Hongbin Gong, and Chunbo Wu. *Dedication the Huawei Philosophy of Human Resource Management.* London: LID Publishing, 2016.

"Huawei Has 56,492 Patents—and It's Not Afraid to Use Them." South China Morning Post. Bloomberg, June 14, 2019. https://www.

scmp.com/news/china/article/3014625/weapons-economic-war-fare-huawei-has-56492-patents-and-its-not-afraid-use.

"Huawei's R&D Investment in 2018 Exceeds $15 Billion." Huawei's R&D investment in 2018 exceeds $15 billion - Chinadaily.com.cn, September 4, 2019. https://www.chinadaily.com.cn/a/201904/09/WS5cac0859a3104842260b5265.html.

Hvistendahl, Mara. "In China, a Three-Digit Score Could Dictate Your Place in Society." Wired. Conde Nast, December 5, 2018. https://www.wired.com/story/age-of-social-credit/.

Inglehart, Ronald F, Bi Puranen, and Christian Welzel. "Declining Willingness to Fight for One's Country." *Journal of Peace Research* 52, no. 4 (March 2015): 418–34. https://doi.org/10.1177/0022343314565756.

Ip, Adrian. "Huawei May Have Largest 5G Patent Portfolio—Starting to Flex IPR Muscle." Wccftech. Wccftech, July 1, 2019. https://wccftech.com/huawei-has-largest-5g-patent-portfolio-starting-to-flex-ipr-muscle/.

Ji, Chengyuan, and Junyan Jiang. "Enlightened One-Party Rule? Ideological Differences between Chinese Communist Party Members and the Mass Public." *Political Research Quarterly*, 2019, 106591291985034. https://doi.org/10.1177/1065912919850342.

Joseph, William A. *Politics in China: an Introduction.* New York: Oxford University Press, 2019.

Kennedy, Paul M. "WWI and the International Power System." *International Security* 9, no. 1 (1984): 7. https://doi.org/10.2307/2538634.

King, Gary, Jennifer Pan, and Margaret E. Roberts. "How Censorship in China Allows Government Criticism but Silences Collective Expression." *American Political Science Review* 107, no. 2 (2013): 326–43. https://doi.org/10.1017/s0003055413000014.

Kolakowski, Leszek. *Main Currents of Marxism: Its Origins, Growth and Dissolution*. Oxford: Oxford University Press, 1978.

Kraus, Charles. "More than Just a Soft Drink: Coca-Cola and China's Early Reform and Opening*." *Diplomatic History* 43, no. 1 (September 2018): 107–29. https://doi.org/10.1093/dh/dhy060.

Lee, Kai-Fu. *AI Superpowers: China, Silicon Valley, and the New World Order*. Boston: Houghton Mifflin Harcourt, 2018.

Li, Changhong, Yulin Shi, Cong Wu, Zhenyu Wu, and Li Zheng. "Policies of Promoting Entrepreneurship and Angel Investment: Evidence from China." *Emerging Markets Review* 29 (2016): 154–67. https://doi.org/10.1016/j.ememar.2016.08.011.

Liang, Fan, Vishnupriya Das, Nadiya Kostyuk, and Muzammil M. Hussain. "Constructing a Data-Driven Society: Chinas Social Credit System as a State Surveillance Infrastructure." *Policy & Internet* 10, no. 4 (February 2018): 415–53. https://doi.org/10.1002/poi3.183.

Lin, Song, and Zhengda Xu. "The Factors That Influence the Development of Entrepreneurship Education." *Management Decision* 55, no. 7 (2017): 1351–70. https://doi.org/10.1108/md-06-2016-0416.

Link, Perry. "China: The Anaconda in the Chandelier." ChinaFile, April 11, 2002. http://www.chinafile.com/library/nyrb-china-archive/china-anaconda-chandelier.

"Live: Huawei Founder & CEO Ren Zhengfei Holds Discussion in Shenzhen." CGTN. CGTN, June 16, 2019. https://news.cgtn.com/news/2019-06-15/Live-Huawei-founder-CEO-Ren-Zhengfei-holds-discussion-in-Shenzhen-HyfoBmbcsw/index.html.

Lloyd, Lloyd George David. *War Memoirs of David Lloyd George.* London: Nicholson & Watson, 1934.

Luft, Gal. "The Palestinian H-Bomb: Terror's Winning Strategy." *Warfare in the Middle East since 1945*, 2017, 475–80. https://doi.org/10.4324/9781315234304-20.

Mai, Jun. "Steve Bannon Says Killing Huawei More Important than Trade Deal with China." South China Morning Post, May 23, 2019. https://www.scmp.com/news/china/diplomacy/article/3011145/steve-bannon-says-killing-huawei-more-important-trade-deal.

Mann, Charles C. *1493: Uncovering the New World Columbus Created.* New York: Alfred A. Knopf, 2015.

Mcbride, James, and Andrew Chatzky. "Is 'Made in China 2025' a Threat to Global Trade?" Council on Foreign Relations. Council on Foreign Relations, May 13, 2019. https://www.cfr.org/backgrounder/made-china-2025-threat-global-trade.

Meissner, Mirjam, Rogier Creemers, Pamela Kyle Crossley, Peter Mattis, and Samantha Hoffman. "Is Big Data Increasing Beijing's Capacity for Control?" ChinaFile, August 12, 2016. http://www.chinafile.com/conversation/Is-Big-Data-Increasing-Beijing-Capacity-Control?.

Meissner, Mirjam. "CHINA'S SOCIAL CREDIT SYSTEM." Merics China Monitor. Merics China Monitor, May 17, 2017. https://www.merics.org/sites/default/files/2017-09/China Monitor_39_SOCS_EN.pdf.

Mundy, Jon, and Kevin Thomas. "What Is Massive MIMO Technology?" 5G.co.uk - UK's Premier 5G Resource, n.d. https://5g.co.uk/guides/what-is-massive-mimo-technology/.

Nathan, Andrew J. (Andrew James). "Authoritarian Resilience." *Journal of Democracy* 14, no. 1 (2003): 6–17. https://doi.org/10.1353/jod.2003.0019.

"Nuclear Posture Review." Department of Defense, February 2018. https://media.defense.gov/2018/Feb/02/2001872886/-1/-1/1/2018-NUCLEAR-POSTURE-REVIEW-FINAL-REPORT.PDF.

O'Kane, Sean. "Audi Taps Huawei to Help Power Self-Driving Cars in China." The Verge. The Verge, October 12, 2018. https://www.theverge.com/2018/10/12/17967320/audi-huawei-self-driving-cars-china.

O'Brien, Kevin J., and Lianjiang Li. "Rightful Resistance." *Rightful Resistance in Rural China*, n.d., 1–24. https://doi.org/10.1017/cbo9780511791086.003.

O'Neil, Cathy. *Weapons of Math Destruction: How Big Data Increases Inequality and Threatens Democracy*. Great Britain: Penguin Books, 2017.

Pan, Chengxin. "The 'China Threat' in American Self-Imagination: The Discursive Construction of Other as Power Politics."

Alternatives: Global, Local, Political 29, no. 3 (2004): 305–31. https://doi.org/10.1177/030437540402900304.

Pan, Jennifer, and Yiqing Xu. "Chinas Ideological Spectrum." *SSRN Electronic Journal*, 2015. https://doi.org/10.2139/ssrn.2593377.

Patrizio, Andy. "Big Data vs. Artificial Intelligence." Datamation. Datamation, May 30, 2018. https://www.datamation.com/big-data/big-data-vs.-artificial-intelligence.html.

Paxton, K. Bradley. "Japans Growing Technological Capability: Implications for the US Economy." *Journal of International Business Studies* 24, no. 4 (1993): 815–17. https://doi.org/10.1057/jibs.1993.57.

Peyrefitte, Alain, and Jon Rothschild. *The Immobile Empire*. New York: Vintage Books, A Division of Random House, Inc., 2013.

Platt, Stephen R. "How Britain's First Mission to China Went Wrong." China Channel, May 18, 2018. https://chinachannel.org/2018/05/18/macartney/.

Platt, Stephen R. *Imperial Twilight: the Opium War and the End of Chinas Last Golden Age*. New York: Vintage Books, 2019.

Popper, Ben. "US Army Reportedly Asks Units to Stop Using DJI Drones, Citing Cybersecurity Concerns." The Verge. The Verge, August 4, 2017. https://www.theverge.com/2017/8/4/16095244/us-army-stop-using-dji-drones-cybersecurity.

Portman, Rob, and Tom Carper. "Threats to the US Research Enterprise: China's Talent Recruitment Plans ." United States Senate PERMANENT SUBCOMMITTEE ON INVESTIGATIONS . United

States Senate PERMANENT SUBCOMMITTEE ON INVESTIGA-
TIONS , n.d. https://www.hsgac.senate.gov/imo/media/doc/2019-
11-18 PSI Staff Report - China's Talent Recruitment Plans.pdf.

Qian, Shanshan. "The Role of Guanxi in Chinese Entrepreneurship," n.d. http://www.diva-portal.org/smash/get/diva2:530871/
FULLTEXT02.pdf.

Qiang, Xiao. "President XIs Surveillance State." *Journal of Democracy* 30, no. 1 (2019): 53–67. https://doi.org/10.1353/jod.2019.0004.

Qiao, Liang, Al Santoli, and Xiangsui Wang. *Unrestricted Warfare.*
Brattleboro, VT: Echo Point Books & Media, 2015.

Rasool, Farhat, Ahmed Gulzar, and Shaheen Naseer. "Drivers of
Entrepreneurship: Linking With Economic Growth and Employment Generation (A Panel Data Analysis)." *The Pakistan Development Review* 51, no. 4II (January 2012): 587–606. https://doi.
org/10.30541/v51i4iipp.587-606.

"Research Starters: Worldwide Deaths in World War II: The National
WWII Museum: New Orleans." The National WWII Museum |
New Orleans, n.d. https://www.nationalww2museum.org/stu-
dents-teachers/student-resources/research-starters/research-start-
ers-worldwide-deaths-world-war.

Rho, Sungho, Keun Lee, and Seong Hee Kim. "Limited Catch-up
in China's Semiconductor Industry: A Sectoral Innovation System Perspective." *Millennial Asia* 6, no. 2 (2015): 147–75. https://
doi.org/10.1177/0976399615590514.

Roberts, Margaret E. *Censored: Distraction and Diversion Inside Chinas Great Firewall*. Princeton University Press, 2018.

Robinson, Darrel, and Marcus Tannenberg. "Self-Censorship of Regime Support in Authoritarian States: Evidence from List Experiments in China." *Research & Politics* 6, no. 3 (2019): 205316801985644. https://doi.org/10.1177/2053168019856449.

Ross, Alec. *The Industries of the Future*. New York: Simon & Schuster paperbacks, 2017.

Rouse, Margaret. "What Is 3Vs (Volume, Variety and Velocity)? - Definition from WhatIs.com." WhatIs.com, n.d. https://whatis.techtarget.com/definition/3Vs.

Rouse, Margaret. "What Is AI Governance? - Definition from WhatIs.com." SearchEnterpriseAI, November 2018. https://searchenterpriseai.techtarget.com/definition/AI-governance.

Ryono, Angel, and Matthew Galway. "Xinjiang under China: Reflections on the Multiple Dimensions of the 2009 Urumqi Uprising." *Asian Ethnicity* 16, no. 2 (2014): 235–55. https://doi.org/10.1080/14631369.2014.906062.

Schwab, Klaus. *The Fourth Industrial Revolution*. Great Britain: Portfolio, 2017.

Schwab, Klaus. *Shaping the Future of the Fourth Industrial Revolution*. Knopf Doubleday Publishing Group, 2018.

Sciglar, Paul. "What Is Artificial Intelligence? Understanding 3 Basic AI Concepts." Robotics Business Review. Robotics Business

Review, April 19, 2018. https://www.roboticsbusinessreview.com/ai/3-basic-ai-concepts-explain-artificial-intelligence/.

Shambaugh, David. "China's Soft-Power Push." Foreign Affairs. Foreign Affairs Magazine, September 3, 2015. https://www.foreignaffairs.com/articles/china/2015-06-16/china-s-soft-power-push.

"Shenzhen, China Population." World Population Statistics, n.d. https://populationstat.com/china/shenzhen.

Sims, Alyssa. "The Rising Drone Threat from Terrorists." *Georgetown Journal of International Affairs* 19, no. 1 (2018): 97–107. https://doi.org/10.1353/gia.2018.0012.

Soubra, Diya. "The 3Vs That Define Big Data." Data Science Central, July 5, 2012. https://www.datasciencecentral.com/forum/topics/the-3vs-that-define-big-data.

"Speech by H.E. Xi Jinping President of the People's Republic of China At the Welcoming Dinner Hosted by Local Governments And Friendly Organizations in the United States." Ministry of Foreign Affairs of the People's Republic of China, September 25, 2015. https://www.fmprc.gov.cn/mfa_eng/wjdt_665385/zyjh_665391/t1305429.shtml.

Statista Research Department. "WeChat: Number of Users 2019." Statista, November 2019. https://www.statista.com/statistics/255778/number-of-active-wechat-messenger-accounts/.

Stern, Fritz. "Fritz Haber: Flawed Greatness of Person and Country." *Angewandte Chemie International Edition* 51, no. 1 (August 2011): 50–56. https://doi.org/10.1002/anie.201107900.

Stern, Rachel E., and Jonathan Hassid. "Amplifying Silence." *Comparative Political Studies* 45, no. 10 (2012): 1230–54. https://doi.org/10.1177/0010414011434295.

Sternberg, Rolf, and Sander Wennekers. "Determinants and Effects of New Business Creation Using Global Entrepreneurship Monitor Data." *Small Business Economics* 24, no. 3 (2005): 193–203. https://doi.org/10.1007/s11187-005-1974-z.

Strittmatter, Kai, and Ruth Martin. *We Have Been Harmonised: Life in Chinas Surveillance State.* Exeter: Old Street Publishing Ltd., 2019.

Su, Dejin, Qixia Du, Dongwon Sohn, and Libo Xu. "Can High-Tech Ventures Benefit from Government Guanxi and Business Guanxi? The Moderating Effects of Environmental Turbulence." *Sustainability* 9, no. 1 (2017): 142. https://doi.org/10.3390/su9010142.

Sun, Bo, and Zhixue Dong. "Comparative Study on the Academic Field of Artificial Intelligence in China and Other Countries." *Wireless Personal Communications* 102, no. 2 (November 2018): 1879–90. https://doi.org/10.1007/s11277-018-5243-2.

Síthigh, Daithí Mac, and Mathias Siems. "The Chinese Social Credit System: A Model for Other Countries?" *The Modern Law Review* 82, no. 6 (April 2019): 1034–71. https://doi.org/10.1111/1468-2230.12462.

Taleb, Tarik, Rolf Winter, Tuncer Baykas, and Farooq Bari. "Telecommunications Standards." *IEEE Communications Magazine* 51, no. 3 (2013): 78–79. https://doi.org/10.1109/mcom.2013.6476869.

Tang, Wenfang. "The 'Surprise' of Authoritarian Resilience in China." American Affairs Journal, February 20, 2018. https://

americanaffairsjournal.org/2018/02/surprise-authoritarian-resilience-china/.

Tao, Li. "What You Need to Know about Facial Recognition Firm SenseNets." South China Morning Post, April 12, 2019. https://www.scmp.com/tech/science-research/article/3005733/what-you-need-know-about-sensenets-facial-recognition-firm.

"THE 5G ECOSYSTEM: RISKS & OPPORTUNITIES FOR DoD." Defense.gov. Defense and Innovation Board, April 2019. https://media.defense.gov/2019/Apr/03/2002109302/-1/-1/0/DIB_5G_STUDY_04.03.19.PDF.

"The Nobel Prize in Chemistry 1918." NobelPrize.org, n.d. https://www.nobelprize.org/prizes/chemistry/1918/haber/biographical/.

"The President Takes On China, Alone." The New York Times. The New York Times, May 15, 2019. https://www.nytimes.com/2019/05/15/podcasts/the-daily/trump-china-trade-war.html.

"The Recruitment Program for Innovative Talents (Long Term)." Recruitment Program of Global Experts, n.d. http://www.1000plan.org.cn/en/.

Thucydides. *History of the Peloponnesian War.* Place of publication not identified: Franklin Classics Trade Press, 2018.

Thum, Rian. "China's Mass Internment Camps Have No Clear End in Sight." Foreign Policy, August 22, 2018. https://foreignpolicy.com/2018/08/22/chinas-mass-internment-camps-have-no-clear-end-in-sight/.

Tocqueville, Alexis de, Arthur Goldhammer, and Olivier Zunz. *Democracy in America.* New York: Library of America Paperback Classics, 2012.

Townshend, Ashley, Matilda Steward, and Brendan Thomas-Noone. "Averting Crisis: American Strategy, Military Spending and Collective Defence in the Indo-Pacific - United States Studies Centre." Averting Crisis: American strategy, military spending and collective defence in the Indo-Pacific - United States Studies Centre, n.d. https://www.ussc.edu.au/analysis/averting-crisis-american-strategy-military-spending-and-collective-defence-in-the-indo-pacific.

"Trained Monkeys and Eagles Ensure Flight Safety for V-Day." Trained Monkeys and Eagles Ensure Flight Safety for V-Day - People's Daily Online, September 1, 2015. http://en.people.cn/n/2015/0901/c90000-8944059.html.

Tse, Edward. *Chinas Disruptors: How Alibaba, Xiaomi, Tencent and Other Companies Are Changing the Rules of Business.* London: Portfolio Penguin, 2016.

Turley, James L. *The Essential Guide to Semiconductors.* Upper Saddle River, NJ: Prentice Hall, 2003.

Twamley, Zachary. *A Matter of Honour: Britain and WWI.* Point Pleasant, NJ: Winged Hussar Publishing, LLC, 2016.

"Venezuela 'Drone Attack': Six Arrests Made." BBC News. BBC, August 5, 2018. https://www.bbc.com/news/world-latin-america-45077057.

Wang, Ying. "Drone-Maker DJI to Develop More Industry Applications." China Daily. China Daily, January 27, 2018. http://www.chinadaily.com.cn/a/201801/27/WS5a6bd252a3106e7dcc1371b0.html.

"Wang Yi's Africa Visit: A New Chapter in China-Africa Cooperation?" YouTube. CGTN, January 6, 2019. https://www.youtube.com/watch?v=lQHBSu9_jOc.

"Weapons on Land - Poison Gas." Canada and WWI, n.d. https://www.warmuseum.ca/firstworldwar/history/battles-and-fighting/weapons-on-land/poison-gas/.

"What Is 5G?: Everything You Need to Know About 5G." Qualcomm, December 15, 2019. https://www.qualcomm.com/invention/5g/what-is-5g.

"What Is Big Data?" YouTube. World Economic Forum, n.d. https://www.youtube.com/watch?v=eVSfJhssXUA.

"What Is Big Data?" Oracle, n.d. https://www.oracle.com/big-data/guide/what-is-big-data.html.

Wilsey, John. "'Our Country Is Destined to Be the Great Nation of Futurity': John L. O'Sullivan's Manifest Destiny and Christian Nationalism, 1837–1846." *Religions* 8, no. 4 (2017): 68. https://doi.org/10.3390/rel8040068.

Wladawsky-Berger, Irving. "The Impact of Artificial Intelligence on the World Economy." The Wall Street Journal. Dow Jones & Company, November 26, 2018. https://blogs.wsj.com/cio/2018/11/16/the-impact-of-artificial-intelligence-on-the-world-economy/.

Wong, Edward. "After Long Ban, Western China Is Back Online." The New York Times. The New York Times, May 14, 2010. https://www.nytimes.com/2010/05/15/world/asia/15china.html.

World War I (1914-1918), n.d. https://www2.gwu.edu/~erpapers/teachinger/glossary/world-war-1.cfm.

Wu, Wendy. "Steve Bannon Helps Revive US Cold War-Era Committee to Target China." South China Morning Post, March 26, 2019. https://www.scmp.com/news/china/diplomacy/article/3003283/cold-war-back-steve-bannon-helps-revive-us-committee-target.

"Xi Jinping: Promoting the Healthy Development of China's New Generation of Artificial Intelligence." Xinhua Net. Xinhua Net, October 31, 2018. http://www.xinhuanet.com/politics/2018-10/31/c_1123643321.htm.

Xiang, Lanxin. "Xi's Dream and China's Future." *Survival* 58, no. 3 (March 2016): 53–62. https://doi.org/10.1080/00396338.2016.1186978.

Xiang, Nina. *Red AI: Victories and Warnings from Chinas Rise in Artificial Intelligence*. Place of publication not identified: Nina Xiang, 2019.

Xin, Zhou, Wendy Wu, and Kinling Lo. "Xi Jinping Sounds Long March Rallying Call as US Trade War Tensions Rise." South China Morning Post, May 21, 2019. https://www.scmp.com/economy/china-economy/article/3010977/xi-jinping-visits-rare-earth-minerals-facility-amid-talk-use.

Yang, Yingzhi. "China's Start-Ups Attract Almost Half of World's Venture Capital Investments." South China Morning Post, July 5,

2018. https://www.scmp.com/tech/article/2153798/china-surpasses-north-america-attracting-venture-capital-funding-first-time.

Yang, Yuan. "China Fuels Boom in Domestic Tech Start-Ups." Subscribe to read | Financial Times. Financial Times, October 22, 2017. https://www.ft.com/content/b63ee746-afc6-11e7-aab9-abaa44b1e130.

Yu, Junbo, Roger R. Stough, and Peter Nijkamp. "Governing Technological Entrepreneurship in China and the West." *Public Administration Review* 69 (2009). https://doi.org/10.1111/j.1540-6210.2009.02095.x.

Zhang, Huai. "How Big Data and AI Will Transform Shenzhen Airport." Huawei. Huawei, December 28, 2018. https://www.huawei.com/en/about-huawei/publications/winwin-magazine/32/shenzhen-airport-digital-platform-and-ai.

Zheng, Yongnian, and Minjia Chen. "China Plans to Build an Innovative State." *China Policy Institute*, June 2006. https://www.nottingham.ac.uk/iaps/documents/cpi/briefings/briefing-9-china-innovative-state.pdf.

Zhong, Zhi-Jin, Tongchen Wang, and Minting Huang. "Does the Great Fire Wall Cause Self-Censorship? The Effects of Perceived Internet Regulation and the Justification of Regulation." *Internet Research* 27, no. 4 (July 2017): 974–90. https://doi.org/10.1108/intr-07-2016-0204.

CPSIA information can be obtained
at www.ICGtesting.com
Printed in the USA
LVHW010937210420
654166LV00009B/3198

9 781641 373760